ROUTLEDGE LIBRARY EDITIONS: POLICE AND POLICING

Volume 16

COMMUNITY, POLICING AND ACCOUNTABILITY

COMMUNITY, POLICING AND ACCOUNTABILITY

The Politics of Policing in Manchester in the 1980s

EUGENE McLAUGHLIN

LONDON AND NEW YORK

First published in 1994 by (Avebury) Ashgate Publishing Ltd

This edition first published in 2023
by Routledge
4 Park Square, Milton Park, Abingdon, Oxon OX14 4RN

and by Routledge
605 Third Avenue, New York, NY 10158

Routledge is an imprint of the Taylor & Francis Group, an informa business

© 1994 E. McLaughlin

All rights reserved. No part of this book may be reprinted or reproduced or utilised in any form or by any electronic, mechanical, or other means, now known or hereafter invented, including photocopying and recording, or in any information storage or retrieval system, without permission in writing from the publishers.

Trademark notice: Product or corporate names may be trademarks or registered trademarks, and are used only for identification and explanation without intent to infringe.

British Library Cataloguing in Publication Data
A catalogue record for this book is available from the British Library

ISBN: 978-1-032-41114-9 (Set)
ISBN: 978-1-032-41216-0 (Volume 16) (hbk)
ISBN: 978-1-032-41230-6 (Volume 16) (pbk)
ISBN: 978-1-003-35693-6 (Volume 16) (ebk)

DOI: 10.4324/9781003356936

Publisher's Note
The publisher has gone to great lengths to ensure the quality of this reprint but points out that some imperfections in the original copies may be apparent.

Disclaimer
The publisher has made every effort to trace copyright holders and would welcome correspondence from those they have been unable to trace.

Community, Policing and Accountability

The politics of policing in Manchester in the 1980s

EUGENE McLAUGHLIN
Faculty of Social Sciences
The Open University

Avebury

Aldershot · Brookfield USA · Hong Kong · Singapore · Sydney

© E. McLaughlin 1994

All rights reserved. No part of this publication may be reproduced, stored in a retrieval system, or transmitted in any form or by any means, electronic, mechanical, photocopying, recording or otherwise without the prior permission of the publisher.

Published by
Avebury
Ashgate Publishing Ltd
Gower House
Croft Road
Aldershot
Hants. GU11 3HR
England

Ashgate Publishing Company
Old Post Road
Brookfield
Vermont 05036
USA

British Library Cataloguing in Publication Data
McLaughlin, Eugene
   Community, Policing and Accountability:
   Politics of Policing in Manchester in
   the 1980s   I. Title
   363.2094273
ISBN 1 85628 488 3

Library of Congress Cataloging-in-Publication Data
McLaughlin, Eugene, 1959–
   Community, policing and accountability : the politics of policing
in Manchester in the 1980s / Eugene McLaughlin.
      p. cm.
   Includes bibliographical references and index.
   ISBN 1-85628-488-3 (hard) : £32.00 ($59.95 U.S. : est.)
   1. Police--England--Manchester--Complaints against. 2. Police
power--England--Manchester. 3. Communication in police
administration--England-- Manchester. 4. Public relations--Police-
- England--Manchester.   I. Title
HV8196.M36M37 1994
363.2'0947'33--dc20   94-163623
                                                         CIP

Printed and Bound in Great Britain by
Athenaeum Press Ltd, Newcastle upon Tyne.

Contents

Acknowledgements		vi
Introduction		1
1	The Politics of Police Accountability	5
2	Theoretical Concerns	21
3	Policing Manchester 1976-81	35
4	Police Committee and Community Liaison	57
5	City Council and Police Monitoring	90
6	Losing the Fight for Police Accountability	104
7	Police Authority and Community Liaison	120
8	City Council and Community Safety	148
9	Unsettled Accounts	166
Bibliography		181
Index		197

Acknowledgements

Thank you to all those friends, colleagues and 'fellow-travellers' (they know who they are) who over many years have suffered from this project being a part of their lives, whether they wanted it to be or not. They helped me to formulate many of the arguments presented in this book, although none of them is responsible for the final form these arguments have taken or any errors. I know that not all of them will concur with my reading of what happened in Manchester in the 1980s and certain of them know the internal histories of the initiatives better than I do. I have no doubt that many of their criticisms will be justified. Finally there are four people who deserve special thanks because their overall advice, encouragement, patience and friendship have literally made this book possible. Kate Lowe has been an astute reader and critic for many years. Tony Jefferson assured me that police accountability was an important research topic and then found himself having to supervise yet another Ph.D! Phil Mole who well 'before the fall' patiently explained to me why socialists had to engage with democratic theory. And finally, Linda Molloy whose well-founded scepticism always put every new political initiative in Manchester in perspective.

Introduction

This book looks back to the 1980s when there was a passionate and extensive public debate about police accountability in Britain. It details and analyzes the origins, key features and outcomes of the different political campaigns around this issue. The first chapter narrates the precise social, political and economic context within which demands for democratic accountability re-emerged in the late 1970s and early 1980s. The riots of 1981 were a moment of political rupture - they pushed the issue of the constitutional position of the police in British society onto the formal political agenda. The nature of the rioting forced a complacent political establishment to confront the uncomfortable truth that in many parts of Britain the police were operating without the consent of significant sections of the public. Consequently, an already heated debate about police powers, racially discriminatory policing and policing the crisis intensified. In the immediate post-riot period, the key question was asked whether it would be possible to construct institutional arrangements which would ensure that those sections of the community most disadvantaged and discriminated against by policework - the policed - had their voices heard directly by those in authority and their complaints acknowledged as legitimate. If the answer to the question was no, it was feared that rioting would become a routine part of British life.

Significant sections of the Labour Party argued that the manifest crisis in police-community relations could only be resolved through fundamental constitutional reform. Provincial Labour-controlled police committees lobbied for a more vigorous role in the determination of policing policies, and in London the radical Greater London Council campaigned for the establishment of statutory local control over the country's largest police force. The left's various proposals and demands for change shared a common aim:

> to secure greater powers for the community, or its elected

1

representatives, to influence or direct the process of selection through which a policy of law enforcement is constructed. Hence, such proposals are all attempts to secure a form of 'democratic accountability' (Jefferson and Grimshaw, 1982, p. 96).

Chief police officers in their turn, with one or two notable exceptions, vociferously defended their autonomy from what they saw as the left's political assault on the police. Although the Conservative government gave its full support to 'the thin blue line', it also established a public inquiry chaired by Lord Scarman to inquire into the causes of the riots. His analysis and recommendations only served to sharpen the debate about policing and police accountability. He rejected the calls for the strengthening of the formal powers of police committees and the establishment of a police committee in London. Instead, Lord Scarman advised the government to establish effective local channels of communication between the police and the community.

The critics were scathing in their reaction, arguing that these consultative or liaison committees would not be able to represent the community on policing issues, and would never be able to elicit the participation of the policed because they were powerless and undemocratic. In response, certain radical Labour-controlled councils controversially decided to boycott Scarman's committees and to set up alternative police monitoring groups and police committees to give representation to the interests of the policed. As a consequence, in the first half of the 1980s, it was possible to find Scarman-inspired police-community consultation committees and radical police monitoring groups, all promising to 'represent the community', 'make the police accountable to the community' and arguing for 'community participation' on policing issues. These respective elements constituted a distinctly new element in the police-community interface. The overall aim of this book is to consider critically the political difficulties and dilemmas of attempting to bring about the representation and participation of those sections of the community who are in conflict with the police. One of its central concerns will be to identify whether the various post-riot arrangements managed to ensure that the voices of the policed were not marginalized or silenced.

What was clear and interesting from the outset was that although the consultative committees and monitoring groups were using the same linguistic concepts, the specific meanings and stresses attached to them differed radically. The second chapter attempts, therefore, to unravel these differences by identifying the wider theoretical questions about 'community', 'representation' and 'participation' which must be addressed by those seeking the democratization of the police. To do so, it utilizes the insights of contemporary post-liberal democratic theorizing and the post-modernist critique to unpick the debates about police accountability, especially the demands for community control of policing. It argues that whilst the above mentioned concepts are easily evoked in political and ideological discourse, there are key problems relating to each concept which must be acknowledged and confronted. These theoretical difficulties have to be faced by any political project having as its aim the democratization of social institutions and practices.

The next three chapters focus on the political struggle over police accountability that unfolded in Manchester between the late 1970s and 1985. Chapter Three considers the overall policing context within which local campaigns for accountability emerged. Chapter Four narrates how, in the aftermath of the 1981 local elections, Labour finally gained control of Greater Manchester police committee and obligated itself to furthering the accountability of the police to the local community. The committee promised to utilize its powers to hold James Anderton, one of the most controversial chief constables in the country, to account. In addition, in the aftermath of the Moss Side riots in July 1981, it decided, despite considerable opposition, to set up Scarman-type community liaison panels to establish a dialogue between the police and those sections of the community in Moss Side who were in conflict with the Greater Manchester Police.

Chapter Five describes how in the 1984 local elections the left of the Labour Party sensationally won control of Manchester City Council. Its manifesto rejected the community liaison model and declared that the council would set up police monitoring groups to make the police more accountable to local communities, and to bring about genuine community participation in policing matters. The result was the creation of an extremely controversial police monitoring campaign. In these chapters, I attempt to illustrate how the two models - community liaison and police monitoring - had to confront and attempt to resolve the structural and conceptual issues raised in the two opening chapters.

Chapter Six discusses the changes that took place in the politics of police accountability at the national level in the latter half of the 1980s. In particular, I look at how, as part of the state's counter-offensive against radical local authorities, the troublesome police committees were crudely abolished. Moreover, a powerful official discourse on crime prevention was constructed and this had a considerable impact on those sections of the Labour Party at the forefront of the campaign for police accountability. I argue that this was the moment when the police accountability campaigns were finally defeated politically and the interests of the policed were marginalized.

The next two chapters document the considerable impact that these national shifts had on the two campaigns for police accountability in Manchester. For a variety of reasons, the police committee's conflict with the chief constable intensified in the late 1980s and moved, with abolition, to a final resolution. Unfortunately for the chief constable, because of its composition, the new police authority was, initially at least, an even more belligerent entity than the old one.

This was the moment when the struggle over policing in Manchester spiralled frighteningly out of control, and when those involved in the accountability campaigns realized that they would pay a high political price for challenging the Greater Manchester Police. Gabrielle Cox, the high profile chair of the old police committee, reflecting on this period, spoke of the 'pressure of death threats and razor-bladed hate mail, of lying awake wondering if a petrol bomb will come through your window, fearful for your children's safety - all because you dared to question the police' (1988, p. 20). And Martin Walker (1986), a journalist, wrote of the fear and loathing of the police that gripped certain Manchester residents in the middle of the 1980s.

It was in this context that concerted efforts were made to revitalize the community liaison panels. Chapter Eight illustrates how the political unpopularity of Manchester City Council's police monitoring initiative reached new heights, and how it was dramatically jettisoned by the council in favour of politically advantageous community safety strategies. The final chapter reflects upon the more general lessons that can be learned from this study of the various attempts to create democratic structures of representation and participation on policing matters in Manchester.

The empirical basis of this book was constructed from the following sources. First, I used the relevant minutes of and research notes from meetings of two local police monitoring groups, Greater Manchester police committee and Manchester City Council police monitoring committee and working party. Second, I had access to documents from Manchester City Council's police monitoring unit and the community safety team and Greater Manchester police committee's community liaison office and community relations unit. Third, personal notes were taken at public meetings on policing in Manchester held during the first half of the 1980s. Fourth, formal and informal interviews/discussions were held with members of police monitoring groups, the police committee, the community liaison officer, the community liaison unit, the police monitoring committee, the police monitoring research unit and the community safety team. And finally, local and national newspapers were scrutinized for relevant information. In the construction of this text, I have attempted at all times to respect the confidences of those who trusted me with politically sensitive material and information.

1 The politics of police accountability

The 1960 Royal Commission on the constitutional position of the police was set up in response to a series of controversial incidents in the 1950s which 'cast doubt on the adequacy of the means of bringing the police to account' (Critchley, 1978, p. 268). Lustgarten (1986) argues that, from the outset, the 'conceptual boundaries of that inquiry were narrowly defined', because they were framed by the general shifts that had taken place in local-central state relations in the post-war period: the general loss of functions by local authorities; the regionalization, centralization and rationalization of local government services and the rise of a managerialist ideology which reinforced the autonomy of the bureau-professionals of the welfare state. In such circumstances, the powers of local elected representatives over policing issues were precariously positioned. There was also the allegation, made most forcefully by Marshall (1960) and Chester (1960), that the state, after the controversies of the 1950s, was making a deliberate attempt to remove policing from the realm of politics.

The Commission report, published in 1962, urged that borough watch committees and standing joint committees should be replaced by police committees which would continue to be responsible for the appointment of chief constables. However, they were to lose: responsibility for the efficient policing of their areas; the power to suspend and dismiss the chief constable and his deputy; and the powers of appointment, promotion and discipline. In addition, the doctrine of constabulary independence received fresh affirmation:

> We entirely accept that it is in the public interest that a chief constable, in dealing with quasi-judicial matters, should be free from the conventional processes of democratic control and influence (Report of the Royal Commission, 1962, para 87).

Thus, a highly questionable reading of constitutional history and law was used to reassert that 'accountability to any principle but the law is incompatible with the ideal of an independent, non-partisan police force' (Smith, 1986, p. 99).

Additionally, it was recommended that the distinction between the county and the borough forces should end and that one third of the new police committees should be composed of magistrates:

> the Royal Commission accepted the argument of the Magistrates' Association that, since local authority decisions were increasingly swayed by political views, it was especially important that a police body contain non-elected persons, and that JPs were suitable because of their close knowledge of police work and problems (Levenson, 1981, p. 46).

The government rejected the centralization proposals and gave the new police committees the duty of securing an 'adequate and efficient' police force in their area. However, the other proposals affecting the governance of the police were accepted, thus strengthening the position of the Home Office and chief constables. Within this 'tripartite arrangement', the accountability of the police to the local democratic political process was to be virtually non-existent. Any formal powers that the police committee was allocated under the 1964 Police Act were subject to the ultimate approval of the Home Secretary. For example, the new police committees were given the power to call for reports relating to the policing of their areas. However, the qualification was added that the chief constable could refer such requests to the Home Secretary if he considered it to be against the public interest or outside the responsibility of the police committee (Jefferson and Grimshaw, 1984, p. 19). Hence, the 1964 Act laid clear restrictions on access to information about policing matters and left the police committees in a position where they had, as Spencer (1985, p. 28) pointed out, wide responsibilities but a conspicuous absence of statutory powers.

Furthermore, although the police committee was to be a committee of the local council, the duties placed upon it were statutory not delegated. The police committee, therefore, had a special and unique status within the structure of local government because it was not accountable in the way other committees were, despite the fact that the council had to pay its share of the police budget. As critics noted, the new arrangements bore a marked resemblance to those which had prevailed in the counties since 1888. The consequence of having an undemocratic policing system available by which to judge and condemn the borough watch committees finally made itself apparent. In addition, because of the 'special' policing needs of London, the Home

Secretary (rather than local government representatives) continued to act directly as the police committee.

The political response to the recommendations was by no means muted. The government's critics claimed that the new arrangements would allow the Home Secretary to evade parliamentary scrutiny and chief constables to circumvent local control (*Tribune*, June 1964). The Commission's dismissal of the need for an independent complaints' process was heavily criticized as were the 'recommendations designed to deprive local authorities of nearly all their few remaining powers over the local police forces'(*Labour Research*, 51; see also Okojie and Noble, 1980). The pointed criticism was made that those serving on the Royal Commission would not 'spring to mind instantly when thinking of those who have resolutely upheld the liberties of the public when encroached upon by the forces of law and order'(*Spectator*, 8 June 1962).

The 1964 Act also provided the Home Secretary with increased powers of amalgamation and by 1969 the number of forces had been reduced from 117 to 47. Instead of separate police committees, joint ones were established, with representation on the authorities being premised upon the size of the populations of the respective counties involved. Marshall had no doubt as to the consequences of such arrangements, arguing that they were likely to be less rigorous than the authority of a single council. The joint board, according to Marshall:

> has no civic spirit to stiffen it, no common interest to unite it and no effective local opinion to support it... This may not matter for the purpose of administering services but for the purpose of securing participation and accountability it matters a great deal (1973, p. 60).

This reorganization of policing recommenced with the 1972 Local Government Act, which resulted in further readjustment of police boundaries to facilitate new county structures. Oliver (1987) has shown how elected representatives, because of their alleged lack of 'expertise', were virtually excluded even from this seemingly 'apolitical' exercise. Prior to the changeover in April 1974, the majority of the planning was conducted by senior police officers, and many police committees found themselves faced with reorganization schemes that had already been agreed upon by the police forces concerned and in which they had played no active part.

Implications for police accountability

As commentators have noted, the crucial outcome of the changes was that senior police officers finally achieved formal recognition and representation within the state (Brogden, 1982). As local government lost its powers, chief constables were correspondingly empowered. No longer constrained by the watch committees, their operational independence assured by the constitutional review and their professional status and power enhanced by the rise of large police bureaucracies, these non-elected public officials claimed the requisite expertise to know and determine local policing needs and policies. Consequently, chief police officers were able to assert their independence and accrue further powers not only from the police committees but also from the Home Office in the post-war period:

> chief constables could debate with the Home Office as equals, with each 'side' supported by its own army of professional advisers. Thus, professionalization not only penetrated deeply into the reshaped structure but augmented the powers granted to both the Home Office and the chief constables under the 1964 Act (Jefferson, 1987, p. 18).

And, as Cain (1972) argued, the 'language of professionalism' further ruptured the discourse of democratic accountability.

The studies that were conducted on the new police committees in this period bear testimony to the worst fears of those who argued that policing had been divested of any pretence of democratic accountability (Marshall, 1973; Banton, 1974; Simey, 1976; Judge, 1976; Cain, 1976; Brogden, 1977; Kettle, 1980). A survey carried out in 1977 indicated that the overwhelming majority of committee members accepted that policing was a 'non-political' function and respected the autonomy of chief constables in operational matters, thus allowing them to take the lead in setting the local policing agenda. Force headquarters also took the lead in dealing with the press and liaising with the public. Certain police committees not only accepted their subordinate role, but had become virtually moribund in terms of overseeing local policing practices. The survey noted, for example, that one English shire county 'never requests information on policing and does not receive regular reports, nor do they [police committee members] give advice on local problems nor have their views sought on social matters' (Association of County Councils, 1977). During a typical meeting of the Merseyside police committee in January 1977, for example:

> The chief constable's report on complaints against the police was briefly 'noted' while considerably greater time was devoted to letters of appreciation, police dog competitions, the Manchester flower show, the Tyneside 'summer exhibition', regional trials for the Sheffield show, police horse shows for 1977 (Loveday, 1985, p. 26).

Kettle ended his research on the Thames Valley police committee with the comment: 'it is hard to avoid concluding that most members neither know nor care much about controlling what is happening'. Instead, these supine committees, for the most part, were content to rubber-stamp the chief constable's requests for more resources.

It is symptomatic of the changes that the only real instances of conflict involving chief constables in this time period were a result of the introduction of corporate management structures into local government. Within the new structures the now dominant professionals, the chief constables and chief executives of the new councils, clashed over who was in control of the police. The police chiefs won the argument (Oliver, 1987, pp. 51-3).

One final point must be emphasized. The active participation of the community in police committee matters, as in other areas of local government, was virtually non-existent. As the 1977 survey noted 'since the 1974 reorganization, relationships with the public had perhaps tended to become more remote'. Through lack of advertising and the development of sub-committees, where the real discussion and decisions took place, police committee meetings were effectively closed off to the public and the media (Cox and Morgan, 1973; Brogden, 1977). Thus, the procedures of the police committees had resulted in the effective privatization of what should have been a public decision-making process.

Nevertheless, there is an important qualification that should be made in relation to the formal position of the police committees. Although the 1964 Act divested them of important powers and they were hemmed in by the powers of the Home Office and the chief constable, the provisions of the act were vague about what the exact powers of the authorities were. For example, although convention dictated that police committees could not interfere in 'operational' matters, the boundary between what was 'operational' and what was 'policy' (and therefore legitimate police committee business) was blurred. Thus as Jefferson and Grimshaw noted, there were 'grey areas' that could be legally contested if any police committee had a mind to do so.

From complacency to concern

As the 1960s and 1970s progressed, policing, despite the attempts to depoliticize it, remained high on the political agenda. This was virtually inevitable because the political and economic climate changed so dramatically that the post 1945 social democratic settlements collapsed amid conflict and strife. As Stuart Hall and his colleagues argued, this had direct implications for the police:

Crises have to be remedied, their worst effects contained or mitigated. They also have to be controlled. To put it crudely they have to be policed (1978, p. 339).

The state and its coercive agencies were, it was argued, repositioning themselves and an authoritarian transformation was taking place. As a result, police powers were being expanded and their public order role prioritized once more. Certain sections of British society were particularly vulnerable to this drift to a law and order society.

Anxieties, covering a wide spectrum of issues, began to surface in this increasingly authoritarian period (Jefferson and Grimshaw, 1984, pp. 1-8; Reiner, 1985, pp. 61-80; Morris, 1989, pp. 144-51). Apprehension was voiced about the increasing gap between the police and the public. Larger, impersonal and professional forces and changes in operational philosophy were the logical outcomes of the structural changes that had taken place in the post-war period. As Phil Cohen (1979) has argued, these technologically proficient forces did not feel the need to negotiate their presence in neighbourhoods, to cultivate the consent of the community or to take the needs of the community into account when formulating policy. The policing needs of the public were defined and decided upon at the professional discretion of the chief constables under the sponsorship of the Home Office. Thus, the technical and organizational changes exacerbated the alienation of the police from certain sections of the public:

> In this way a variety of valuable and non-crime related contacts with the public were lost to be replaced by those involving a greater possibility of inquisitorial and potentially coercive relationships (Stephens, 1988, p. 9).

These constitutive changes also enhanced the autonomy of the occupational culture because, as Manning (1988, p. 35) has noted, 'the dispersal of officers in space, their diverse duties, the wide range of situations that they are expected to encounter' impacted negatively on the effectiveness of internal control and supervisory systems. There was also concern about: an expanding catalogue of grave police malpractice; the 'heavy' and increasingly coercive policing of public order situations and industrial disputes; the deployment of specialist 'troubleshooting' units and aggressive policing strategies in black neighbourhoods; and controversial 'anti-subversion' and intelligence gathering activities (Bunyan, 1976; Hain, 1979 and 1980).

Furthermore, in the 1970s civil liberties groups began to fear that the public statements and actions of senior police officers indicated that the doctrine of 'political impartiality' was being seriously undermined. Freed from the strictures of political accountability, certain of the corporate managers of the police, both as individuals and through the Association of Chief Police Officers (ACPO), began to believe that they had the right to voice their authoritarian opinions on the state of the nation. The resultant politicization process expressed itself in a challenge to any encroachment upon their powers, a refutation of demands for public accountability of 'their' officers and, through the manipulation of people's fears about crimes such as 'mugging' and social unrest, their lobbying for, and exaction of, unfettered powers and resources (Mark, 1979; McNee, 1980). As Gilroy has argued, the appearance of senior police officers in the political arena in this time period should be seen as 'a 'morbid symptom' of the crisis of political representation so vividly described by Gramsci' (1982, p. 166).

However, it was not only chief officers who were making what Punch (1979) has described as the 'swing to right wing radicalism'. The Police Federation, representing rank and file officers, transformed itself into an 'organized and open faction of the populist right' (Hall, 1982, p. 67). In 1975, for example, supported by the Superintendents' Association, the Federation launched a reactionary law and order campaign. In 1979, through a national press campaign, it intruded into the democratic process by asking voters in the forthcoming election to consider where the candidates stood on law and order. Unsworth (1982, p. 68) argues that these rebellious interventions were manifestations of a closed institution which was estranged both from the government, because of the protracted battle over pay and conditions, and from the 'liberalizing and pluralizing social tendencies of the 1960s and 1970s which complicated policing by challenging the absolutism of its conservative social and moral values'. In many respects this publicly funded 'unrepresentative bureaucracy' was increasingly at odds both with society and itself.

What needs to be stressed is that, as Stuart Hall (1980) pointed out, many of the above mentioned reframing of police discourse and police work took place without any form of democratic discussion. And when those concerned about controversial shifts in policing demanded an explanation, they had to face the fact that the British police had 'slipped the leash' of accountability to become, in certain instances, state-sponsored vigilantes. An ineffectual complaints' procedure, which had no element of independent scrutiny, combined with the virtual absence of effective managerial controls and sanctions, meant that individual officers could not be called to account internally for wrongdoing (Walters, 1981). The rule of law seemed to facilitate highly questionable police practices rather than curbing them. Moreover, because of their constitutional position in relation to the police committees and the Home Secretary, there was no effective public forum within which chief constables could be publicly questioned or held responsible, over either the behaviour of their officers or for the manner in which particular locales and social groups were policed. As Jefferson and Grimshaw have argued:

> At this point, when general criticisms of chief constables' overall policies began to appear alongside specific criticisms of particular officers' practices, the questions of who decides the nature of policing, and of how to call those responsible to account for controversial decisions, became paramount (1984, p. 8).

Renewed demands for democratic accountability

During the 1979 election campaign in Britain, the bi-partisan consensus on law and order finally broke down when the Conservatives made the Labour government's record on crime a key issue. The Conservative Party and right-wing media successfully established in the eyes of significant sections of the electorate that the Labour Party was soft on law and order and anti-police (Taylor, 1981; Kettle, 1982; Gilroy and Sim, 1987). To illustrate its ideological commitment to law and order, the incoming authoritarian populist Conservative government dispensed generous increases in police pay and personnel. As Hugo Young (1989, p. 238) has noted, cynics, not all of them anti-Conservative, viewed the radical right's patronage of 'the boys in blue' as 'prudent preparation for the civil breakdown that seemed implicit in high unemployment and anti-union practices'.

In the same 'moment' that the radical right was bracing the police for battles to come, new left sections of the Labour Party and civil liberties' pressure groups attempted to place the interests of those who were being subjected to intensified discriminatory policing practices - the marginal, the dispossessed, the criminalized - at the centre of the political agenda (Levenson, 1981). Highly localized campaigns were organized around incidents of police racism, violence and corruption, deaths in police custody and controversial policing strategies (Scraton, Sim and Gilroy, 1987). The immediate outcome of the campaigns in the conurbations was the development of a variety of police monitoring groups. Some of the groups were organized while others were loose coalitions; some were affiliated to the Labour Party, others consciously stood outside the formal political process; some were group based while others were issue based. What they all had in common, however, was that they 'watched' local policing practices, collected independent data on local police work, developed systematic knowledge about police and community relations, provided support and advice for those in difficulties with the police, held independent inquiries and campaigned for changes in the structure of police governance and the complaints' procedures. In effect, they policed the police.

Their objectives were:

> to defend the community against police attack, malpractice and inefficiency, and the incursion of racists. These two objectives overlap and are prioritized by virtue of the geographic area which the group is in and the nature of their workers (Walker, 1986, p. 45).

This monitoring work linked into, and overlapped with, a wider political campaign for 'a new form of accountability - democratic accountability - which would be characterized by prospective control by a local democratic authority over a chief constable's general policies of law enforcement' (Brogden et al, 1988, p. 161). In 1979 and 1980, Jack Straw MP unsuccessfully introduced parliamentary bills proposing amendments to the 1964 Police Act to ensure that chief constables consulted with police committees on general policies and priorities and to establish a police committee for London (Jefferson and Grimshaw, 1984, pp. 150-6; Oliver, 1987, pp. 68-70).

Between March 1980 and the local government elections of 1981, the issue of police accountability and demands for a police committee achieved recognition within the electoral manifesto of the London Labour Party (Bundred, 1982; Spencer, 1985; Lansley, Goss and Wolmar, 1989). After the victory of the latter in the 1981 elections, the Greater London Council set up a non-statutory police committee and support unit as part of its election manifesto promise to campaign for accountability, which was defined as:

> limiting police powers to those which are strictly necessary (for example, by repealing powers framed in statute), controlling the exercise of discretionary powers and providing effective remedies for the abuse of that discretion when it occurs (a complaints' system and civil actions, for example) (Greater London Council, 1983).

For this to happen there would need to be a democratically elected police committee which would have the powers 'to determine the overall operational policies and practices of the Metropolitan police' (Greater London Council, 1983). Within this initiative, administrative and financial support was made available to monitoring groups to enable them to act as the 'eyes and ears' of the police committee, to articulate the concerns of the community and to link the committee to the community (Walker, 1986). Through this 'deep' and relentless independent monitoring the local community would be able to hold the police to account. After the 1982 borough elections, Labour controlled local authorities in London also set up their own non-statutory police committees (Jefferson, McLaughlin and Robertson, 1988).

Elsewhere in England, the county council elections of 1981 resulted in radicalized 'municipal socialist' administrations securing control of the local state. They too believed that policing was a legitimate brief of local government and were determined, like their counterparts in London, to have a real voice in the manner in which policing was carried out in their areas. Most of the Labour parties in the metropolitan areas had manifestos which argued that effective, consensual and accountable policing would only be achieved through greater community representation and participation and the development of an independent and effective complaints procedure. Thus, they too demanded changes to the 1964 Police Act to empower police committees in relation to policy and personnel issues (Kettle and Hodges, 1982; Loveday, 1985; Scraton, 1985). In addition, local Labour parties promised to create meaningful communication channels to ensure that community needs and priorities, and force policies and practices, corresponded. Thus, the previously hidden decision-making processes were to be made transparent to the community's elected representatives at force, divisional and individual officer levels.

The momentum for change was maintained when, after the elections, the Association of Metropolitan Authorities passed a resolution to campaign for additional powers which would enable police committees to exercise closer control over local policing, and for the removal of non-elected magistrates.

'Riot' and reaction

However, it was the nation-wide urban rioting of 1981 that infused a sense of urgency into the campaigns for community representation and participation in policing matters. The fault lines of British policing became crystal clear in the intense glow generated by the torching of the inner cities. As Reiner has noted:

> The riots of the spring and summer of that year, and the Scarman Report on the Brixton disorders, were a turning point in the increasingly politicized debate about police organization and strategy, and the accountability and constitutional position of the police (Reiner, 1985, p. 170).

The response of the British state and the intense debate about 'race', policing and criminal justice was formally extensive but framed, in the final instance, by the definitional parameters of the constitutional status quo. Support was given to the enhancement of the paramilitary response capabilities of the police and the 1984 Police and Criminal Evidence Act and 1986 Public

Order Act were eventually passed, legislatively extending the range of coercive discretionary powers available to the police (Zander, 1985; Hillyard and Percy-Smith, 1988).

In addition, Lord Scarman's inquiry into the disturbances - 'the form in which the state would talk to black communities' (Joshua and Wallace, 1983) - was set the task of producing a set of rational and realistic recommendations that would: curb crime, maintain social order, restore 'policing by consent' and impact positively on the problems of the inner city and a multi-racial society. Thus, as Stuart Hall has argued, Scarman was faced with:

> The social democratic dilemma - how to square all interests, without having to make hard choices, engage power or introduce radical changes. It is better known as 'having your cake and eating it', or the politics of the easy choice, or perhaps 'squaring the circle' (1982, p. 69).

He did acknowledge and inscribe in official discourse: the complaints levelled by black people against the police; the links between accountability and consensual policing; and the demands for greater community representation and participation in policing matters. However, he could not, given the philosophical and juridico-political space he inhabited, accede to demands for the democratization of policing because this would compromise the sacred principle of operational independence. Thus, he opted for the constitutional status quo, arguing that police committees should utilize the powers given to them by 1964 Police Act to the full and for the adoption of more sensitive policing strategies. This left him with only one pathway out of his dilemma:

> If you want consent without the passage of power, and 'a sense of accountability' without the exercise of strategic control, then you must have mediation which squares the circle. The name for this operation is *consultation* (Hall, 1982, p. 70).

Accordingly, community consultation - 'the wavy line that squares circles' - became the touchstone of Scarman's remaining recommendations. He urged the creation of nation-wide statutory divisional police-community consultation committees, on which police officers, elected representatives and 'community leaders' would sit. These committees would compel the police and the community to engage in 'constructive dialogue' to lift the veil of misunderstanding and reveal a coincidence of interests, namely, the formulation of effective 'crime control' strategies. In this moment of dialogue consensual policing could be realized and Scarman warned community leaders not to jeopardize the potential for consensus by engaging in 'extravagant language or ill-informed criticism' or questioning the police about operationally sensitive issues.

After considerable public debate and the right's neutralization of Scarman's more 'radical' proposals, Scarman's consultation recommendations were formalized by Home Office Circular 54/1982 and the 1984 Police and Criminal Evidence Act (for details see, Morgan and Maggs, 1985; Morgan, 1987).

1981 was also a defining moment for left criminology in Britain because, in response to Thatcherism, the uprisings, the extremely limited nature of the Scarman proposals and the civil liberties issues raised by the release of the report of the Royal Commission on Criminal Procedure, it entered the debate about police powers, democratic accountability and community policing. As a consequence of both the political space which opened up briefly in the aftermath of the riotous disorder, and the election of radical metropolitan Labour administrations committed to campaigning for police accountability, left criminologists were able to feed off and into the immediate political situation which rapidly unfolded during the first half of the 1980s. They also split irrevocably into 'realist' and 'critical' camps.

Left realist and critical criminologists were in general agreement, along with many Labour-controlled local authorities, that the intrinsically political nature of policework demanded effective structures of democratic accountability rather than the false solution offered by Scarman's 'unrepresentative' consultation committees. However, they disagreed on why policing was in crisis and what alternative institutional arrangements were needed to improve police-community relations. The realists' claimed (in a manner similar to Scarman) that the inability to control crime was the motor of the policing crisis in the inner city and that a democratically accountable police force was the instrumental touchstone for effective and consensual crime control strategies. Taylor asserted that:

> our task is to argue for a police force that is authentically responsive to a highly polarized and pluralistic society, via the thorough going subjugation of the police to the broad control of democratic forces at local and national level (1981, p. 46).

While Lea and Young, in their reformist manifesto insisted that a:

> rigorous system of local democratic accountability of the police is vital for restoring mutual respect and trust between the police and community, restoring the flow of information between the two and...for creating a political structure in which the most deprived

16

sections of the working class community can articulate their interests (1984, p. 231).

Their immediate reformist vision was of a post-Thatcher social democratic city where there would be a democratically elected, and thus reconstituted, police committee which would play a mediatory role between the police and the community, and local consultative arrangements where all sections of the community would be actively represented and have a say in a realistic discussion with the police about local crime priorities. In the far off future socialist city, these interim arrangements would be developed to allow 'full political discussion as to the proper character and the legal scope of police action' in the fight against crime (Taylor, 1981, p. 163). In this moment authentic community policing would become a reality. However, the left realists also repeatedly cautioned against 'a fully accountable, non-autonomous police force' (Kinsey and Young, 1982, p. 134) because of the perilous consequences for impartial law enforcement of direct community control. As Lea and Young put it:

> One of our constant nightmares is that if there was a completely democratic control of police in areas such as Hackney, the resulting police force would look exactly the same as the present (1984, p. 270).

A neurotic fear that in a highly fragmented and unequal society direct community control of and participation in policing matters would give rise to unregulated militias, right-wing vigilante groups and destructive intolerance explains the left realists' obsession with ensuring that the police committee had a lead role in representing community interests. Because of their stress on democratic accountability rather than political control, for reasons discussed in the next section, their proposals can be defined as falling within an indirect conception of democracy.

Critical criminologists were much more sceptical about the possibility of building upon and working within and through a framework of enhanced representative democracy, particularly at an apocalyptical moment when the British state was moving definitively to the right. As far as they were concerned, the authoritarian state would never countenance the democratization of its repressive agencies because they were historically mandated to play a key role in suppressing any group that opposed the new unfolding economic order (Bunyan, 1982). Despite warnings from Stuart Hall that careful analysis was required because Scarman was inhabiting the a complex political space momentarily created by 'the very nameless and spontaneous ones into whom he was inquiring' (1982, p. 67), critical criminologists opted for a position that condemned the proposals as a trick - the means by which the community would be made accountable to the police.

The proposed consultation process was castigated as a retread of the colonial-style liaison strategems that the British state had been using since the 1960s to communicate with self-appointed black community 'leaders' and moderate organizations. The defining features of these schemes was their unrepresentativeness and powerlessness - they, and this included the senior police officers sitting on them, had not been able to exercise any influence on the routine policing of black neighbourhoods. Furthermore, because they operated on the principle of 'commonality of interests', it was impossible for the liaison schemes to acknowledge that the escalating war of attrition being waged by police officers and black youths meant the 'quest for consensus' was doomed to failure. Scarman, as far as critical criminologists were concerned, had conspicuously failed to recognize these specifying truths and was, in essence, offering more of the same. Thus, there was every likelihood that his consultative arrangements were 'likely to amplify fundamental difficulties or to ignore them; they are unlikely to resolve them in situations similar to that in Brixton' (Jefferson and Grimshaw, 1984, p. 104). There was no possibility that those individuals and groups in conflict with the police would agree to participate in 'talking shops' that were geared towards helping the police to legitimate crime control operations. Hence, those 'community leaders' who did consent to sit on the toothless consultative committees would never be able to represent 'the community' or bring a halt to the discriminatory policing of black neighbourhoods.

Critical criminologists, unlike the left realists, were also deeply suspicious of the multi-agency community policing initiatives advocated by Scarman. As far as they were concerned, multi-agency initiatives would lead to welfare agencies, such as housing social services departments, being colonized to carry out territorially based 'crime' control functions under the direction of the police. Hence, a concerted effort was being made to replace the local welfare state with an authoritarian and disciplinary one in which social control and civil functions would be integrated in an overarching attempt to manage crisis-ridden black neighbourhoods. This meshing would permit the police to:

> to wield a frightening mixture of repressive powers, on the one hand, and programmes of social intervention, on the other, as mutually reinforcing tools in their efforts to control and contain the political struggle of the black and working class communities (Bridges, 1982, p. 184).

Embedded in their critique was the skeletal notion that genuine accountability would only be realized if communities had direct control over the fixing of policing policies, priorities and practices. Gilroy and Sim expounded this radical conception of democracy most forcefully in the conclusion to their extensive and scathing appraisal of left criminology's attitude towards policing:

> Socialists must begin to affirm and extend the belief that people are able to regulate their own community space and protect their lives and property without lapsing into vigilantism (1985, p. 50).

In the absence of this moment of authentic communitarian policing, critical criminology asserted that communities had the right to pursue 'a strategy of opposition to oppressive policing' (Scraton, 1985, p. 11). And in this context they viewed autonomous police monitoring initiatives as the 'only effective means by which police operational policies and practices can be opened to public scrutiny' (Scraton, 1985, p. 176). They were, in effect, arguing for a socialist 'popular justice' which could realistically challenge the authoritarian populism of Thatcherism.

Conclusion

Re-reading the left's debates over policing and police accountability, it is apparent that embedded in the different positions is a series of intriguing questions concerning the relationship between 'community', 'representation', 'participation' and democracy. However, for the most part, the participants in this debate, with the notable exception of Jefferson and Grimshaw (1984), devoted little real time and space to analysing their demands critically. Theoretical reflection took second place, on both sides, to the stated urgent need to construct a vigorous politically situated criminology which could challenge the law and order project of the hegemonic 'new right'. In the left realist master narrative, there is the message that many of the difficulties relating to 'community', 'representation' and 'participation' could be resolved by legislatively ensuring that 'the political and organizational structure of the police force is open, democratic and accountable' (Kinsey, Lea and Young, 1986, pp. 145-6), and that policing did not fall under direct community control. By contrast, critical criminology's counter narrative stated that truly democratic policing involved the community, rather than the police or politicians, deciding on its own policing needs, and indeed forms of policing.

However, the problematical nature of their demands and proposals should have been acknowledged and confronted in a more rigorous manner because they, in effect, constituted the theoretical and empirical terrain on which radical discourses and initiatives (revitalized statutory police committees; non-statutory municipal police committees and research units; police monitoring groups) challenged state discourses and initiatives (Scarman inspired consultation committees and community policing strategies) in the 1980s. A delineation and deconstruction of the intricate theoretical issues arising from the demands for community representation and participation in policing matters form the core of the next chapter.

2 Theoretical concerns

Theorists of democracy have identified a 'slew of slippery' and 'essentially contestable' first order concepts that need rigorous clarification before they can be fully analyzed in practice (Held, 1984; Berki, 1989; Massumi, 1992). There could be no more problematic a constellation of concepts than those foregrounded in the campaigns for police accountability detailed in the previous chapter. It is necessary, therefore, to disentangle the concepts of 'representation', 'participation' and 'community' and to highlight the theoretical difficulties of employing them uncritically. In order to do so, it is necessary to consider the findings of a variety of political and social writers who, in the course of the 1970s and 1980s, began to think through the theoretical prerequisites for a post-marxist and post-liberal radical pluralist democracy.

Community

Considerable discussion has taken place concerning the difficulties of using 'the community' as the basis of demands for any progressive political project. First of all, a seemingly unresolvable problem relates to the virtual impossibility of providing a satisfactory definition. If one examines the extensive sociological literature on 'community', it is possible to identify a complex overlay of spatio-temporal, sentimental and interpretative meanings and boundaries (Nisbet, 1970; Plant, 1974; Thorns, 1976; Fish, 1980; Cohen, 1985; Midgley, 1986; Wilmott, 1988). However, these categories, in themselves, are not neatly delineated and the concept continues to plague theorists and researchers who hanker after a more precise definition.

Stacey (1969) argues that community should be treated as a non-concept precisely because it is incapable of exact definition - it has no 'essence'. Pahl

(1970) maintains that because of its vagueness and malleability, it has served more to confuse than to illuminate, while other writers have referred to the 'fig-leaf' of community, an imaginary consensual device which when imaged onto lived realities conceals all kinds of contradictions, conflicts and confusions:

> To speak of a community when working politically on issues such as housing, health, play or welfare can cause great confusion, since, however one looks at it, no community exists: on the contrary one is confronted with a cluster of class positions, conflicts and interests, some of which are irreconcilable (Cowley et al., 1979, p. 5).

If this critique is extended to include race, gender and generational divisions, then the concept of 'the community' becomes even more problematical in terms of realizing policies premised upon it.

Second, it is important to note that concern about 'community' constantly expresses and replays itself in relation to urban social processes. A fundamental sociological debate continues to rage over whether it is possible to discuss the concept of community, whatever its definition, in the context of highly fractured urban industrial and post-industrial formations. Is community compatible with the modern and postmodern city? The 'whither/wherefore community?' and 'lost but longed for community' debates continue to dominate urban sociology at both theoretical and empirical levels (Harvey, 1990). It should also be noted that heightened debate and concern about community tend to surface during periods of serious social crisis.

A third problem, as Williams (1976) has pointed out, is that although difficult to define theoretically and examine empirically, community, unlike most other terms of social organization, is rarely used in a negative manner. This characteristic has led Titmus to caution against using such a positive concept:

> All kinds of wild and unlovely weeds are changed by statutory magic and comforting appellation into the most attractive flowers that bloom not just in Spring but all year round (1968, p.104).

However, despite the lack of agreement about this magical configuration and whether its existence can be verified or not, community remains a powerful ideological organizing principle. Precisely because it is a floating signifier, all political positions have attempted to claim it as their own. For sections of the left, 'community', as opposed to the state, continues to signify 'not just a distinctive political ideology but a particular set of values and norms in everyday life: mutuality, co-operation, identification and symbiosis... [a]

powerful means to co-ordinate action and create solidarity' (Gilroy, 187, pp.234-7).

But Plant cautions that 'community' is a core organizing concept within right-wing communitarian thought and as such it has a dangerous essentialist pedigree. The right-wing version with its racially inscribed notions of territorial belonging and homogeneity:

> will be unable to make sense of a multi-racial form of community when 'multi-racial' implies that not all values are shared and not all ends are recognised, and this is why, with perfect if manic consistency, the new conservatives formulated the Volkgemeinschaft idea (1974, p. 46).

This is why left-wing critics of participatory democracy are worried by those who uncritically promote communitarian control mechanisms. If careful attention is not paid to patterns of representation and participation, the community in control could be extremely reactionary in nature and empowered to define who is and who is not of the community and which interests should be prioritized. As Samuels (1993, p. 16) argues, an evocation of community that does not recognize the 'totalitarian shadow of community' will be, 'thin, desiccated, morally elevated classroom civics and socially useless'.

Loney's (1983) important study of the community development programmes of the late 1960s also illustrates the ease with which the state is capable of responding effectively to radical anti-statist 'community' campaigns for democratic participation and representation in a way that subverts the radical nature of those campaigns. There can be little doubt the 'community' is both an ideological terrain that the state is capable of 'mapping' and 'knowing', and a political space that it is willing to contest.

Representation

Political theory distinguishes between two models of democracy, representative (indirect) and participatory (direct), which have been traditionally constructed in opposition to each other. Liberal or representative democracy is, 'a system of political rule embracing elected "officers" who undertake to "represent" the interests and/or views of citizens' (Held and Pollitt, 1986, p. 7). However, in complex social formations there are considerable difficulties in an individual, institution, political party, government or state claiming to 'represent' the wishes of 'the people','the community' or the 'working class'. On the point of assumed, pre-given and fixed correspondence, Foucault (1981) has raised crucial questions about whether discourses and practices can ever be assumed to correspond and coincide. Building upon this point, other theorists have argued that radical social theory in the 1990s must confront (a) the problematical issue of the very production of representational subjects, and recognize the contingent character of social, political and self identities, and (b) the notion that interests are anchored in time and space. As a consequence, key problems with representative democracy relate to the mis-representation and non/under/over-representation of particular interests, issues, identities and 'selves':

> Representation involves the surrender of control over decisions to others, so that any control is only exercised indirectly; it constitutes a condition of inequality, whereby only a few are entitled to take part in the decision making and the vast majority are excluded (Beetham, 1993, p. 62).

> Definitions of democracy and good governance that focus on electoral participation are a potent instrument of social control. Elections offer the illusion of participation in exchange for political quiescence. In sum, they limit and constrain ones interaction with our government - substituting subordination for the promised liberation of participative democracy (Petrecca, 1990, p. 121).

It is within this context of indirect democracy that the normative issue of the accountability of the representative individual or institution takes on paramount importance:

> Political accountability begins when individuals are given responsibility for carrying out tasks on behalf of their fellow citizens. The division of civic labour, the delegation of particular roles to individual citizens, creates the demand for political as distinct from personal accountability (Day and Klein, 1987, p. 6).

In a situation of partial participation, where the community must depend upon stewards, there must be mechanisms for ensuring 'truth-telling' and 'securing conformity between the values of a delegating body and the person or persons to whom powers and responsibilities are delegated' (Robertson, 1985, p. 3). However, 'accountability', as a concept, is also deeply problematic. Day and Klein have argued that it is necessary to recognize and distinguish between different levels and often competing forms of accountability. The political level necessitates being held to account for and justifying policy decisions; the legal level for adhering to statutory procedures, rules and regulations; and the managerial level for ensuring that those with delegated authority are 'answerable for carrying out agreed tasks according to agreed criteria of performance' (Day and Klein, 1987, p. 27).

However, it has become increasingly difficult to separate and rank these different levels of accountability. In relation to public services and activities, citizens in a liberal democracy may view the political as the overarching and deciding form of accountability, but legal duties and requirements can override, determine or constrain any policy proposal. Policy implementation must remain within the law, irrespective of the democratic mandate. Similarly, within an organizational setting, 'the managerial' may challenge rather than be subordinate to 'the political' because of the level of legal and auditing expertise needed to assess the viability of policy proposals.

Given that accountability has been traditionally premised on having clear ideas about who can be called to account, to whom and for what, the blurring of the lines between political, managerial and legal forms of accountability has had serious consequences in complex representative democracies. The reality is that it has become increasingly difficult to realize accountability, especially prospective accountability, in any form. Impunity has become the norm. And in many respects the erosion of democratic values and the crisis of representative democracy are directly connected to the crisis of accountability. It is precisely these crises which can be identified in a variety of 'advanced' social formations in the late twentieth century.

In the case of Britain, it is possible to identify the dramatic post-war structural changes as the root cause of these contemporary crises. The edifice of liberal democratic citizenship was constructed upon the welfare state (premised upon notions of universalism), the adaptation of capital and labour to the notion of a mixed economy and a political consensus about the continued existence of capitalism (Hall et al, 1978, p. 228). An historic settlement was reached 'under which all citizens enjoyed certain civil, political and social rights' (Gamble, 1988, p. 11). Hence, a framework of full formal rights of representation was characteristic of the advanced liberal democratic state form.

However, the post-war settlement also constituted an incomplete process of democratization both in itself and because of the nature of the settlement. Jordan has argued the British establishment remained 'fundamentally suspicious of democratic principles'(1985, p. 341). And Arblaster (1987, p. 63) maintains that, despite claims to the contrary, in the twentieth century concerted efforts were made to restructure democracy so that popular participation was treated with suspicion, 'if not regarded as positively undesirable'. It is within this context, he argues, that 'thin' procedural notions of representative parliamentary democracy became hegemonic, with politicians claiming to 'know' intuitively the interests of their constituents. Thus, at the same time as the state negotiated over formal institutionalized rights of representation, a concurrent process of de-democratization was taking place. Non-democratic institutions such as the House of Lords, the monarchy, the security services, the military and the judiciary remained outside of the structures of democratic accountability, as did key sectors of decision making, most significantly economic ones (Hindess, 1983; Bentley, 1984; Leys, 1984; Arblaster, 1987; Hirst, 1988).

The rise in the 1960s of corporatism, and the corresponding concentration of decision-making powers in the hands of powerful elites, were the most visible manifestations that the formal democratic process was becoming substantively meaningless. The state, in its attempt to represent both the interests of capital and class, entered into a compact with those groups whose consent was seen to be central to the effective management of the economy. While such an historic class compromise benefited those powerful groups who had gained additional and substantive representation, the interests of the powerless found no meaningful expression within the new consensus (Lindblom, 1977; Jessop, 1980; Offe, 1980; Lash and Urry, 1987). As was indicated in the discussion of the reconstitution of the police committees, the move to a corporatist state also had serious consequences for local democracy because local government was restructured to act as an apolitical mechanism for the realization of central state policies. The end result of this shift 'was a centralized local government system heavily bureaucratized and professionalized, remote from a local public who often showed so little interest in electoral participation' (Bassett, 1984, p. 94).

Corporatist modes of representation, both locally and nationally, also produced new contradictions, antagonisms and sites of struggle. By the prioritization of certain powerful interests, the powerless were systematically marginalized and excluded from the edifice of citizenship (Held and Krieger, 1982). Thus, it became manifestly clear that there was a considerable discrepancy between formal and substantive rights of citizenship. This took on particular significance in Britain's inner cities because they had been subject to constant redevelopment and were the first to experience the fall out of the economic downturn in the late 1960s. As Friend and Metcalfe (1981) documented, it was the unskilled, the semi-skilled, the immigrants, the old and one parent families who bore the brunt of urban de-industrialization and social dislocation. The result was a much more fragmented social structure than the one upon which the post-war consensus had been initially premised.

Another consequence was the collapse of confidence in and acceptability of the political parties and institutions which had championed such corporatist policies (Held, 1984). Manifest favouritism resulted in the erosion of the electoral support among those social groups not represented by the special negotiations. Furthermore, the corporatist arrangements were not 'delivering' to the satisfaction of those groups whose interests were supposed to be formally represented in the various arrangements. Consequently, the two main political parties attracted an ever smaller percentage of the total vote. Low levels of participation indicated that the parliamentary representative process was being consciously rejected. The institutions of the British state thus faced in the inner cities a legitimation crisis with critics condemning it for being unresponsive, invasive, inefficient and unrepresentative.

It is possible to identify two outcomes of this deep disenchantment and disillusionment. Baudrillard (1983) argues that in the last decades of the twentieth century - the 'most degenerated, artificial, and most eclectic phase in history' - the masses ceased to participate because the 'signs' of the political and the social ceased to have meaning - they were effectively drained of all content. Consequently, there is:

> no longer any political investiture because there is no longer even any social referent of the classical kind (a people, a class, a proletariat, objective conditions) to lend force to effective political signs. Quite simply, there is no longer any social signified to give force to a political signifier (1983, p. 19).

He argues that the masses effectively declined to speak and therefore refused to be manipulated any longer by politicians and the media. As a consequence of this disinterest in the process of public representation:

> No one can be said to represent the silent majority and that is its revenge. The masses are no longer an authority to which one might refer as one formerly referred to a class or to the people (1983, p. 22).

And it is here that we can locate the origins of the potency of radical right critiques of social democracy and the concurrent commitment to free the sovereign individual from the bondage of the state.

The second more 'positive' response was the renewed effort to realize alternative localized forms of radical participatory democracy which could secure unmediated forms of accountability (Pateman, 1970; Richardson, 1983; Barber, 1984; Held and Politt, 1986; Mouffe and Laclau, 1986; Bachrach and Botwinick, 1992; Fishkin, 1992):

> Fresh demands for participation were put forward, and these generated fresh discussion about this supposedly obsolete concept. Trends towards the centralization and bureaucratization of power, far from being accepted with resignation, generated an opposition which stressed the virtues of smallness, accessibility, openness and decentralization (Arblaster, 1987, p. 57).

Participation

Participation is universally seen to be an essential component of democracy on several grounds. To begin with, it is an inclusive process and as such it empowers citizens to become involved equally and directly in the processes which affect their lives. Second, it is a transformative process because the developmental and educative effects of participation enable citizens to ascertain and articulate their needs and interests. Third, it is the only possible basis for legitimate legal authority. Fourth, it is the process through which human social solidarity can be created. And finally it acknowledges that 'democracy' describes a dynamic ideal not a politically existing institution, but a political project (Pateman, 1970). These are the powerful reasons why advocates of direct democracy argue that it is the only fully valid and legitimate democratic form:

> That is what democracy was originally understood to mean: the people governing themselves, without mediation through chosen representatives, directly or, if necessary, by the rotation of governing offices among the citizens (Arblaster, 1987, p. 62).

Rustin (1984) maintains that face to face deliberative decision making, after due discussion must be the proper socialist definition of democracy while Mouffe argues that radical socialism must deepen and expand liberal democratic ideology in order to create a radical, vigorous and emancipatory polity where:

> everyone, whatever his/her sex, race, economic position, sexual orientation, will be in an effective situation of equality and participation, where no basis of discrimination will remain and where self-management will exist in all fields - this is what the ideal of socialism for us should mean today (1984, p.143).

Participatory theory also posits that it is only through direct democratic deliberation that the problems of accountability identified in the previous section can be effectively confronted. From this perspective, representative democracy stands accused of being intrinsically incapable of creating meaningful citizen involvement. It is, therefore, antithetical to the survival of a healthy public domain:

> representation destroys participation and citizenship...representative

democracy is as paradoxical an oxymoron as our language has produced; its confused and failing practice make this ever more obvious (Barber, 1984, p. 43).

However, the proponents of participatory democracy have also conceded that a series of problems have to be confronted, although by definition never resolved, if their 'political imaginary' is to be furthered. To begin with, there is the issue of active versus passive forms of participation. For many theorists it is crucial to recognize that social and political relations are dynamic and in constant flux. Consequently, notions of democratic participation must be constantly re-imagined and re-embedded in new times and new spaces (Rustin, 1984).

But feminist epistemologies, which have maintained that the abstract 'public' rights inevitably 'authorize the male experience of the world' (MacKinnon, 1983) and have been at the forefront in advocating decentering, non-hierarchical, pre-figurative networks of self-organization, have also noted that an undue emphasis on active participation can result in coerced participation or the effective disenfranchisement of those unable or unwilling to participate (Sunstein, 1990; Phillips, 1991; Iannello, 1992). An active 'political' realm, as well as being potentially emancipatory, is intensive and arduous in terms of resources and time, and remains a gendered space:

> the very notion of the active citizen presumes someone else is taking care of the children and doing the necessary maintenance of everyday life (Phillips, 1993, p. 100).

It would seem then that procedures have to be put in place to ensure that absence does not mean exclusion - absence just complicates the process of representation of interests.

A further source of difficulty relates to the inter-connected matter of mobilized versus voluntary participation. Should 'top-down' projects and structural arrangements consciously sponsored by the state, at whatever level, or its institutions and para-agencies, be designated as active participation or as distortion and manipulation? Should definitions of authentic participation be restricted to spontaneous 'grass roots' activities initiated by citizens in pursuit of their own interests?

It is also necessary to acknowledge the structural constitution of power which 'prohibits, which refuses, and which has a whole range of negative effects: exclusion, rejection, denial, obstruction, obfuscation' (Foucault, 1977, p. 183-4). Foucault also reminds his readers that power is 'not an institution, and not a structure; neither is it a certain strength we are endowed with; it is the name that one attributes to a complex strategical situation in a particular society' (1979, p. 93). This leads him to argue that power is not a concrete commodity that can be given away or bestowed. It is only through resistances to power that alternative forms of power come into being.

On this point, Pateman (1970) has identified two forms of participation: full, where individuals are equally empowered, and partial where multiple forms of subordination ensure that one party/group retains ultimate control. And Richardson (1983, p. 25) has argued that effective power 'the combination of resources which groups mobilize in their cause [is] the critical variable determining who gets what in the end'. It must therefore be borne in mind that:

> Groupings vary in cohesiveness, territorial dispersement, skills and experience, resources (especially money), size, the intensity of feelings of support they engender, and even in their sheer ability to use techniques for their own advantage (Spitz, 1984, p. 138).

Therefore, complex normative notions of equality of: opportunity, ability to participate and power to affect the outcome of any given issue must be given serious consideration. Dahl (1989) argues that if people are not empowered or do not have the resources or status to affect outcomes or veto policy decisions that specifically disadvantage them, they will not voluntarily and actively participate. The fullest possible forms of democratic deliberation therefore necessitate the operationalization of specific structures and principles of 'justice', 'equality' and 'fairness' that will address positively the processes of structural, cultural and psychological disempowerment, and mediate between competing needs and interests. As Young has argued:

> the inclusion and participation of everyone in social and political institutions therefore sometimes requires the articulation of special rights that attend to group differences in order to undermine oppression and disadvantage (1990, p. 120).

If power is not re-articulated and re-constituted within a radical democratic framework and inequalities of power are not subject to democratic justification and actively resisted, there is every possibility that participatory structures will be manipulated through the 'ventriloquized voices' of the traditionally empowered. As Arblaster cautions:

> Accessibility and a readiness to listen are not...incompatible with a fundamentally authoritarian structure of power and government. Nor is making a show of consultation and participation, when what is being looked for is essentially a ratification of decisions already taken (1987,

p. 43).

It was this problematic that led the pre-war East London Claimants Union to warn its members:

> any of this 'participation' would be a sell out to the system and an attempt on the part of the establishment to absorb our militancy. To the establishment, participation merely means that a few of us will help them make decisions about us (quoted in Richardson, 1983, p. 59).

However, if the rights of particular groups and individuals are 'overprivileged' in order to achieve such an 'equalization', by definition, this constitutes a deviation from the core principle of all perspectives and experiences having equal validity. If restrictive rights of access and veto are brought into play in order to promote a just dialogue and democratic outcomes, there is the danger of constituting an essentialist privileging of certain interests and groups.

In order to ensure adequate representation of 'the authentic self', if indeed this is possible, those participating must also be in full and equal possession of the relevant information upon which to consider alternatives before reaching a decision:

> Compounding inequalities in the opportunity or ability to participate in the early part of the policy making process is the unequal distribution of information (Spitz, 1984, p. 138).

Arblaster argues that access to information and expertise is fundamental to any participatory project:

> it also requires a distribution of the resources for propaganda and persuasion which ensures that the power to influence our minds is distributed roughly in accord with the degree of diversity of opinion within society (Arblaster, 1987, p. 96).

On this point, Foucault (1979) has sought to demonstrate theoretically the critical connection between knowledge and power and identified the discursive processes through which certain knowledges have been subjugated, disqualified and defined as 'the infidel'. And, in these deliberations, the work of Habermas on the role of 'rational' and 'undistorted' communication in the construction of a 'truly' democratic discourse and vibrant public realm is of direct significance. Habermas recognizes that in any given situation there are inequalities between parties and substantive restraints affecting the capability to participate effectively.

The critical point of participation is to bring interests into 'being' and to arrive at a meaningful and abiding decision 'through discursive will formation, with adequate knowledge of the limiting conditions and fundamental imperatives of society' (Habermas, 1976, p. 113). Any possibility of individuals and groups becoming aware of what their real needs are can only be achieved through participation and rational procedures of free and unconstrained communication:

> The goal of coming together to an understanding is to bring about an agreement that terminates in the intersubjective mutuality of reciprocal understanding, shared knowledge, mutual trust, and accord with one another. Agreement is based on the corresponding validity claims of comprehensibility, truth, truthfulness, and rightness (Habermas, 1979, p. 3).

Genuine consensus, defined as the co-operative search for truth and a resolution of conflict, can only be brought about through unimpeded communication where external constraints do not prevent participants from evaluating evidence and argument. Each citizen must have an open and equal chance of entering into a debate in which they willingly observe the force of democratically grounded reasoning. The opposite situation is where participants are engaged in pseudo-communication which generates 'a system of reciprocal misunderstandings' or 'systematically distorted communication'. Arato and Cohen have argued that Habermas' modernized rational 'life-world' would necessitate the use of no force except the force of better argument and:

> the communicative opening up of the sacred core of traditions, norms and authority to processes of questioning and discursive adjudication. It entails the replacement of a conventionally based normative consensus by one that is reflexive post-conventional and grounded in open processes of communication (1992, p. 202).

However, postmodernists warn that the distinction between 'real' and 'false' needs embedded in the Habermasian notion of rational communicative action is no longer tenable because of the 'implosion of the real'. The fracturing and problematizing of the social and the political means that there are no longer any collective points of reference, public vocabulary or commonality of interest that can be 'uncovered' through speech participation. Lyotard (1984) also condemns Habermas' modernist project as oppressive, and argues that what is needed to avoid repression, manipulation, incorporation and domestication, is not a quest for rational conciliation but the preservation of dissent, antagonism and difference. There must be the recognition of a multiplicity of equally valid perspectives and experiences and not just a bourgeois obsession with 'others' having to 'learn' how to participate and be represented in the structures of the powerful.

Other postmodernists such as Lyall and Soutter (1993) have celebrated the healthy political import of violent 'archaic', 'irrational' 'ruptures' rather than the quest for stifling institutional (and ultimately disempowering) consensus, describing, for example, the 'flaming' of south central Los Angeles in 1992 as the 'pleasurable madness of the day'. For such writers 'the carnival of the riot' and 'that petrol emotion' (the continuation of politics by other means) are ultimate, if fleeting, moments of empowerment. This important critique echoes the seminal work of Piven and Cloward (1977) on 'dissensus politics'. They argue that the powerless can only influence matters through systematic 'institutional disruptions', ranging from lawful protests through to violent confrontations, which unmask fundamental and often irreconcilable contradictions and conflicts. It is only the legitimate threat of 'no justice, no peace' that brings about meaningful dialogue (see also, Aya, 1990). Thus the implication is that if the powerless play the game by respectable Habermasian rules, they will inevitably be co-opted, neutralized or compromised. The right not to participate by conventional means must, therefore, be acknowledged and accepted.

Discussion

From this discussion of the problems of democratic theory and practice, it would seem that a series of complex issues have to be confronted by those who argue that in a democratic society accountable policing can only be achieved through community representation and participation. If these issues are not addressed satisfactorily, the project will be flawed, and there is every possibility that marginalized and dissenting voices will not participate or be adequately represented. The central issue is whether it is possible, to imagine flexible, spontaneous arrangements, processes and necessary conditions that: first, work with a complex concept of community that recognizes inequality, plurality, fragmentation, heterogeneity, antagonism and conflict of interests; second, ensure adequate representation of interests by producing open, genuine and ongoing dialogue about 'real' needs and concerns; and finally facilitate direct and maximum participation by being empowered to bring about visible and meaningful transformations.

It must be stressed that, given the far-reaching and disparate theoretical problems identified in the course of this discussion, that it may not be possible to ever realize such ideal democratic arrangements, particularly if the sceptical postmodernists are accurate in their analysis of the 'death of the public' and the un-representable 'silent majority'. And, has been indicated previously, there is evidence to suggest that the crisis in representative democracy has led to deep cynicism with and alienation from 'the political' in the case of key sections of society. What this means is that any radical democratic project or imagining needs to start with an awareness and acknowledgement of these problems because, as the research findings reported in the rest of this book indicate, it will have to confront them in practice.

3 Policing Manchester 1976–81

In April 1976 James Anderton, who started his career in the Manchester City Police in 1953, became the chief constable of the Greater Manchester Police, the largest provincial police force in Britain. Anderton in many respects remains the prime example of a new breed of post-war professional police chiefs who adopted a high political and media profile in order to shape public opinion on policing, crime and the social order, because they regarded policing as an 'ideology in its own right' (Kettle, 1979; see also Reiner, 1991). This particular cohort of chief police officers were the fortunate beneficiaries of the legal, organizational and political changes detailed in chapter one. They also came to power at a moment when Britain was descending rapidly into serious social, economic and political crisis and tumultuous change (Hall et al, 1978). This crisis was to be the background against which they constructed and lived out their professional careers. For most of the 1980s, James Anderton and the Greater Manchester Police were never far from the centre of the maelstrom. And it was Anderton's controversial public pronouncements and actions that provoked a sustained campaign for police accountability in Greater Manchester. Hence, in order to understand the origins of this campaign, it is necessary to examine the chief constable's policing philosophy.

The Greater Manchester Police and the community

Until his retirement in 1991, James Anderton consistently voiced his concern about the moral state of British society, vociferously defended the autonomy of chief police officers from political interference and labelled those who dared to demand a strengthening of the structures of accountability as subversives. Although his statements achieved national and international prominence, it was in the local policing context that they had most impact.

The following fundamental beliefs about the community underpinned this policing philosophy. First, Anderton repeatedly stressed the 'traditional and unique partnership between the community and its police force', and compared the nature of the relationship 'to that which operates in a well conducted family where there is complete trust and confidence and an absence of any kind of deception whatsoever' (Annual Report, 1979, p. xiv). In his numerous speeches and statements it is possible to detect the clear idea that, for the chief constable, 'the community' was made up of those respectable people, irrespective of class, race, gender and age, who both supported and respected the police and the law of the land.

Second, as far as he was concerned, the chief constable and the police force were 'fully accountable to the community both directly and through the business of the police committee' (Annual Report, 1979, p. viii). Anderton always claimed that he was willing to provide the police committee with reports and answer questions as long as committee members accepted the legal, technical and constitutional ground rules laid down by the 1964 Police Act. He made it clear that it was the duty of the police committee to support its police force and that he would oppose any attempts by elected representatives to 'interfere' in operational matters. Third, the chief constable emphasized that there was an ever-present conspiracy to undermine the relationship between the community and its police force. Fourth, a 'loss of community' thesis also informed his statements about the inner city areas of Greater Manchester. Anderton, in his statements, harked back constantly to a time 'when life was rather less complicated than it is today' (Anderton, 1985b). The police, he was convinced, had the impossible task of handling blighted inner city urban areas where there was 'a dispirited and trammelled populace', moral decline, diverse standards of living, large scale unemployment, poor housing and multi-cultural values, and where crime was endemic, actively involving whole communities. Of such neighbourhoods he asked, 'how on earth do we reach these people'?

Finally, given his analysis of the nature of the relationship between the police and the community, the chief constable believed that it was the duty of the police to intervene actively to halt the 'drifting morality' and improve 'the quality of community life'. This was particularly important when politicians and community leaders had 'reneged' on their responsibilities and had lost the trust of the people. Anderton quite correctly sensed that there was considerable community alienation from the agencies, personnel and practices of the local state. His conviction that civilized democracy was on the point of collapse in Britain led him to state that:

> our police will be the one body left to erect an umbrella of public confidence and safety under which all social agencies can shelter; the

one truly trusted profession attracting the unwavering support of the public *(Manchester Evening News,* 12 March 1982).

Thus, the chief constable's view of the community and the police was one where both he and his force were of the community, intuitively acting in the best interests of the community and being inherently responsive to the needs of the community. Within this schema of things, those who were critical of the police were, by definition, not representative of the community, and whether through naivety or malice were not acting in the best interests of the community. In many respects, they were not of the community at all.

At the heart of the chief constable's statements and actions there was, therefore, a coherent ideological understanding of the proper relationship between the police and community that provided the context for routine policework in Greater Manchester. Anderton consistently stressed that policing in Greater Manchester was community-based and argued that effective protection of the community required the deployment of hard and soft strategies. Residents of inner city Manchester soon became aware after his appointment that James Anderton's force operated with both a gentle touch and an iron fist.

The gentle touch

Because of the chief constable's views on the role of the police in the community and the loss of community in inner city neighbourhoods, community involvement was strengthened to compensate for the previous fifteen years in which the police had not been members of the community (Kettle, 1979). Police contact was established with the various district council departments, particularly those of Manchester City Council. The chief superintendent of each division was allocated liaison responsibility for each of the key local social service departments. Thus a police initiated professional multi-agency approach was informally established as part of the community work of the force.

During 1976-7 a fully fledged Community Contact department became operational and subsumed within it the traditional focus of police-community relations, young people and 'ethnic minorities'. This department became one of the best resourced and most innovative in the country and the nature of its work gives an indication of how the Greater Manchester Police dealt with 'problem' groups. By 1980, the Greater Manchester Police had constructed a community policing infrastructure, which was both an expression of the chief constable's beliefs about the vanguard role of the police in the community, and designed to show that the Greater Manchester Police was a caring police force, in tune with the community and committed to policing by consent. Almost inevitably, it was the police force itself rather than the police committee that assumed frontline responsibility for liaising with the public.

Young people

The chief constable laid particular emphasis on making contact with young people, as he believed that society had failed in its duty to provide proper guidance and discipline for its young, particularly those living in the inner cities:

> The Police Service in the past has adopted a relatively passive policy in the matter of direct intervention in social affairs, but I am now practically convinced that we are as well equipped as any institution to help in guiding and influencing society in what is best for young people...the police must take such action as appears to them appropriate before it becomes too late (Anderton, 1976).

It became force policy in Greater Manchester to concentrate on young people because they were easily led into crime and anti-social activities, and because through the young people the force was able to make contact with the parents. Police officers attempted to foster special relations, for example, with single parents who were characteristic of the inner city, and reported that 'to the very young children police officers take the role of the father figure' (Community Contact, 27 July 1981). Community Contact also arranged summer adventure playgrounds, soccer competitions and holidays, as well as joint work experience programmes with the Manpower Services Commission for inner city youth. On 6 June 1980, the force opened a highly controversial police-run youth club which had a sub-station on the premises, in the north of Manchester. The club was proudly viewed by the force as 'the pinnacle of the most intensive youth policy of any force in the country' (*Scene*, 1981, p. 8).

Community Contact had a very clear understanding about the purpose of its youth club. Police involvement was officially geared towards: helping to compensate for the 'inadequate' home backgrounds of deprived youth; giving young officers an opportunity to participate in the community that they worked in but did not live in; breaking down the barriers between police and young people and, in the long run, reducing the crime rate. Another important role was to counter the 'anti-establishment' progressive youth work supposedly being practised in other clubs in the vicinity. Community Contact officers openly expressed 'distaste for some of youth work's theories and practices', and stressed that the proper role of youth clubs was to instill discipline and order in young people. In addition to their youth work, Community Contact had regular contact with education establishments, presenting lectures on the history of the British police and 'Police Weeks' devoted to explaining the role of the police in society, and the duties and responsibilities of the general public.

Ethnic minorities

Considerable attention was also paid by the Community Contact to ethnic minorities because, as the chief constable made clear, 'occasionally, as a result of language barriers and lack of understanding, problems arise in which the police are involved' (Anderton, 1980, p. 56). Building upon links that had first been established in the late 1960s, contact was formalized through a special Community Relations Unit. Greater Manchester Police was thus represented on the committees of minority organizations and 'community leaders' were appointed onto the force training programmes. However, the force made it clear that it would not liaise with politically motivated community groups. Therefore, there were clearly delineated limits to its consultation process.

There was considerable overlap between the initiatives that focused on ethnic minorities and the ones that focused on young people. In both cases, community police officers limited those to whom they were prepared to talk. As a result, youth and community workers and community organizations which did not accept the official line that problems between police and blacks and young people were the result of communication and cultural difficulties were excluded. These individuals and groups were eventually identified as central participants in a conspiracy to discredit the chief constable and undermine the Greater Manchester Police.

The iron fist

In the same time period, the force showed itself to be a formidable and highly controversial presence in its dealings with certain sections of the community. After Anderton became chief constable, the police committee agreed to the acquisition of expensive and sophisticated computer and surveillance equipment, and by 1979 the force was reputed to have the most extensive police arsenal in Britain (*State Research*, 1981). Anderton also prepared his officers for a high profile war against crime. In 1976, at the same time as the Community Contact branch was becoming operational, an elite paramilitary unit, the Tactical Aid Group (TAG), initially comprising seventy-two officers, was formed, which was to be the source of regular controversy. Concern about this unit was subsequently heightened by the disclosure that ninety-five per cent of its officers were trained and authorized to use hand weapons (Annual Report, 1978). There were also blitzkrieg crackdowns on prostitution, illegal drinking, gay clubs and pornography.

The impact was immediate. In 1976, for example, fifty-five search warrants were executed under the Obscene Publications Act and there were proceedings in twenty-five cases. The comparable figures in 1977 were 287 warrants and 134 proceedings. 'War' was declared on 'muggers', particularly in the Moss Side area and, following the example of the New York Police Department, police decoys were deployed in an attempt to lure 'muggers' into the open. In the autumn of 1977, without informing either the police committee or local residents, paramilitary anti-terrorist manoeuvres were held in the Collyhurst area of north Manchester which effectively sealed off the area for the duration of the exercise. Despite local protests, the chief constable refused to discuss the operation (*Guardian*, 2 November 1977; *Morning Star*, 3 November 1977).

During this period, Anderton also dealt with National Front marches in Greater Manchester in a highly contentious manner. In October 1977, after initially banning a proposed National Front march, he met secretly with leaders of that organization and agreed to allow a march to take place if the location were kept secret. In order to control anti-fascist demonstrators, the force was placed on emergency stand by, reinforcements were called in from nine other forces and helicopters with air-to-ground cameras were deployed. The estimated cost of the most sophisticated public order operation seen in Britain up to that date was £250,000 (*Times*, 11 October 1977). In January and February 1978, two more massive policing operations allowed Front meetings to take place in Hyde and Bolton town halls, with Anderton making it clear that there would be no repeat of the violence that had marred Front marches in Ladywood (Birmingham) and Lewisham (London) earlier that year.

The chief constable, although he did not inform them of his plans, was publicly supported by both his police committee and Merlyn Rees, the Home Secretary. However, concern was expressed by community groups, local Labour MPs and trade unionists about his facilitation of fascist marches in parts of Greater Manchester with significant ethnic minority populations, and the policing styles that were devised to protect such marches. It was noted that in the course of the three operations, the Greater Manchester Police had become more tactically skilled and effective in dealing with counter-demonstrators. In addition, the protection afforded to the National Front was specifically contrasted to the lack of police protection offered to victims of racist attacks in these communities. Because of the chief constable's actions, Tameside Trades' Council organized an 'Anderton Must Go' campaign. For his part, Anderton subsequently stated that he should not have been placed in the position of having to consider seriously curbing the freedom of speech and the right to protest because of the threat to public order from political extremists:

> it is completely unjust when a chief constable, acting with due discretion and independence under the law and free from political pressure and control, takes a proper and lawful course in line with his duty... [and is] wrongfully accused of bias, prejudice and political motivation (*Times*, 11 April 1978).

The difficulties Anderton encountered in policing the National Front marches prompted him to call for parliament to reform the 'outmoded' public order legislation.

In 1979, the conduct of vice squad officers in Moss Side came under scrutiny when Darcus Howe, a black journalist, was arrested for supposedly obstructing police officers. In the aftermath of this arrest, a group of black community organizations started a campaign both to support Howe and to highlight the policing of black people in Manchester. The trial itself brought into the public gaze some unsavoury aspects concerning the policing of Moss Side and Howe was found not guilty, with costs being awarded against the police (*Race Today*, May 1980).

This incident was indicative, as far as police critics were concerned, of the type of policing to which people in Moss Side had been subjected for decades (Humphrey and John, 1971, pp. 36-7). It needs to be remembered, for example, that in the early 1970s at an in-service training session, police officers informed a representative from the Manchester Council for Community Relations that black people were:

> dirty, immoral, bring down the value of a house, live on immoral earnings, live off crime, bring down the tone of neighbourhoods, are uneducated, have no right to be here and should be sent home (quoted in Banton, 1973, p. 115).

From 1977 onwards there was a widespread belief that the local police were out of control. Complaints about arbitrary stop and searches and arrests, threats and street justice, corruption, drug dealing and the use of illegal weapons by officers based at the Moss Side station were intensifying, and there was no adequate means of redress. This was not helped by the fact that in 1979 the chief constable seemingly gave the seal of approval to such policing by stating publicly that he would 'clean up' Moss Side. During this period, black youth built up clear profiles of the type of treatment they thought they would receive in the assorted police stations encircling their neighbourhoods. 'Communal memory' insisted that Longsight station was the place where juveniles were beaten up, Stretford station was notorious for 'nigger bashing' and there was a deep resentment for the type of treatment meted out at Moss Side's Greenheys station. It is no coincidence that during the disturbances:

> The youth attacked the station with such ferocity that police officers abandoned ship. Revolts of this kind always contain within them violence of equal intensity to that experienced by those in revolt. It was proof positive of the intolerable violence that had been heaped upon generations of Irish and black immigrants by officers who manned that station (*Race Today*, May 1985).

Complaints about the policing of Moss Side continued (particularly from the Manchester Black Parents' group) and there was another march in August 1980 protesting about police harassment of black people. Thus, the implementation of hard policing policies brought forth complaints from various groups in Manchester on the receiving end of such methods, particularly gays, blacks, the young and trade unionists.

Crisis in police-community relations

The focus of both the hard and soft policing strategies was the same - young people and black inner city neighbourhoods of Greater Manchester. While Community Contact officers were communicating with those organizations they defined as respectable, and meeting youth and youth workers who would accept their definition of youth work, their colleagues on ordinary policing duty, including those in the Tactical Aid Group, were 'reaching' young people and black people in very different circumstances.

Home Office research carried out in October 1980 provides 'objective' evidence about the policing of Moss Side in this period. Although the research findings did 'not appear to support a picture of widespread police misbehaviour or of police oppression of minority groups', certain focal points of conflict and discontent were identified. The report notes that the range of anti-police sentiment was more extensive in relation to all West Indian age groups. There was also a statistically significant tendency for West Indians in the 35-54 age group to be stopped, searched and/or arrested more often than their white counterparts. And there was a high frequency of stop and searches, with one in three males between 16-24 having been stopped, searched or arrested in the year prior to the study (Tuck and Southgate, 1980).

Because the Greater Manchester police committee, under the control of the Conservative Party, was practically moribund in terms of questioning the policies of the chief constable, it was left to inner city youth and community workers, along with community groups, to take the lead in complaining about policing practices. For his part, the chief constable viewed his local critics as part of an extensive left-wing conspiracy to overthrow British democracy. He argued that in order for such a conspiracy to succeed, the police had to be weakened and made subordinate to politicians. Thus, criticisms of the police and demands for police accountability were part of the strategy to bring about such political control. As far as he was concerned, all demands for accountability and public inquiries had to be rejected and he reiterated that 'the paramount truth has to be faced that it is the duty of the state to protect the police' from such demands. If the state failed to do this, the police would not be able to protect it from the conspirators.

In his 1979 annual report, in response to criticisms of his policing of Greater Manchester, he argued that the police were being asked to 'defend what need not be defended; to answer what did not have to be questioned; to explain what was already known and abundantly clear; and to account for matters to an exceptional and unreasonable degree'. He specifically refused to countenance any criticism of the Tactical Aid Group and denied that it was a 'tough, hard-hitting paramilitary force':

> Apart from the rather exacting nature of their training, their exceptional physical fitness, their iron discipline and ability to withstand stress and provocation - attributes sought in every police officer - there is really nothing special about the group (*Daily Telegraph*, 15 October 1979).

Between this period and the county council elections of May 1981, Anderton's political interventions became more pronounced, and he aired his conspiracy theory at every opportunity, most notably on BBC *Question Time* (16 October 1979), when he stated that in the 1980s the primary role of the police would not be crime prevention, but quelling attempts to overthrow democracy and subverting the authority of the state. His response to the police bills introduced by Jack Straw was to reiterate that seemingly innocuous demands for accountability were a front for those whose real objective was to gain political control of the police:

> We are witnessing and passively acquiescing in a quiet but hardly bloodless revolution...If disciplined and established institutions like the police service which embody commonly accepted values and stability can somehow be discredited and neutralized, the way is set to demoralize and vanquish the public. Indeed the police service in the United Kingdom represents the largest single obstacle to politically

contrived domination and ultimate totalitarianism (*Times*, 13 May 1980).

This in turn led him to argue, to the consternation of his critics, for the creation of ten regional police forces which would enable an elite group of chief police officers 'to speak with one voice' and defend the institution of the police against its political enemies.

Anderton's accusations linked into allegations about the corrupt nature of local politics and his belief that he was the subject of a local smear campaign:

> There has been a political campaign in the Greater Manchester area, certainly for the past three years...purposefully engineered and clearly designed to discredit me in the eyes of the public...to try to persuade responsible people, well-meaning people...to turn against the police force in general and the chief constable in particular (*Manchester Evening News*, 12 January 1981).

The dispute about the policing of Manchester escalated to a different level, politically, when, after the May 1981 county council elections, a Labour administration which was committed to campaigning for police accountability took control of the Greater Manchester Council, and serious anti-police disturbances broke out in Moss Side in July 1981. As a consequence, those apprehensive about the chief constable's policing strategies finally forced their views onto the local political agenda.

The May 1981 Elections

As part of the Labour Party's election campaign in Manchester, candidates in those areas where policing was an issue stated that they believed that the locally elected council should have strategic responsibility for policing policy and promised that if elected there would be a campaign:

> to make the police accountable to locally elected representatives -so that YOUR views on how the police should spend their limited time and resources can have real importance to ensure all members of the community are treated fairly (Moss Side Labour Party).

On 9 May 1981, Bernard Clarke, the new leader of the Greater Manchester Council, stated that under the new administration the police committee would cease to be a 'mutual appreciation society', and that the chief constable could expect a more rigorous examination of policing practices. James Anderton was also advised that if he did not cease making controversial political statements, he would be subject to the same disciplinary procedures as other senior officers of the council (*Manchester Evening News*, 9 May 1981). The clerk to the committee prepared a paper on the statutory powers and duties of police committees and at the first meeting after the election, the Labour group argued for the removal of the magistrates, a widening of remit of the committee in relation to its jurisdiction and the appointment of senior police officers, and the full integration of the committee into the county council structure. One of the first 'symbolic' actions of the committee was to cut one per cent from the police budget for reallocation to other council services suffering under the first wave of Thatcherite cuts. Thus, from the outset the newly constituted police committee asserted itself in relation to the policing of Greater Manchester. However, no sooner had it taken office than Moss Side erupted on 8 July 1981 and the police committee suddenly found itself in a situation where they had to account publicly for the actions of the forces for which they were formally responsible.

Moss Side, July 1981

It is difficult to piece together an accurate picture of exactly what happened in Moss Side, and in parts of Greater Manchester, between the 8-11 July. One has to rely on partial, selective and 'forgotten' memories of participants and eye witnesses, as well as media reports and official statements, and these are directly linked to multiple ways of 'seeing', 'hearing' and 'remembering'. The trouble started in Moss Side in the early hours of 8 July with shops being spontaneously looted and 'torched'. The following night a large crowd of approximately 2,000 people, which had congregated during the day, launched a serious attack on Moss Side police station and later nearby shops. At the same time, reports were circulating of serious disturbances in Salford as well as 'incidents' in Reddish Bridge, Clayton and Rusholme. It was this 'escalation' that led to a major police offensive to clear the streets of Moss Side and, after another night of skirmishes, the disturbances officially ended on 11 July.

The policing strategy used embodied both the soft and hard approaches documented above. After initial trouble, which the chief constable played down as 'a case very simply of arson and serious looting', there were what turned out to be highly controversial meetings between senior officers of 'E' division in Moss Side and community leaders. The purpose of the discussion:

> was to bring together the community and the police so that older members of the various ethnic groups could help the police to influence

the younger people and avoid an escalation of violence (Anderton, 1981, p. 1817).

An instructive insight into how the chief constable looked upon community representation on policing issues is provided in his report on the disturbances. He recounted that when a group of young blacks demanded access to the meetings as representatives of the black youth of Moss Side, senior police officers in charge could not accommodate the request because it was force procedure to 'have discussions only with the elders of the community'. Given this procedure, it is not surprising that Anderton had also to report that despite this community consultation, further disturbances took place and 'demonstrated in a very real way that representatives of the community in the area had little or no influence or control over the people concerned in this rioting' (1981, p. 3).

The chief constable subsequently implied that the 'fact' that the community leaders had no control over the situation was one of the reasons why he had been forced to switch from a low profile approach to the use of hard policing tactics in order to re-establish control of Moss Side. Anderton was also under considerable pressure to act in a decisive and firm manner for two other reasons. Many of the officers he had sent to Merseyside on 5-6 July had suffered extensive injuries in Liverpool 8 - such a casualty level on home territory would have seriously damaged the force psyche. In addition, rumours abounded that the police had lost control and that 'the mob' was threatening to attack surrounding neighbourhoods, especially the nearby city centre business district and the shopping arcades. The headlines in the *Manchester Evening News* did nothing to allay community fears: 'LOOTING BLITZ IN MOSS SIDE'; 'PARADISE LOST...FROM HAVEN TO GHETTO'; 'HOOLIGAN ARMY'S ORGY OF LOOTING'; 'CRIME ORGY'; 'GUERILLA WAR IN MOSS SIDE'; 'LIKE A SCENE FROM DANTE'S INFERNO'; 'STREETS OF BLIND FURY'.

Anderton proclaimed that his officers were now facing systematic 'guerilla warfare' on the streets. Thus, spontaneity and mindlessness had given way to orchestration and conspiracy in the police view of events. His message for the people of Manchester was that the youth of Moss Side should desist because:

> The police do not want a war with the young. That can never be the answer. Nobody wants a war. The victors become complacent through success and the vanquished nurse their grievances for ever (*Guardian*, 10 July 1981).

However, despite such sentiments, the 'Force Contingency Plan' was executed. The city centre was 'secured' against rioters, extra personnel carriers were made available and 'mobile charge centres' were set up to process the anticipated mass arrests (for a discussion of the 'mass arrests' strategy, see Vogler, 1991, pp. 150-6). The police, in newly acquired riot gear, then 'swamped' Moss Side, with the Tactical Aid Group spearheading the response. However, the tactics used in Moss Side were different from elsewhere. It was decided not to deploy officers in a traditional manner (as had happened in Bristol, London and Liverpool), because it would encourage predictable set piece large scale confrontations and inevitably heavy police casualties would result. Instead, police support groups were deployed in vans in order to ensure a rapid and flexible mobile response. The result was that, at all times, the police retained the initiative and the element of chaotic surprise:

> Twenty-four police wagons, each manned by ten steel-helmeted riot police, roared around the shopping and housing area pinning black and white youths to the walls and arresting them. Several youths were knocked to the ground by the wagons...The rioters moved on to take up positions in high rise flats and flyovers to hurl down rocks on the wagons. Later snatch squads of police moved into the flats. Youths - black and white - were kicked to the ground before being taken away (*Daily Mirror,* 10 July 1981).

Thus, the Greater Manchester Police, as in its handling of the National Front demonstrations, proved itself to be at the forefront in developing 'positive' riot control tactics which were suited to the 1980s. As Anderton subsequently stated, the logic behind the new strategy was:

> When trouble arises and violence occurs on the street, you hit it fast and hard. And that's what we did the following night. We hit the rioters fast and hard with all the force at out disposal - legitimate and lawful force - and we crushed the riots in Manchester in twenty-four hours (Anderton, 1992).

The chief constable was subsequently praised for the manner in which he had brought the Manchester disturbances to a swift conclusion, with William Whitelaw, the Home Secretary, describing the operation as a 'conspicuous success'(*Times,* 11 July 1981). There had been few police casualties and the Greater Manchester Police did not have to face the ignominy of having to retreat as had the forces in other cities. Crucially, for the morale of officers on the ground, the authority of the force had been maintained - Moss Side did not become a no-go area.

Initially, certain community leaders emphasized that the disturbances were not anti-police and the 'copy cat' theory was much in evidence in the comments of these representatives. However, bitter recriminations about the way in which the disturbances were handled and the conduct of police officers were gradually voiced.

Demands for a public inquiry

Questions were initially asked by local shopkeepers about why the police, during the first night of the disturbances, had not intervened and had been seemingly content to let Moss Side, and their shops, burn. It was alleged that the police had deliberately let Moss Side 'go up' to teach the people of the area a lesson, and to mobilize support for the implementation of the Force Contingency Plan. However, this initial concern was lost amongst widespread allegations about the behaviour of police officers during the second night. The Moss Side Defence Committee emerged to mobilize opposition to racist policing and to defend those who had been arrested during the uprising (Moss Side Defence Committee, 13 July 1981). Youth and community leaders refused to meet the Home Secretary during his visit to Moss Side in the aftermath of the disturbances because of his statements about co cat disturbances.

Community Contact faced serious opposition in their attempts to re-establish relations. A proposed 'police week' at a local school in Moss Side had to be aborted because pupils opposed the presence of police in their school and parents threatened to keep their children at home if the event took place. Considerable anxiety was expressed about their proposals to take as many youngsters as possible from Moss Side on a hastily constructed police holiday to the Lake District. A series of police initiated 'clear-the-air' meetings with local youth had to be cancelled because of allegations that the police were attempting to pressurize local youth into attending the meetings. Letters were also sent to the chief constable from residents of one of the local housing estates where the policing had been heaviest, complaining about the racist and brutal behaviour of officers.

The complaints took on even more force when ultra-respectable community leaders and representatives voiced their anxieties about the policing of Moss Side. The Bishop of Manchester, during a service on 19 July 1981, said he believed the allegations that police officers had used 'abusive language and undue force' when dealing with black people. The chair of the Manchester Council of Community Relations also expressed concern about the policing of Moss Side. The vice-chair of the police committee, Gabrielle Cox, who was the elected representative for the area, made similar allegations and officially complained to the chief constable, whilst a local doctor released case details of the injuries he had treated and said that in the light of them he now had to recognize that the past allegations of police brutality in Manchester were probably true. The Haldane Society also expressed dissatisfaction about the manner in which magistrates were dealing with cases arising out of the disturbances. Thus considerable pressure was forthcoming from various respectable quarters for the setting up of an independent inquiry which would examine the causes of the disturbances and the policing of Moss Side.

The chief constable did little to allay the growing concern about the policing of the disturbances. Predictably, he repeated his allegations that people from outside the community had been involved, that there had been a conspiracy to 'torch' Moss Side and that his officers had to deal with organized guerilla warfare on the streets of Manchester. He repudiated the accusations that his force was racist in its policing practices and rejected initial demands for an inquiry, saying that if he had to hold one every time there were rumours of dissatisfaction with the police:

> It would be open to anyone with more malicious intent to create severe internal problems for the police. That surely is desperately unfair. There is an established procedure and it is open to members of the public to use it (*Times*, 21 July 1981).

His only concession was to give his personal assurance that if people used the proper complaints' procedure, all grievances would be investigated.

However, as the pressure mounted, both locally and nationally, assistant chief constable John Stalker was appointed to head an internal inquiry into allegations of police misconduct. He gave the ominous warning that everyone who had made a complaint would be interviewed by the investigative team, and those deemed guilty of making unfounded or malicious complaints would be subject to criminal proceedings. It is hardly surprising that this promise of an internal police investigation did little to assuage the intensifying demands for an independent inquiry. Those insisting on such a course of action looked to both Manchester City Council and the Greater Manchester Council to authorize such an inquiry.

The Hytner inquiry

Certain Labour representatives, particularly those representing Moss Side, pressed for Manchester City Council to discuss the policing of the disturbances. These demands were initially rebuffed by the right-wing Labour leadership and instead an all-party statement was released, supporting the police in their efforts to maintain law and order. However, the requests for a public discussion continued, with Moss Side Labour party calling for the setting up of an independent joint inquiry between the city and county councils to investigate both the causes of the disturbances and complaints of heavy-handed policing. After bitter argument between the left and the right of the Labour Party, Manchester City Council finally agreed in July 1981 that Lord Scarman should be asked to extend the range of his inquiry to include Manchester.

In the meantime, as a matter of urgency, the Greater Manchester Council hosted, with the Greater Manchester Youth Association, a conference of community and political representatives on 15 July 1981 to discuss what could be done to prevent further disorder. On 22 July 1981 it was announced that there would be a county council sponsored inquiry, made up of representatives of ethnic minorities and youth organizations. The Hytner Inquiry (named after the chair of the inquiry, Benet Hytner QC) was scheduled to start hearing evidence on 17 August 1981 and its brief was to examine the causes of the disturbances, the way in which they were dealt with and the steps that could be taken to ensure that there was no repeat in the future.

Despite the fact that there was widespread agreement that there should be an independent investigation, there was considerable disquiet about the nature of the inquiry that was agreed to by the council and the police committee. A public meeting of approximately 300 people in Moss Side on 12 August 1981 discussed a boycott of Hytner. Subsequently a statement was issued by the Moss Side Defence Committee saying that such a course of action was necessary because the nature and the structure of the inquiry had been decided upon in total disregard of the wishes of the community in Moss Side. It was stressed that the inquiry membership did not represent the community and that the racist policing of Moss Side and the operational policies of the chief constable should be the real focus of attention.

The Defence Committee warned that the inquiry could not guarantee immunity from prosecution, and as a result any information given to it could find its way to the police. As an alternative it urged people, including councillors and council officers, to give information concerning police attacks on the community to the Defence Committee. Subsequently, the youth section of Manchester Labour Party and the Haldane Society and various other local groups joined the boycott of the inquiry. Thus, because of the manner in which the county council had proceeded, the inquiry faced the possibility of the non-participation of those who had fought with the police on the streets of Moss Side.

However, it was not just radical opinion in Manchester that was opposed to the Hytner Inquiry. The local Conservative Party questioned the quality and reliability of the evidence upon which the inquiry would be dependent. Manchester City Council, although co-operating, continued to demand that an inquiry 'with teeth', under Lord Scarman, be set up, arguing that Hytner had no formal statutory powers. The chief constable stated that he was not prepared to allow any of his officers to give evidence in person or to be subjected to cross questioning. Although every effort was made to persuade local people to attend the hearings, the public gallery remained by and large empty as the boycott took effect.

Nevertheless, those who did co-operate provided confirmation of a crisis in police-community relations in Moss Side. Testimony was given relating to the heavy-handed policing of the area, the ineffectiveness of the complaints' system, the work of Community Contact officers being undone by aggressive street policing and the chief constable's unwillingness to accept criticism of his force or policing tactics from community representatives.

When the report was finally released in October 1981, one month before Lord Scarman's report on Brixton, it confirmed what critics of the chief constable's policies had been claiming. After exploring what role the 'myth of Moss Side' - 'visions of vice, high crime, racial friction and poor social conditions' - had played in 'triggering' the disturbances, the report decided there was enough evidence to suggest that the young people of Moss Side deeply resented, and in certain cases, hated the police:

> What is alleged is that over the past few years the police have developed a new style of 'stop and search' operation. It is said that young and inexperienced officers in Panda cars or vans tour areas of Greater Manchester at night stopping youths whether walking singly or in groups; that they physically manhandle them; that in the case of blacks they racially abuse them; that they sometimes are actually physically violent to them; that they not infrequently push or otherwise manhandle them into a police vehicle and that they rudely question them. It is further alleged that in many cases, particularly if the youngster responds to this treatment by 'giving cheek', he is taken to the police station and kept overnight before being released without a charge but a threat that he will 'be got next time' (para 25.9).

The report conceded that it was not just young people who had made these allegations, but that evidence had been forthcoming from respectable members of the community, that is, from solicitors, youth workers, the clergy and community leaders. It also noted that despite the considerable efforts of Community Contact officers, links had been forged only with the older and more 'respectable' community representatives. In its conclusions, it recommended that the chief constable would be well-advised to take note of the high levels of hostility towards the police that had been had uncovered, and to realize 'that in Moss Side among young blacks the feeling is intense':

We appreciate that the chief constable may believe that such a scenario is a figment of the imagination but we believe that he and the Police Committee should be most concerned that it is a figment of very many people's imaginations and we believe that policing in Manchester will never be wholly effective until young people cease to believe it (para 49.3).

Hytner identified the inadequacies of the complaints' system as one of the major sources of community dissatisfaction, and suggested that practical and immediate steps could be taken to improve the local operation of the existing system. The report recommended that a 'community representative' be appointed to receive complaints and communicate them to the police. However, before passing on the complaints, the 'community representative' would screen them to ensure that only the strongest cases were submitted to the official complaints' system. The hope was that, as a result of strict screening, the proportion of successful complaints would rise, with a resultant improvement in public confidence in the system. Those complaints defined as being too weak for official processing would be taken up informally in an attempt to alleviate public concern.

It was emphasized that for this revamped complaints' system to work, three things were essential. First, the 'community representative' would have to enjoy the full confidence of the community, especially young people. Second, this confidence could only be sustained if the 'representative' achieved a real measure of success with any complaints that s/he deflected away from the official system. And finally, the chief constable would have to agree to the appointment of a senior officer who would be, in effect, 'independent' of the force structure, and authorized to receive direct complaints from Moss Side. This officer and the 'community representative' would work in tandem to build up an atmosphere of trust, sift out the serious complaints, deal with informal complaints, and closely monitor local police-community relations.

'Hytner myths' and police monitoring

Such recommendations substantiated the misgivings of those who had boycotted the inquiry. The central idea of appointing, in a top down manner, yet another professional community spokesperson, as 'the' community representative, proved to the critics that Hytner and the police committee were incapable of either understanding the source of the problem or learning the lessons of the past. The Moss Side Defence Committee reiterated in its counter report, 'Hytner Myths', that the Moss Side uprisings, like the ones in Brixton and Liverpool 8, were a specific and 'legitimate protest' against many years of 'indiscriminate beatings, raids, frameups and harassment laced with racist abuse, which the police have been dishing out in this community', and the deliberate mapping of Moss Side 'as a dangerous and alien colony, full of actual or potential criminals, which demanded forceful and repressive policing'. The counter report concluded:

> What we have seen from the Hytner Report doesn't give us the confidence to believe that any future official inquiry will unearth the reality of policing in Moss Side (14 October 1981).

In the immediate post-uprising period, little effectively changed with regard to the police-community relations in Moss Side. There were complaints about coercive policing operations and rumours of alleged 'revenge' police raids and 'street justice' that had been orchestrated by certain police officers as soon as journalists and news crews had left the area. An indication of the state of policing in Moss Side in this period is provided in an open letter from local youth and community workers to a national newspaper in December 1981. It claimed that police officers in Moss Side had embarked on a systematic campaign of harassment and intimidation of the young people of the area. Additionally, it asserted that this campaign had been extended to youth and community workers and tensions remained high. The signatories to the letter stated that as a result they were no longer prepared to work or co-operate with the police in any capacity:

> We cannot, in all conscience, work with a police force which allowed vans to career through our streets with uniformed hooligans beating their truncheons against the vehicles, and chanting slogans such as 'Nigger, nigger, nigger - Oi, oi, oi' (*Guardian,* 9 December 1981).

Tension between police officers and youth workers had intensified during the disturbances because certain youth clubs chose to remain open all night rather than allow their members on to the streets where they would have to run the gauntlet of the police vans. As far as the police were concerned, the youth workers had deliberately provided sanctuary for criminals. In the heated disputes that followed, one youth worker was arrested and charged.

The concern expressed by the workers also extended to the work of Community Contact. It was alleged that not only were police officers harassing youth and community workers on the streets, but that Community Contact was moving into youth and community work in an aggressive imperialist manner, and allocating resources and patronage to those individuals and organizations who accepted its philosophy. At one and the same time, Community Contact was publicly identifying and denouncing those youth and community clubs and workers who would not co-operate with police initiatives. As far as a significant number of inner city youth and community workers in Manchester were concerned, the connections between the policing of the streets and the actions of Community Contact were clear. A concerted effort was being made, through harassment and intimidation, to break those who had dared to criticize and oppose the policies and actions of the Greater Manchester Police.

It was the considerable dissatisfaction with Hytner's analysis and recommendations and ongoing conflict with the police that gave rise to the first independent police monitoring group in Manchester. A meeting of approximately eighty youth and community workers took place in July 1982 to discuss how to respond to increasing police involvement in youth and community work. By August 1982, as a result of the meeting, a report, 'Police and Youth Work', had been drawn up, which presented a systematic critique of the work of Community Contact. It was argued that community policing initiatives were placing youth and community workers in an impossible position. They were being publicly labelled as anti-police if they refused to co-operate with Community Contact. But if they co-operated with and facilitated such police-led initiatives, they would lose their credibility and authority with the young people with whom they worked. Thus, they demanded that the ethical basis of their work be recognized, as well as their professional right to disagree with Greater Manchester Police's understanding of the world. In addition, they asked the council to explain why the police were being allocated resources to engage in youth and community projects at a time when professional youth and community work was suffering from drastic cuts in funding and valuable schemes were being closed down.

The report concluded by demanding that police involvement in youth and community work and the harassment of youth and community workers cease. It was stated that the only way to realize this, given the chief constable's attitude to such matters, would be through campaigning for wider changes in the policing of Manchester:

> Community policing cannot be appended to an otherwise unchanged police force. There must be real changes in the balance of power between the various communities and groups and the police force in a region as socially diverse as Greater Manchester (Youth and Allied Workers' Police Monitoring Group, 1982, p. 7).

Thus, the emergent Youth and Allied Workers' Police Monitoring Group committed itself to campaigning for the complete overhaul of the structures of police accountability and the establishment of an independent complaints' procedure. In order to further their demands, the group decided on three courses of action. First, they would refuse to co-operate with community policing initiatives and those agencies and authorities that participated in multi-agency activities. Second, every effort would be made to ensure that the 'true' meaning and significance of community policing was placed on the agendas of as many relevant organizations, authorities and groups as possible. And, finally, efforts would be made to support the establishment of a network of local community-based police monitoring groups.

Two incidents in particular heightened the determination of concerned youth and community workers to campaign for police reform in Manchester. In September 1982, a black community worker was stopped for questioning by drug squad officers outside Moss Side Shopping Precinct. During the ensuing arguments, another well-known black youth worker was arrested and charged with assault and obstruction. When he was released from the local police station, he had extensive eye injuries. This caused an immediate outcry.

In October 1982, a youth worker who went to his office on a Sunday afternoon stumbled across what turned out to be an undercover police surveillance team operating video equipment from the vantage point of the office. The youth worker was bundled into another room and informed that permission had been obtained to use the offices for an anti-mugging operation. In follow up inquiries, it was established that permission had not been obtained and that the real focus of the surveillance was a gay pub directly facing the youth office. Specific concern was generated by the fact that the particular offices which had been broken into belonged to an organization that the police would have defined as being non co-operative, and whose confidential files would have been open to police inspection. Despite prolonged correspondence between this organization and the police, no satisfactory explanation was forthcoming (Cox and Scott, 1984). Although no-one knew it at the time, the 'facts' surrounding this police surveillance operation would correspond with many others that were uncovered in Greater Manchester in the 1980s.

Further meetings of the youth and community workers took place in response to these incidents, and various statements were released reiterating that as far as Youth and Allied Workers' Police Monitoring Group was concerned, police interventions into youth and community work in Manchester were part of a policing strategy whose objective was neighbourhood-wide surveillance and information gathering. Consequently, the group argued, community policing initiatives should be seen as part of the problem rather than as a solution to the breakdown in police-community relations in the inner city. The group also reiterated its policy of non co-operation, because as far as it was concerned there was no point in entering into dialogue with Greater Manchester Police as the chief constable was incapable of responding constructively to criticism.

In October 1982, one of the statutory organizations approached by the monitoring group issued a press release criticizing police involvement in youth and community work, and asked local authorities to provide clarification on the exact extent and nature of such involvement. The chief constable replied immediately, stating that the criticisms were unfounded and 'not worthy of comment' (*Manchester Evening News*, 8 October 1982). However, as more local organizations and groups began to express concern, Greater Manchester Council finally agreed to set up a working party to examine police involvement in youth and community work. The issue was also recognized by Manchester City Council when its education committee established a working party in September 1983 to produce a set of guidelines which would strictly govern legitimate contact between youth and community workers and the police and hopefully protect workers, schemes and clubs from unwarranted police attention.

Discussion

Anxieties that had existed about James Anderton's policing philosophy since he took control of the Greater Manchester Police in 1976 coalesced in the political space opened up by the outcome of the county council elections and the 1981 uprisings. A concerted campaign for police accountability rapidly unfolded and the eventual result of the debates, proposals and counter-proposals was the construction of two distinct pathways to police accountability. One pathway, envisioned by the police committee, was based upon utilizing the existing provisions of the 1964 Police Act to the full in order to make the chief constable accountable to the elected community representatives. It also involved utilizing the recommendations of both the Hytner and Scarman reports to encourage community representation and participation in liaison committees. The alternative route, placed on the local political agenda by members of Youth and Allied Workers' Police Monitoring Group, and eventually taken up by Manchester City Council, was premised upon a rejection of what they viewed as wholly inadequate police committee proposals. It opted instead, in the absence of meaningful constitutional reform of policing, for a strategy of opposition to unacceptable and unaccountable policing through the campaigns of community-based police monitoring groups. As a consequence, as we shall see in the next chapters, 'the community' became a site of struggle as both the police committee and Manchester City Council attempted to realize their proposals.

4 Police committee and community liaison

Between 1981 and the passing of the Local Government Act in July 1985 the Labour-controlled police committee and the chief constable clashed over virtually every aspect of the policing of Greater Manchester. It is worth 'memorializing' this conflict because it remains, in many respects, a prime example of the struggles between chief constables and police committees which characterized the 1980s. As will be seen, the committee attempted to use its powers to the full to call upon the chief constable to report to it on any matter connected with the policing of the force area. In addition, in order to fulfil its statutory responsibility to maintain 'an adequate and efficient' force, and to act as a watchdog for the ratepayers of Greater Manchester, it also endeavoured to take the lead on certain policing issues. In this sense, its Labour members were attempting to create a pro-active committee where elected representatives held the chief constable to account by overseeing policing, just as they oversaw other council services.

James Anderton, in turn, made it clear that the role of the police committee was to fulfil its duties by working within the existing tripartite structure, and that he would fend off all unconstitutional 'encroachments' into 'operational' matters. In inflammatory statement after inflammatory statement, he denounced those whom he saw as challenging his operational autonomy, accusing them of fighting an 'acrimonious and secretive' battle to undermine the institutions of the British state:

> The current concern over policing being expressed by certain political factions has got precious little to do with better community participation in policing affairs or the improvement of democracy - rather it is the first conscious step manifesting itself towards the political control of the police, without which the dream of a totalitarian, one party state in this country cannot be realized (*Times,*

18 March 1982).

His beliefs led him finally to demand that the government reconstitute police committees as 'non-political' entities, either by giving magistrates at least half the membership or by replacing them with non-elected police boards. And, as Anderton must have been aware, given the role being played by the police in the birthing of post-industrial Britain, any chief constable 'holding the line' against anti-police elements was guaranteed the unquestioned public support of the Conservative government.

As a consequence of this 'divergence of opinion' on the proper role and responsibilities of police committees, the monthly committee meetings became media spectacles, characterized by scenes of disorder, motions of no confidence, crisis adjournments for constitutional clarifications and the wholesale abandonment of proceedings. They were also accompanies by striking front page headlines in the *Manchester Evening News* (the local newspaper) which left the people in Greater Manchester in no doubt about the intensity of the struggle over police accountability: 'ANDERTON IS WARNED: STAY OUT OF POLITICS'; 'TIGHTEN GRIP ON POLICE BID BY WATCHDOGS'; 'RIOT STORM: POLICE PROBE STARTS'; 'ANDERTON CRISIS AS COUNCIL CHIEF LASHES OUT'; 'WHO IS BOSS? POLICE STORM'; 'CRISIS TALKS ON POLICE BUDGET'; 'ANDERTON STICKS TO HIS GUNS'; 'ANDERTON STORM GOES TO THE TOP'; SIGN A PLEDGE ORDER TO JIM'.

There were, of course, lulls in the conflict. In December 1984, for example, as a result of a series of private meetings with the Home Office, the chief constable and the committee pledged that they would endeavour to fulfil their respective duties without acrimony. The proposed abolition of the metropolitan county councils also unified both the chief constable and the committee, momentarily, in their opposition to the bill. But, overall, consensual relations were the exception rather than the norm.

This turbulent situation constituted the context within which the police committee attempted to set up the second part of its accountability package - the police-community liaison panels. The outcome of the clashes and the uncompromising stance of the chief constable had serious ramifications for the success or otherwise of the consultation initiative, especially in key areas of Greater Manchester.

The police committee and the chief constable

As indicated in the last chapter, under Conservative Party leadership the Greater Manchester police committee had made no attempt to 'interfere' with the policing of the area. According to councillors and council officers, the committee was the quietest of all the council's committees. Symptomatic of the lack of scrutiny of policing matters was the fact that there had been just one 'rubber stamp' subcommittee which concerned itself with financial matters.

However, in the period prior to the 1981 elections, through involvement on the Association of Metropolitan Authorities' working party on accountability, and awareness of the struggles in neighbouring Merseyside, a younger generation of Labour councillors began to formulate ideas on how to counter the pre-May 1981 practice of the chief constable setting the agenda (Cox, 1985). As a consequence, after May 1981, the police committee was gradually restructured to neutralize the presence of 'non-political' non-elected magistrates and mirror the internal organization of the Greater Manchester Police.

The magistrates

As documented in chapter one, police committees, unlike their sister council committees, were skewed by the presence of non-elected members. This was particularly problematical in the Greater Manchester case, because after the decimation of the Conservatives and Liberals in the 1981 elections, the magistrates took on the role of being the 'official' opposition to the Labour members. They immediately began to vote, as a block, with the Conservatives, giving unquestioning support to the chief constable. The chair of the police committee was acutely aware that the vote on any given issue always looked closer than on other council committees because of the presence and voting behaviour of the magistrates. It always looked as if decisions had 'only just' been agreed to. Furthermore, there was always the possibility that if Labour members did not attend meetings, Labour motions would be lost. Because of the difficulties of the situation, the Labour Party leadership at full council level endorsed the use of the party whip to ensure that all Labour members attended meetings and that there was no dissension from the party line (Cox, 1985).

Eventually the Labour members announced that the community had the right to know that: the magistrates were non-elected and non-accountable; certain of them did not even live in Greater Manchester and although they were appointed as individuals, they organized as a partisan faction which uncritically supported the chief constable. As a consequence, a procedure was introduced whereby the names of those voting for and against particular motions was recorded under the headings elected and non-elected, so that the community could see the voting patterns of the magistrates. However, this only heightened the conflict between the magistrates and Labour members of the committee.

Restructuring the police committee

This involved the setting up of standing sub-committees for each of the operational function of the force to allow members, and especially the committee chair (who sat on all the committees) to:

1. Develop a direct and independent relationship with the assistant chief constables.
2. Be able to influence the agenda by requesting detailed reports on items 'not volunteered' by the chief constable.
3. Follow up on specific issues.
4. Acquire an expertise on the 'nuts and bolts' of the internal workings of the force and specific aspects of police work.
5. Move away from the dramatic setting of public committee meetings.

Through this restructuring, the committee was saying to the chief constable 'we want to be involved, we want to know what you are doing, we want reports' (Cox, 1985). In so doing, Labour was recognizing that if any measure of accountability were to be realized, it would be necessary to challenge the chief constable's monopoly on information concerning the policing of Greater Manchester. Anderton initially agreed to the new structure (and indeed encouraged its extension in 1983) and it should be made clear that much of the 'unseen' work of these sub-committees was uncontroversial: committee members had good working relations with senior officers and, as the chief constable subsequently conceded, worked to improve the force by upgrading the telecommunications system, computer facilities, divisional control rooms and section stations. Nor should it be forgotten that despite campaigning for changes to the 1964 Police Act, Labour-controlled police committees during this period consistently attempted to protect their police budgets from the Conservative government's onslaught on local government finances. Greater Manchester police committee, for example, spent substantially over the Grant Related Expenditure Assessment set by central government. As a result, the County Council incurred significant grant penalties on the 'overspend'.

However, inevitably, Anderton began to take exception to certain of the suggestions of the sub-committees. For example, in September 1984, he condemned a sub-committee's proposal to produce a prisoners' rights leaflet (as part of the lay visitors' scheme) as unacceptable because it was 'inaccurate, biased and possibly legally dangerous'. The Labour members were completely wrong-footed by this reaction since the leaflet had been prepared by one of the sub-committees over the previous five months and agreed to by one of the assistant chief constables and the Home Office.

Anderton was subsequently advised by the committee chair to develop proper channels of communication with his senior managers, so that when they attended sub-committee meetings as his representatives, they would know his views on the issues under discussion. The chief constable replied that he could not do this as it would mean that they would have the power to bind him to operational positions with which he might not agree. In November 1984, he announced that:

> whatever the police committee choose to do I feel under an obligation to put it back to the Home Office to see what the legal implications are for chief constables. It will also be put to Association of Chief Police Officers. There's a long way to go on this yet.

This dispute over the prisoners' rights leaflet continued into 1985, with the committee periodically asking the chief constable whether he would make it available in police stations. Anderton stonewalled by saying that he was perturbed by certain sections of the text and would continue to seek advice from the Home Office, the Inspectorate and Association of Chief Police Officers.

As his altercations with the police committee intensified, the chief constable began to protest publicly about the amount of time the senior management of 'his' force was having to spend servicing the sub-committees. Finally, to the consternation of the committee, he disrupted their work in 1985 by instituting a major internal re-organization of the force without consultation. When pressed on the matter, deputy chief constable John Stalker informed the committee:

> it is not practical or the chief constable's intention to go back and discuss this matter. These are operational decisions, part of the normal senior management where chief officers get on with decision making. I agree with consultation but when it comes to deployment it's an operational matter, not administration. When it comes to deployment and movement of men, it cannot be done by bargaining and bartering.

Labour members of the committee also broke with tradition by attempting to obtain independent assessments of policing in the county. Such probing brought a sharp response from the chief constable who accused them of interfering in matters which were outside their jurisdiction.

The Moss Side disturbances

In late 1981, the chief constable declared that he was troubled both by the attempts of certain police committee members to interfere in what he defined as 'operational' decisions during the disturbances, and the subsequent setting up of a committee sponsored inquiry. When he was asked during a police committee meeting in September 1981 why he had not co-operated with the Hytner Inquiry, he replied that he should have been consulted 'to discuss the full implications for police and determine acceptable lines of inquiry' before the terms of reference were drafted (*Times*, 5 May 1981). However, the committee had not done so and consequently could not expect senior police officers to submit themselves to a non-statutory tribunal or to be subjected to questioning based upon the hearsay and unsubstantiated allegations of 'any Tom, Dick or Harry'.

At the beginning of this meeting, Labour councillors refused to allow the chief constable to read from his paper on the disturbances, because he had not submitted it beforehand. In response, Anderton's aides distributed a document, *The Truth about the Moss Side Meeting*, in which he claimed that, among others, Gabrielle Cox, the deputy chair of the committee, had asked him, during the disturbances, to make an apology to the black community and to relieve the divisional chief superintendent of his duties:

> I was absolutely dismayed by the appalling proposition, the like of which I have never previously received in my whole career...We hear a lot nowadays about the much heralded concept of 'democratic community policing'. Well, if this was a practical example, then all I can say is - God help us (*Police Review*, 18 September 1981).

On *The World This Weekend* (BBC, 6 September 1981) Anderton claimed that there had been a 'calculated attempt' by the police committee to force him to speak against his will to the Hytner Inquiry. He also asserted that because he had refused to do so, he was being 'gagged' from speaking the truth about what had happened. The arguments continued at a specially convened committee meeting, with Labour councillors denouncing the chief constable's report into the policing of the disturbances as deficient because of its lack of detail concerning key moments of the policing operation. However, the chief constable refused to elaborate on what he defined as operational matters and stated that he would not provide any further information (*Times*, 12 September 1981).

During the November and December meetings, Anderton rejected Hytner's 'evidence' of: a breakdown in relations between the police and black youth; the discriminatory use of 'stop and search' operations in Moss Side; and Scarman's proposals concerning ethnic minority recruitment and racial prejudice within the police. He also ominously informed the committee that he would not hesitate to employ rapid dispersal tactics in any future public disorder scenario. In the force newspaper, he reassured his officers that the majority of the community in Greater Manchester supported the policing action in Moss Side and that, unlike their critics, they worked for 'the benefit of the community' (*Brief*, December 1981). The chief constable provoked further controversy by issuing a force statement publicly praising his officers for:

> quelling the riotous, disorderly and criminal behaviour widespread in Toxteth, Moss Side and elsewhere in July 1981, and...effectively and speedily restoring the Queen's Peace throughout the County of Greater Manchester for the benefit and protection of all its citizens (*Manchester Evening News*, 7 December 1981).

Despite periodic requests, the chief constable never produced a more detailed report for the police committee.

The police band

In January 1984 the police committee decided to abolish the full-time police band as part of a wider £1.5m package of economies, which included stopping recruitment, leaving posts vacant, reducing overtime and cutting the vehicle replacement programme. The intention was to maintain establishment levels by returning officers to essential policing duties. The chief constable declared that the committee had departed from the normal practice of consulting him on financial matters affecting his force:

> There is simply no precedent in this force for a police committee virtually to order or require the chief constable uncompromisingly against his carefully considered opinion and advice and without proper consultation practically to close a long established unit. I view this shift of policy and posture with grave concern.

The chair of the committee refuted the assertions, stating that the chief constable had been informed of the proposed cuts and that his alternative had been to delete from the budget three new section stations and reduce the operational staff by forty. As far as the police committee was concerned, this was not acceptable, as it had a legal responsibility to maintain the operational strength of the force and viewed the new section stations as an important part of its community policing plans. After an adjournment, the clerk to the committee gave a ruling that under the 1964 Police Act it was the duty of the police committee, not the chief constable, to determine the establishment of the force.

The media was subsequently informed by the chief constable that this decision raised the constitutional issue of whether a police committee had the right to disregard a chief constable's views on important operational matters. He stated that he intended to refer the issue to the chief inspector of constabulary and the Home Office, and until he received their advice, he would allow himself the discretion to deploy his officers as he pleased. A further meeting took place between Anderton and the County Council to review the issue, with the chair of the police committee subsequently going to the Home Office to discuss the cash crisis facing the force on 11 January 1984.

At the October 1984 meeting, the chief constable informed the committee that he had met privately with the chief inspector of the constabulary and the deputy under secretary of state, and that they had asked him to request the committee to defer any decision about the band:

> until I, as chief constable, have had a proper and fuller opportunity to appraise them of the implications of the police committee's proposals, and of the legal and constitutional points which are of issue.

He also informed the Home Office that the police committee was attempting to use its financial powers of control:

> in order selectively to restrict or prevent the deployment by the chief constable of a manpower resource within the force for which budget provision has already been made in respect of which a Home Office grant is paid. According to advice I have received this morning, I must seriously inform the police committee that the action they now propose to take may well be ultra vires and I would suggest they look again at this matter.

The meeting was adjourned and the advice of the county legal clerk once more sought on the constitutional position. The clerk reiterated that the band was not within the chief constable's operational remit. The Labour members viewed the chief constable's actions as an act of deliberate provocation, especially when he informed them that the reason why he not informed them earlier about his meetings was because he did not 'consider it opportune or necessary to explain'. One member summed up their feelings when he said that the chief constable disregarded the work of the committee and was constantly provoking constitutional crises. As a consequence, the police committee seemed to find itself in its dealings with the chief constable always 'in the small print of the law and that there was no spirit of co-operation':

> we have gone very far from the band to the issue of constitutional control. Now is the time to seek central confirmation of our powers as

advised by the Home Office.

The chair accused the chief constable of being in breach of the duties of a chief officer of the council. By the end of this meeting, resolutions had been passed to dissolve the police band and to censure the chief constable for his behaviour. Both Anderton and the police committee appealed to the Home Office for a definitive clarification of the powers and responsibilities of the chief constable.

In October, the Home Office advised the chief constable that the band could not be considered necessary to the efficiency of the force. He subsequently agreed, in 'the best interests' of the relationship between the police committee and himself, to 'accede' to the request to return members of the police band to active police duties. Nevertheless, he also warned the committee that the legal opinion he had obtained confirmed that:

> the deployment of personnel is the sole prerogative of the chief constable and that any decision by the police committee to oust his jurisdiction in that matter should be resisted by an application for judicial review.

Called to account

At the same time as the police committee was attempting to be an active participant to the decision-making process, it also had to respond to a series of controversial policing incidents involving the Greater Manchester Police which tested its commitment to extract retrospective explanations from the chief constable to the full. This proved just as problematic as its struggle to intervene pro-actively in the policing of Greater Manchester.

The Laurence Scott dispute

The manner in which a dispute at the Laurence Scott engineering works in Openshaw, Manchester in April 1981 was policed became a source of serious disagreement between the chief constable and the police committee. In October 1981 the management's unsuccessful attempt to re-open the factory generated complaints about the policing tactics used. The chief constable publicly intervened in the dispute, guaranteeing protection for those workers who wished to cross the official picket line. In November 1981, a dramatic joint operation between police and management rescued goods and equipment enabling Scott's to meet their existing contractual obligations. This decisive policing action, involving 300 officers, helped to undermine the workers' occupation. The Labour group of the police committee was highly critical of the chief constable for 'conniving' in an asset-stripping operation by using the force to break the workers.

For the chair of committee, the Laurence Scott dispute was in many respects more straightforward than the Moss Side disturbances, in terms of accountability issues.This was a legitimate industrial protest by respectable white members of the community, and despite documented police provocation, there had been no picket line violence. In addition, there was considerable local support for the workers with residents complaining at a public meeting, convened by the police committee, that ordinarily it was impossible to locate a police officer in the locality. The chair of the committee informed this meeting that there was nothing she could do because the chief constable had defined it as an 'operational' matter. In March 1982, the committee ratified a resolution stating that the chief constable's deployment of over 300 officers during the dispute constituted an unwarranted over-reaction. The chief constable, in turn, repudiated all criticism, accusing certain Labour councillors of fermenting trouble by 'working very hard in the area to canvass opinion against the police'.

Arming the force

In September 1981, the committee questioned the chief constable's seeming determination to turn the Greater Manchester Police into a force with a full paramilitary capability. The origins of this row lay with the discovery that the force had secretly acquired two modified Heckler and Kock HK33, SAS style sub-machine guns (*Observer*, 20 September 1981). When challenged, police spokespersons had denied any such purchase and the county legal officer, acting on behalf of the police committee, had publicly supported this denial. With media confirmation that the guns had been procured, Bernard Clarke, the leader of Greater Manchester Council, condemned the chief constable for making the clerk 'look a fool and a liar'. He also stated that if any other officer of the council had behaved in such an unaccountable manner, s/he would have been sacked (*Manchester Evening News*, 1 October 1981).

Such protests had little effect. In April 1983, the chief constable once more made national headlines, given the controversy surrounding the Metropolitan Police shooting of Steven Waldorf in 1982, by disclosing that armed police were patrolling Greater Manchester because of the supposed increase in the number of armed robberies in the region. As far as the police committee was concerned, the decision to issue firearms as a matter of routine represented a major and unacceptable change of policy. However, the chief constable made it clear that, for (unspecified) operational reasons, he had no intention of reversing this policy decision or disclosing to the committee the number of police vehicles or officers who were now armed (*Manchester Evening News*, 6 April 1983).

Policing the miners' strike

The 1984-5 coal dispute resulted in the 'greatest and most prolonged mutual aid that has occurred in the history of the police in the UK, involving officers from almost every force' (Oliver, 1987, p. 212). As '1984' unfolded, police committees, especially Labour-controlled ones, found themselves in an impossible situation. The financing of the most expensive policing operation in the history of the British police raised a series of fundamental constitutional questions for those police committees sending the aid. The central question was whether 'the costs be contained within the budget and, if not, who would pay? Knowing the limits of the budget, could the chief constable nevertheless ask for, or send, mutual aid as he saw fit, irrespective of cost?' (Spencer, 1985, p. 8).

Second, what were the effects of losing so many officers likely to be for the day-to-day policing needs? Third, what were the reinforcements from Greater Manchester being used for and who was in charge of them? Finally, how would these 'battle-hardened' officers behave when they returned from prolonged public order duties? As the police committee was to find out, given that all of these questions could be cloaked under the 'operational' shroud or defined as a legal obligation, it was virtually impossible to locate a legitimate political 'space' to articulate these questions.

During April 1984, one month after it started, the policing of the miners' strike was first discussed by the police committee. The chair argued that a working party should be set up to assess whether the scale of the response of the Greater Manchester Police in sending 400-500 officers to other parts of the country was justified. James Anderton, in reply, demanded to know whether it was being suggested that emergency meetings should be called before he could dispatch his officers to carry out their lawful duties. The chair stated that whilst she was not suggesting that the chief constable needed to ask permission, she wanted him to recognize and acknowledge that his operational decisions were likely to bankrupt the committee and have a detrimental effect on local policing needs. By the July meeting, the full financial implications of the coal dispute were becoming apparent. The chair announced that due to the resources being spent on policing the dispute, the overtime budget would be exhausted by August, and that Derbyshire refused to reimburse other police committees.

As far as Gabrielle Cox was concerned, too much money was being spent on one particular law and order issue, and the dispute could have been resolved in a completely different manner. She re-emphasized that no other chief officer of the council would be able to carry out her/his duty irrespective of cost. This illustrated, once more, the urgent need for some form of real police accountability, because as it stood once an issue was defined as 'operational', the committee lost any right to ask questions:

> Chief constables do not have the right to spend, spend and spend when other areas of policy are cut. There is the constitutional anomaly of chief constables being able to spend and no body being capable, legally, of stopping them.

For Labour councillors the strike proved conclusively that the chief constable, the Home Secretary and ACPO had more say over policing that the police committeese. Anderton refused to respond to these questions and complaints. Instead, in a speech at the Institute of Housing conference in June 1984, he compared mass picketing and violent demonstrations to 'acts of terrorism without the bullet and the bomb'. He also, once more, expounded his conspiracy theory, arguing that 'certain political ideologues recognize that power over the people requires first that the police be publicly controlled' (*Guardian*, 18 June 1984).

Labour responded to this speech by presenting a motion of censure at the July 1984 meeting:

> It is exceptionally unfortunate when we are in the middle of a difficult industrial dispute that comments are made which aggravate the situation. It does not help this police committee or police officers. I propose that this police committee deplores the provocative partisan nature of part of the speech. I do not expect [council] officers to intervene in political issues in this bipartisan way as it erodes the idea of police impartiality.

She subsequently informed the people of Greater Manchester that the policing of the strike was rendering the police committee's statutory responsibilities 'meaningless':

> Not only can the chief constable do what he likes but he can spend all our money doing it and bankrupt us, and potentially bankrupt the County Council. In theory, we should have to cut back on fire services and everything else to pay for this.

The miners' strike, and particularly a confrontation that had taken place with the Home Secretary over who was responsible for the financing of the policing operation, dominated the October 1984 meeting. Only the

Conservative councillors disagreed with the chair's stance, affirming their support for the Home Secretary's stand, and demanding that the council find the money to sustain the police budget.

No sooner had the November 1984 police committee meeting commenced than it withdrew into private in an attempt to resolve 'the discrepancy between the chief constable's understanding of the meeting and the committee's'. When it resumed in public, the first item discussed was the effect of mutual aid arrangements on local policing. The question was put to the chief constable:

> When is the point at which the police committees can say stop, the policing of our own area is more important? At the moment it is out of our hands because of the operational discretion of the chief constables. What about law and order within our own communities?

Anderton replied that he was legally mandated to provide whatever level of aid was necessary to keep the peace.

During the January 1985 meeting, the chief constable did acknowledge that the length of the coal dispute was having a detrimental effect on the policing of the county. By this time Greater Manchester had provided approximately one thousand police support units to eleven other forces, at a cost of hundreds of thousands of pounds. The local policing implications were also becoming clear - in one randomly chosen area the levels of cover were down to sixty-four per cent of the usual number of officers. A motion was passed to the effect that the committee 'deplores the lack of control it has over its own force, the loss of service to the people of Greater Manchester and the failure of the government to solve this long and costly dispute'. The March meeting began with the chair reporting back on the disappointing meeting with Leon Brittan, the Home Secretary, during his visit to Manchester and that, given the government's position that financing should remain local, the committee would have to take court action to recover the financial costs of the anti-strike operation.

In May 1985 the chief constable did provide a retrospective 'factual' report on the local effects of the policing of the coal dispute. However, he informed the committee that he was not prepared to enter into any further dialogue about operational issues. This report prompted Gabrielle Cox to make a final statement on the matter in which she expressed her outrage about the 'draining' of the committee's financial resources, to pay for the 'restoration' of public order in other parts of the country. For the committee, the policing of the coal dispute:

> has been frustrating, demonstrating the inability of the police committee to deal with its own budget and its own area. There is the

whole question of accountability and the issues of policing public order situations. A lot of the issues of policing are not about practicalities and technicalities but how we want our communities to be policed. What liberties and rights do we want upheld. And how we prioritize. There are issues about the preservation of peace being the key concern for the police. These issues are for the community to decide, not the police alone. Its not just for the Association of Chief Police Officers. I am concerned that the police force will be demand-led and that everything will be secondary to public order in future.

There was also one other issue that the strike had bequeathed. The March visit of the Home Secretary had provoked a demonstration at the university and there was evidence that the police officers on duty, fresh from their clashes with the miners, over-reacted and used excessive force to clear the students. Approximately forty people were injured, of whom at least four required hospital treatment and forty people were arrested mainly for public order offences.

However, because it resulted in a Police Complaints' Authority investigation, the 'Battle of Brittan' (like the Jackie Berkeley case) never became a source of public conflict between the police committee and the chief constable. In April 1985, the incident was discussed briefly, with the chair informing the committee that the Home Secretary had turned down its request for the establishment of a public inquiry. Anderton, replying to a question about whether he would furnish a report explaining the policing of the incident, stated:

> I cannot give you a full report of all that transpired, not even concerning the deployment of police officers, because that is germane to the proceedings. What I will do, and it is all that I am prepared to do, is let you have a brief report containing such information as I deem it proper for you to have.

Community liaison

In November 1981, the police committee agreed to appoint a community liaison officer to act as 'the' community representative to deal with complaints in Moss Side and to establish a police-community liaison panel in Moss Side. Further community involvement in local policing was envisaged by implementing Lord Scarman's lay visiting proposals.

The liaison panels were to be 'an essential part of any accountability structure...an attempt to involve the community in making the police more accountable' (Cox, 1985). They were to be more than 'talking shops' and were not to concern themselves solely with crime prevention problems. The police committee had two terms of reference for its liaison panels that were very different to those listed in the Home Office circular 54/1982. First, they were to promote co-operation between the police and the community in the determination of priorities and the formation of agreed strategies to deal with specific local problems. Just as the chief constable and senior ranks would be expected to consult with the committee, so local police divisions would be expected to consult with the local community. By breaking down force-imposed barriers and initiating a real and equal dialogue between police officers and the communities they served, it was hoped that a new 'service' style of policing could develop which would ensure that police policies and operations were decided upon on the community's terms. Gabrielle Cox argued that the force should recognize that police professionalism should not be defined in relation to exercising their autonomy to make decisions on behalf of the community but:

> in skills relating to presenting and discussing policing dilemmas in ways which assist the community to agree policies and strategies which are both operationally sound and carrying community consent (1985, p. 13).

This was why community liaison would be different to the force's Community Contact department:

> It is not enough for the police to consult only those with whom they agree or to whom they wish to speak. A key role for the police committee must be, we believe, to provide the opportunity to be heard to all groups in society, including those who have deep reservations about or hostility to police actions or role...consultation is designed to include all the community, not only that section (albeit, no doubt, the large majority) which feels itself well-disposed towards the police (1985, p. 14).

Second, as the 'eyes and ears' of the police committee, the liaison panels would provide crucial 'on the ground' information about the different types of policing being practiced across the various divisions. It was also hoped that they would eventually mature into devolved 'mini police committees', asking questions of local police officers and pressurizing for change.

Moreover, the initiative would enable the committee to forge direct links with local communities and any requests that the panels might make would provide the police committee with extra leverage to press for change. Because the panels would be representative of the community, it would be much more difficult for the chief constable to dismiss their demands in the same way he dismissed the police committee's by claiming they were politically motivated. Thus, the committee was envisaging establishing a three way dialogue between itself, the police and the community.

The police committee also set up the first lay visiting scheme in the country. However, from the outset the police exercised tight control over this particular initiative, which became operational in May 1983. The force drafted the guidelines and assumed sole responsibility for the training of the lay visitors. After considerable negotiation, each liaison panel was allowed to having three visitors who were shortlisted and agreed to by the police committee and the chief constable. Panel members ceased to be lay visitors if they resigned or were removed from the liaison panel, and the chief constable had the right to terminate an appointment if conduct fell below 'required standards'. All visitors had to sign a document promising confidentiality concerning information collected during the course of the visits, in any report submitted to the police committee or to the police or to a police officer investigating a complaint against another police officer. Additionally, it was recommended that visits should be undertaken alone, only to local police stations, and visitors should only speak to detainees in the presence of a police officer. Significantly, the community liaison officer did not gain any rights of access to police stations in the force area.

While the Labour group saw the post-Hytner and Scarman inspired initiatives as a way of making the police more accountable to the community, other sections of the police committee had different ideas. The Liberal councillors, whilst supporting lay visiting and community liaison, wanted the latter to be extended to the 'whole' of the community, and saw the initiatives as contributing, primarily, to the control of crime. The Conservatives and the magistrates were completely opposed to the changes, viewing them as a Left-wing ploy to hinder the police in the fight against crime. The chief constable, whilst supporting the appointment of the community liaison officer and the lay visiting scheme, expressed concern about the panels becoming unrepresentative 'mouthpieces' of the police committee. He also made it clear that the police would continue with its own avenues of consultation because different communities required different approaches. There is every reason to suppose that he would have opposed these initiatives if they had not corresponded to government and Home Office thinking. The local Police Federation, for its part, rejected totally the appointment of the community liaison officer.

This 'official' opposition was mirrored by the rejection of the proposals in Moss Side. As was documented previously, the Moss Side Defence Committee had successfully organized a boycott of the Hytner Inquiry precisely because of its unrepresentativeness. Despite this and the fact that the Defence

Committee had subsequently rejected the recommendations of the inquiry, the police committee proceeded with the recommendations. To compound its problems, the committee appointed Linbert Spencer, a member of the Hytner Inquiry panel, as the community liaison officer. Thus, someone who had been publicly defined previously as unrepresentative was appointed as 'the' community representative. This policy decision had serious ramifications because the Inquiry had stressed that 'active community support' would only be achieved if an acceptable representative were selected. The disapproval of key community groups meant that it would be extremely difficult to establish a liaison panel in Moss Side.

Furthermore, the reaction to the lay visiting scheme was scathing. Lay visiting was one of the few real powers promised to those willing to participate in the liaison initiative, but the chief constable had ensured that the police retained control. In this situation, there was little chance that the worries of those concerned about what happened in police stations surrounding Moss Side would be assuaged.

The work of the community liaison officer was complicated by additional problems. First, his efforts were constantly undermined by routine police work in Moss Side in particular. A series of controversial incidents consolidated opposition to police-community liaison, confirming the view of those who believed that the police committee was incapable of influencing the policing of the area. Second, the prototype liaison panel that was established elsewhere in Greater Manchester confirmed the scepticism of those who opposed such arrangements. Third, the general philosophy informing the work of the community liaison officer further alienated those groups grid-locked in struggle with the police. The overall consequence was to lend support to those such as Youth and Allied Workers' Police Monitoring Group who argued that the police committee was incapable of representing the interests of those for whom the police were a problem, and that an alternative to community liaison should be found for Manchester.

The community liaison officer: representing the black community

The community liaison officer, who was based in Moss Side, had to face a boycott from significant sections of the community whose interests he was supposed to be representing. Thus, when he attempted to attend the first meeting of Youth and Allied Workers' Police Monitoring Group, for example, he was asked to leave on the grounds that his role and function made it impossible for him to be 'a legitimate member of the group'. Despite this dismissal Linbert Spencer persevered, and there is little doubt that he took his representative role seriously and attempted to ensure that the needs of black people were prioritized in his work. He focused specifically on: the police response to racial attacks; complaints about police malpractice; racism in the force and ethnic minority recruitment. He believed that if he could 'deliver' in these disputed areas, it would be considerably easier to 'sell' the idea of a community liaison panel in Moss Side.

Racial violence

The community liaison officer held meetings with departments of Manchester City Council and police representatives about how to activate a multi-agency approach to racist attacks. Spencer was a consistent advocate of multi-agency approaches on the grounds that they were the most effective response to complex social problems, and because they allowed non-police agencies the possibility of discovering what operational police policies in a given area actually were and subsequently influencing them. In the case of racial attacks, council departments began to gather information on the extent and nature of the problem and to pass it to the police. In addition, the police agreed to monitor incidents of racial harassment by filtering all reports, including those where no formal complaint had been made, to an assistant chief constable who, in theory, had a direct remit to ensure that they were investigated.

In September 1983, in response to Linbert Spencer's work, the chief constable presented a report on force monitoring of racial incidents to the police committee's crime sub-committee. It was agreed to hold a conference to produce a joint approach to the problem. However, Anderton subsequently decided that the force would hold its own symposium with limited community participation. The community liaison officer was particularly concerned about the nature of the chief constable's proposal because of its narrow community base. He argued that any conference on the issue should be open in terms of representation and participation so that the community could 'be given more opportunity of understanding the nature of police monitoring being done, and have an opportunity to participate in structuring any changes' (2nd Annual Report, p. 10). However, this did not happen. Thus, the community liaison officer quickly realized that the chief constable constantly redefined problems in order to exclude those 'unrepresentative' members of the community who would be critical of the police. Not being able to challenge such redefinitions, the community liaison officer confirmed his critics' point about the futility of his role.

Ethnic minority recruitment

The community liaison officer argued that 'all...institutions should reflect the communities they serve and if black people are part of the community they should be part of the institutions'. He argued that the Greater Manchester Police - a force in which ethnic minority officers made up less than one per cent of the authorized establishment - must recognize that the way their actions were viewed by the black community influenced whether black people would join the force. If changes were not forthcoming:

> it is hard to see that there is going to be a reflection of the black community population in the Greater Manchester Police before the year 2400 (lst Annual Report, p. 5).

To bring about a more ethnically representative bureaucracy, Linbert Spencer worked with the force to improve its race relations' training. He attempted to move the force policy away from classroom lessons to 'on the job' and 'on the division' based training. Additionally, he urged that the training programme be restructured to acknowledge that racial prejudice and discrimination existed within the force:

> This is the central issue that concerns people on the street. I don't care whether the police officer is familiar with the place where my parents were born; I want the officer to exercise his discretion towards me without being influenced by racially motivated prejudice (1st Annual Report, p. 7).

He argued that the police should also think about two further reforms. First, there had to be an unambiguous statement from the force that they were prepared to act to 'eliminate the use of inappropriate assumptions in the organization based on national origin or colour'. And second, that force orders and anti-racist training had to be followed up by effective supervision, and if need be, disciplinary action against racist officers:

> unless the profile of the Greater Manchester Police in the eyes of ethnic minority groups, particularly Afro-Caribbean groups, is radically changed, then ethnic minority recruitment, despite the efforts being made by the police, will never increase beyond the trickle at which it stands now...The fact that the police may perceive themselves to be neutral or even anti-racist is almost irrelevant, because the action of the minority groups and individuals is based on their own perception of the police, and not on the police perception of themselves (lst Annual Report, p. 16).

However, as indicated previously, the chief constable rejected all allegations concerning racism in the force and there was no attempt to address the criticisms and suggestions of the community liaison officer. When, for example, the police committee formulated an anti-discrimination code of ethics for the force, the chief constable made it clear that he would have nothing to do with it.

Complaints against the police

The community liaison officer hoped that if complaints involving police officers were dealt with in a satisfactory manner, the tenor of police-community relations could be changed. However, the chief constable refused to appoint an officer to work with the liaison officer and Linbert Spencer was left to deal with the force's existing complaints' department. He dealt only with those complaints submitted directly to him and was not involved with any complaint made directly to the police under normal statutory arrangements.

Linbert Spencer saw his 'casework' on those complaints which were not strong enough to be dealt with under the formal procedure as central to constructing 'community confidence' in the police. This informal conciliation process was intended to allow members of the community with grievances to work with the liaison officer to resolve their problems rapidly and satisfactorily. 'Complainant' and 'complained about' were to be brought together in an attempt to achieve mutually satisfactory reconciliation:

> The accent is on the achieving of understanding through a personalized focus and not necessarily on the obtaining of testable evidence so as to mete out punishment (1st Annual Report, p. 13).

If clear and valid complaint patterns did emerge, these would be taken up with the local police commander.

While the community liaison officer expressed satisfaction with his informal casework method, he recognized that a series of outstanding issues needed to be addressed if community concerns were to be assuaged. In his first annual report, he noted that half the total of formal complaints recorded by him had been subsequently withdrawn, compared to one quarter of the informal complaints. He had also assumed that the formal complaints coming through his office would have a higher completion rate than ones which had been processed by the formal police complaints' department. In fact, as it happened, the withdrawal rate for both was comparable. Feedback he received from complainants indicated that they felt themselves to be under considerable pressure when they were interviewed by police officers. In his second annual report, Linbert Spencer noted that the withdrawal rate was down to twenty-five per cent, and explained this by reference to his being more closely involved in the cases:

I have tried to stay much more closely in contact with the complainants and in doing so have, hopefully, enabled them to feel more confident during the generally long, tedious and often fruitless wait which they endure after having given their statements (2nd Annual Report, p. 19).

It was precisely because the official complaints' system was so arduous, and often pointless in terms of outcome, that Spencer placed so much emphasis on the informal dispute resolution mechanism. However, even with regard to this imaginative mechanism, he was worried that one third of the informal complaints were not followed up by complainants.

This part of the community liaison officer's work took him to the heart of the matter as far as policing in Moss Side was concerned. In his last report to the police committee, he concluded that 'the high proportion of complaints from black or brown people may point to the need for an in depth look at policing on the ground'. He also emphasised that if community liaison were to stand any chance of success in Moss Side, complaints against the police would have to be a priority concern and be included within the remit of the liaison panels. In addition, a means would have to be found to overcome the serious problems associated with attempting to use the formal police complaints' process.

Thus, Linbert Spencer did attempt to articulate and represent the interests of Moss Side by addressing policing issues that concerned people living in that locale. However, the manner in which he did so, and the outcomes of his interventions, reinforced the opposition of key community groups in the area. He had no power to challenge the way the police dealt with these issues and as a consequence the force could ignore criticisms with which they disagreed. His informal complaints structure was viewed as lending legitimacy and support to a completely discredited and ineffective official complaints' procedure. His efforts were, it was argued, diverting complainants into a completely impotent system where the objective was to achieve not justice but reconciliation. In addition, the liaison officer was criticized for refusing to recognize that whole sections of the community, not just individuals, were being systematically criminalized by the Greater Manchester Police.

Furthermore, his response to racist attacks advanced multi-agency policing and did not acknowledge community claims that certain police officers were responsible, in their everyday contact with the community, for carrying out racial assaults. Therefore, not only could he not challenge existing police policies and practices, but he was accepting uncritically police definitions of the problems, facilitating multi-agency policing strategies and lending legitimacy to the Greater Manchester Police.

In addition, there was no identifiable change in the policing of Moss Side as a result of his work. Compounding the routine allegations arising out of the policing of the area were a series of highly publicized incidents which continued to heighten tensions. There were ongoing allegations by youth and community workers that they were being harassed and threatened in their places of work, in their professional contact with police officers and in certain instances also in their homes. The resultant court cases, during 1983, arising from an incident outside Moss Side Shopping precinct in September 1982, resulted in the two youth workers involved eventually winning their cases against the chief constable.

To make matters considerable worse, in April 1984, a young black woman, Jackie Berkeley, complained officially that she had been racially abused, beaten and raped by police officers during her detention in Greenheys (Moss Side) police station. She, in turn, was charged with assaulting police officers and criminal damage. The ramifications of this complaint for police-community relations were staggering:

> Here was an allegation, more serious than any so far, being made about Moss Side Police just at the time when the chief constable of Manchester, James Anderton, and the police establishment of the city, are desperate to prove that since the mass revolts against the police in 1981, all is rosy in the garden (*Jackie Berkeley Defence Committee*, 1985).

Such incidents also seriously hindered all efforts to set up a liaison panel in Moss Side.

Community representation

The community liaison officer looked towards the Lambeth consultative committee in London as a possible model for the Greater Manchester liaison initiative. However, he was concerned about adopting a format which, in the absence of a statutory police committee, encouraged a 'chaotic participatory process'. This convinced him that although flexibility was essential to ensure 'genuine' representation of all sections of the community, it was important to have structured terms of reference and precise agendas to keep meetings manageable (Ist Annual Report, p. 2). Hence, the critical impressions gleaned from London, in conjunction with Home Office guidelines on consultation, determined the initial formula for the community liaison panels.

In order to set up the liaison structures, the police committee negotiated with the constituent district councils and the Council for Voluntary Organizations. They were notified that there would be automatic representation of the police committee, the police and the constituent councils. Additionally, all community groups and residents within the sub-division would be invited to attend inaugural meetings 'to decide who they wanted to have as members of the liaison panel'. The meetings would be open for anyone to attend as observers, and after the formal business was concluded, all present would have the opportunity to air their views on policy issues.

Hence, community participation was to take place through invitation within a highly formalized setting, and be primarily indirect in nature, through community representatives. The purpose of participation was also very clearly delineated:

> consultation is the idea of the police consulting the community or meeting with the community to discuss all aspects of policing so that they will be better informed about public feelings and ideas and as a result be better able to make decisions about policing the community ...consultation is not about the community making decisions affecting policing, but it should lead to the police taking better decisions affecting the community (Community liaison officer, 1983).

Moss Side

There were intensive 'unseen' negotiations between key individuals on the police committee, local political representatives, local police officers and more radical community representatives during 1982 to sell the idea of police-community liaison in Moss Side. However, little progress was made. In addition, between 1 February and 30 March 1983, fourteen meetings were held in ten different venues in the area. Two of the meetings had to be cancelled for lack of interest but the people who did attend the other meetings were 'earmarked' as the potential core for a liaison panel. They were invited to another meeting to discuss what kind of consultative machinery would be appropriate for that subdivision. This meeting was attended by eighteen members of the public, five police officers and the community liaison officer. A draft proposal suggested that there would not be a formal panel with a formal membership. Instead, liaison would be premised on open public meetings. There would be a core membership (consisting of the elected representatives for the area, those individuals who had been involved through the area meetings and interested others) who would organize meetings, set the agenda, 'proselytize' and manage the publicity.

Thus, despite the views of the community liaison officer concerning the need for tight formal liaison structures, the urgent political imperative to establish a panel in Moss Side meant that he, and the police committee, were willing to agree to loosely structured arrangements. More meetings took place in January 1984 and March 1984, with very few members of the public attending. It was agreed at this meeting that there should be a meeting between the chief constable and the community to 'clear the air' about the policing of the area. However, this proved difficult to realize.

The meeting of the 17 September 1984 was Linbert Spencer's third attempt to get Anderton to come to Moss Side. However, to the anger of the police committee and the liaison officer, the chief constable did not turn up. Instead deputy chief constable John Stalker and the divisional chief superintendent were present to deal with an audience of less than twenty in 'an open and frank way'. John Stalker was questioned about a wide variety of local policing issues. He denied allegations of racist policing and that certain police officers were 'fitting people up' on a regular basis. He said that he was worried that there was 'a feeling of paranoia in Moss Side' and that nothing could be gained by 'raking up the past'. He also defended the complaints' system, saying that the community liaison officer and lay visiting scheme would be able to assuage any outstanding community concern. A complete stalemate was reached over a whole range of contentious issues, with allegations being made from the floor and the police representatives denying their validity.

No panel materialized in Moss Side. Despite meetings being held in a variety of settings, 'the black community' was not participating in the proposed structure. Furthermore, while respectable community leaders were prepared to continue to meet with the police in other established situations, they were not prepared, especially in the context of the Jackie Berkeley case, to identify publicly with the liaison initiative.

A clear indication of the gap that existed between the authorities and local people is provided by juxtaposing the turnout to the liaison meetings, with those initiated by issue-based groupings in Moss Side. Youth and Allied Workers' Police Monitoring Group, for example, attracted approximately eighty people to its first public training day on policing and youth work in November 1983. Throughout this period, there were also large turnouts to meetings held by the Manchester Campaign Against the Police Bill. Public meetings concerned about the Home Office's illegal immigrant trawls in Moss Side were also well attended, and approximately 150 people attended a public meeting to support Jackie Berkeley in December 1984. By comparison the community liaison officer could not muster more than twenty people, including councillors and police officers, to any of his meetings.

The constituent councils

Throughout late 1982 and 1983, negotiations took place between the police committee, individual district councils and the Greater Manchester Association of Metropolitan Authorities to establish liaison throughout the force area. By October 1983, the negotiations were complete, except in the case of Tameside and Manchester, which were fundamentally opposed to community liaison. The opposition of Manchester City Council was of particular significance because Moss Side lay within the city's boundaries and, as indicated, the police committee's intention had been to establish the first panel in Moss Side.

There were constant efforts to cajole and persuade the two 'maverick' councils to sponsor the liaison structures. However, Manchester, spurred on by the rejection of liaison panels by Moss Side, in February 1984 passed a resolution stating that community liaison panels would not strengthen the democratic accountability of the police and therefore the council 'would be unwilling to participate' in such powerless, unrepresentative and enforced structures. Eventually, as will be discussed in the following chapter, the city council decided to set up an alternative police monitoring initiative. The police committee, in an attempt to overcome Manchester's opposition, stated that liaison panels could be set up in such a way as to supplement the proposed police monitoring groups. However, this was rejected. Subsequently, both councils were notified that the committee intended to establish the liaison panels with or without their co-operation. By November 1984, it had been decided to set up a community liaison meeting in Tameside which would include representatives from the Tameside Volunteer Bureau and the Tameside Council for Racial Equality. Liaison panels were subsequently set up without council representation because Tameside was seen to be 'a weaker political animal' than Manchester. It was also hoped that when the panels were thriving throughout the rest of Greater Manchester, people in Manchester would pressurize the council to change its position.

The first community liaison panels

By September 1984, sixteen panels had been established. The first panels set up in Greater Manchester were in Leigh in December 1982 and Salford in August 1983, areas of the county where there was no public controversy about policing. A review of their first year of operation, by the community liaison officer, identified key problems of representation and participation. According to panel members, there were too many councillors who exercised undue influence, and too few representatives of the young, unemployed and working class. The community liaison officer's report also acknowledged the disproportionate over-representation of white, middle-aged males.

Members also stated that they had no real understanding of what they were supposed to be doing, other than 'representing' the organizations and groups who had nominated them to attend meetings. In terms of active participation, members felt constrained by the agenda, the lecturing manner of certain police officers, the refusal of officers to share information and the size and format of the meetings. The suitability of using the police sub-division as the basis for the panels was queried as it was felt that this was too big a geographical area to be defined as 'a community'. General scepticism was also expressed about the effectiveness of such fora as a means of influencing policing. Panel members acknowledged that they were not in touch with those people who were in conflict with the police, and recognized that their positive relationship with the police, which had been built up during panel meetings, would not necessarily translate into better police-community relations. As one member put it:

> Things might have changed on the street, but I don't think they can put that down to us (Community liaison officer report, July 1984).

Thus, questions of adequate representation and participation surfaced immediately as practical issues for the newly established panels. Linbert Spencer recognized that, whilst in theory the whole community was supposed to be represented in the panels, certain important sections of it were 'absent', namely, ethnic minorities, young people and women.

The lack of representation and participation of key groups was reflected in the types of issues upon which the panels focused. There were demands for more beat policing, queries about victim support schemes, questions concerning effective crime prevention measures, demands for neighbourhood watch and constant complaints about juvenile delinquency. Thus, as the Home Office envisaged, discussions about the extent of crime, fear of crime and crime prevention dominated the agenda of the liaison panels. The issue that had inspired the initiative, the total breakdown in consensual relations between the police and black people, rapidly disappeared from the liaison panel agenda. Linbert Spencer recognized the dilemmas posed by the change in focus:

> Are the community liaison panels local machinery where the police are part of a process which addresses and seeks to find ways of tackling policing issues; or are community liaison panels local machinery where the police are party to a process which addresses and seeks ways of tackling the police? (Community liaison officer, July 1984).

He also expressed concern about the 'lack of clarity, sometimes confusion and even ignorance' among panel members. He concluded that unless the police committee provided structured support, the 'confusions', 'contradictions' and 'absences' mentioned above would result in the panels operating and ultimately degenerating 'in an isolated void'.

Resolving problems of representation and participation?

The community liaison officer did not believe that non-participation of ethnic minorities in the liaison initiative could be because there was a lack of faith in such structures. Instead, he viewed non-participation as a technical problem that could be resolved by setting up a special supplementary consultative forum where ethnic minority representatives would have the time and space to articulate their views on the policing issues that concerned their community:

> It is possible that issues relating to policing and its effects or implications for ethnic minorities will never be adequately aired or dealt with in a localised forum. The localized forum will have many other pressures on its time and if they are to be adequately aired and dealt with, this might have the effect of making an imbalance in the work of any local or division wide forum (Community liaison officer, 1982).

To this end, he had continual discussions with the various community relations councils throughout Greater Manchester, proposing that any such panel should have representatives from all ethnic minority organizations in the county and should be attended by senior police officers. A discussion document was distributed to relevant community groups but a positive response was not forthcoming.

Moss Side

Other ways were imagined to foster the consultation process in Moss side. First, there were ongoing discussions between the police and 'authentic' community leaders. Second, the force deployed what it described as 'omnicompetent' community police officers in the area. Third, monthly meetings were held between the divisional commander, the community liaison officer and the Community Contact inspector to discuss the general situation in Moss Side. Finally, Linbert Spencer initiated a multi-agency crime prevention panel which did not require direct community involvement.

In June 1983 the liaison officer convened a meeting of area managers of recreation, housing, employment, education and social services departments and a senior police officer to formulate a corporate approach to what they defined as the pressing social problems in Moss Side. This group collated and shared all available data on one particular housing estate in the area 'to test whether a co-ordinated approach can have an impact on some of the issues identified as leading to a fear of crime' (Community liaison officer, May

1984). Consequently, an open day took place in September 1984 'to inform the community about the approach that the local services are taking in trying to co-ordinate the services better and also to test out the effect of focusing on a well defined area' (2nd Annual Report, p. 16). Although the community response was 'disappointing', a second day was held in March 1985 in the Moss Side Shopping Precinct. Although it was conspicuously unsuccessful in terms of mobilizing community interest, this 'professional' liaison panel provoked considerable anger because of the way it was meeting in an unaccountable manner and because it was furthering a multi-agency approach.

Young people

In his second annual report, Linbert Spencer repeated his concern about, 'the almost total lack of young adult involvement in the work of the panels' and warned that, 'if the panels are to be at all effective, then this section of the community must be enabled to have their say' (2nd Annual Report, p. 22). The lack of youth representation was confirmed by those attending the first two county-wide liaison fora:

> Everyone is talking about young people yet look around here there is a lack of youth. There's a lack of cross sectional representation. Where's the young people on the panels? Eighteen to twenty-five year olds' views should be heard. These meetings are mainly for councillors, there's not enough people from where the problems are.

> At our first meeting there were twenty-four young people and we got six representatives from youth groups. However, they didn't come to the following meetings. There's a lack of youth. People of our age bracket are identifying the problem of youth yet the youth aren't here.

> How do you incorporate young people who don't want to come? How do you incorporate old people who only come to moan about young people? We must incorporate youth but it can't be done.

One representative said that his panel had found an effective, if undemocratic, means of achieving youth representation and participation:

> We go to the youth clubs and physically get the youth to come to our meetings!

The liaison officer attempted to bring about 'more consistent involvement of young adults in public consultation about policing' by proposing that a weekend forum be set up with youth 'representatives' from each district. The participants, young people aged between sixteen and twenty-one, would be contacted through general advertising in the local media and through youth officers, community relations councils and voluntary youth organisations.

The chief constable immediately intervened, arguing that the focus of the forum should be changed from policing and young people 'allowing the young people to discuss their views of current social issues' and that it be held not at a weekend rural 'retreat' but at the force training school. The police committee opposed Anderton's intervention, maintaining that the point of the forum was to enable young people to discuss their relationships and attitudes to, and with, the police, rather than general more social issues.

The eventual 'compromise' reached reflected the demands of the chief constable. It was agreed to hold a one day conference at the force school, with the 'emphasis to be put on allowing the young people to identify those issues most important to them.' This was a notably different proposal from the liaison officer's original proposal.

Women

The under/non-representation and participation of women was another issue that was addressed as a matter of urgency:

> If the membership of the panels offers us any clues as to who they might influence in terms of police/public relationships, then relationships between women and the police will be unaffected (2nd Annual Report, p. 5).

Linbert Spencer was concerned that there had been no real attempt by the panels to 'address the balance and increase the number involved in this work'. Overall, out of the initial thirteen panels, there was a total of 445 members, of which 102 were women. Furthermore, at some of the meetings there were no women present. Spencer noted with apprehension the view within one of the panels that 'the fact that there are very few women involved is irrelevant and makes no difference'.

The liaison officer also identified the issue of the special policing needs of women through his casework. He noted an increasing tendency within local police work to define domestic violence incidents as 'domestics' in order to not become involved and/or to suggest civil action. As far as Spencer was concerned, this was not acceptable because 'the casualties are weak, usually female of sometimes frighteningly violent relationships' (2nd Annual Report, p. 20).

The outcome of the liaison officer's concern was a police committee women only conference on women and policing. This conference, held in June 1985, provided a further example of how the committee sought to deal with the problematic question of representation and participation. All women's groups and organizations in the county were invited to send representatives. The conference itself was divided into separate workshops on issues relating to black women, domestic violence and sexual offences. With regard to the latter two workshops, splits emerged between the representatives of the more traditional and conservative women's organisations, for example, the National Council of Women and Victim Support, and the more radical ones, most notably, Black Womens' Group, Rape Crisis, Womens' Aid and Taboo. However, it was during the discussions in the black women's issues' workshop that the real problems with the police committee's format became apparent. This workshop had to be abandoned after two of the councillors dismissed black women's complaints of police racism as exaggeration and hearsay. As a consequence, a black women only workshop was hastily reconvened. The point was made to the conference chair that the very fact that there had to be a separate workshop was indicative of the police committee's practical inability to address the black community's complaints about police racism.

During the plenary session, there were further problems when the black women's workshop attempted to report back. One of the key concerns it raised was how difficult it was for black women, who were victims of domestic violence, to complain to the police, because it provided racist police officers with a legitimate opportunity to arrest black men. During the ensuing discussion, a councillor from Greater Manchester Council's Equal Opportunities sub-committee stated that she failed to see what relevance race had in the police response to domestic violence. She argued that at one time all human beings had been black but that 'by the grace of God some of us had lost this pigment from our skin' (Report to the Police Monitoring Committee, July 1985). The meeting ended in uproar. At a subsequent police-committee initiated 'women and policing' working party meeting, radical women's groups withdrew from discussions after a vote of censure against the two councillors was overruled by the committee chair.

Discussion

The Labour-controlled police committee tested to the full the assertion that the 'tripartite structure' provided an effective form of local accountability. When the committee found itself in open conflict with the chief constable, the severe limitations placed upon it by the 1964 Police Act quickly became apparent. The various disputes indicated that the police committee had no powers to ensure that the chief constable consulted with them before finalizing policing priorities and policies. Furthermore, as Morgan (1985) noted, the blank cheque given to the chief constable by the Home Office during the miners' strike demonstrated conclusively that committee members had no control over police expenditure. This meant that there was no means of holding the chief constable to account under the existing constitutional arrangements. As the chair of the committee acknowledged:

> people assume that somewhere there is someone who can say 'you can't do that', they assume that somewhere there is accountability. Laurence Scott showed that there isn't - the chief constable is in control (Cox, 1985).

It was against this background that the committee attempted to establish its community liaison initiative.

This chapter has recorded the nature of the problems encountered, and generated, by the community liaison officer in his attempt to represent the black community and establish liaison panels. He faced a series of difficulties in his role as the 'community representative'. First, his 'top-down', ascribed 'representative' status was rejected by significant sections of 'the community' he was supposedly representing. Second, the multi-agency philosophy underpinning much of his work, and his inability to have any seeming impact on the policing of Moss Side, confirmed his unrepresentative status in practice. This illustrated his powerlessness in relation to effecting change in the policing of the area. Such problems impacted directly on his attempts to set up a liaison panel in Moss Side.

Furthermore, the expressed hope of the community liaison officer and the police committee that the setting up of successful panels in the rest of Greater Manchester would persuade people in Moss Side to change their minds was misplaced. Problems of adequate representation and participation surfaced immediately. The formulaic liaison structure emphasized community representation as opposed to community participation. As a consequence, all formal community organizations and representatives were invited onto the panels. However, such an approach was inherently problematic. First, there was no recognition of the possible power inequalities that existed between the different groups that were supposed to have equal representation. Second, there was no acknowledgment of the questionable representative status of many of these community groups and individuals. Third, there was no appreciation that certain sections of the community did not have formal community representatives. Fourth, invitations were given to community groups and representatives who had no necessary relevance to police-community relations. Finally, the police committee, the police and local councils were given a privileged status in that they enjoyed automatic rights of representation, despite what the other community representatives might think.

The representative structure that unfolded was tightly controlled, with limited rights of participation. Direct community participation was limited to contributions at the end of meetings. In addition, there was a highly formalized structure and tightly structured terms of reference governing the purpose of participation and representation. Participation was mobilized by the Home Office for the specific purpose of helping the police to control crime. Also, the panel meetings were, in Pateman's (1970) terms, situations of partial participation with power residing firmly with the police representatives who had their operational autonomy enshrined in the terms of reference. Moreover, they kept control of the information and knowledge that would have been a pre-condition for an open discussion about policing, or indeed about crime.

Thus, the manner in which issues of community representation and participation were dealt with reproduced existing power inequalities. The initial community liaison model facilitated the over-representation and participation of white, middle-aged males who acted as respectable community representatives. The liaison officer did realize that important sections of the community - black people, women and young people - were non/under-represented. However, in order to redress the situation he recommended that all-encompassing additional structures of representation, based on the notion of the whole community of ethnic minorities, the whole community of young people and the whole community of women, be superimposed.

It is not surprising that even the respectable black community leaders rejected the proposed ethnic minority liaison panel. Effectively, what Linbert Spencer was suggesting was that they participate in a special forum to compensate for the fact that the panels had failed to represent the interests they had originally been established to represent. Even if this forum had been agreed to, the liaison officer would undoubtedly have had to encounter the problems of the non/under-representation of black youth and black women.

The recommendations concerning young people suffered from similar difficulties. The liaison officer recommended that ten young people be given the mantle of being the representatives of young people in their districts. The problem with such a proposal was that it was not these young people who were in conflict with the police. Furthermore, by the time that the chief constable had finished restructuring the proposal, not only was the meeting of the youth representatives convened within police premises, but discussion of policing and young people was no longer on the agenda.

The non/under-representation of women was given considerable attention by the liaison officer and the police committee. However, the all-encompassing format of structured representation failed to give recognition to the fact that there are racial and class inequalities between women, and that certain women's groups work within and articulate dominant ideologies. As a consequence, the interests of those powerless women's groups which challenged dominant ideologies concerning women and policing were in constant danger of being excluded.

Thus, not only did the original structure of community representation reproduce existing power inequalities and social divisions, but the additional arrangements, set up to counter-balance those inequalities and provide adequate representation of all interests, reproduced further divisions between, for example, 'respectable' youth and 'disreputable' youth, and 'respectable' women and 'disreputable' women. Hence, the interests of those in conflict with the police were, in effect, being marginalized by the liaison structures.

In February 1985, Linbert Spencer publicly reaffirmed his belief in the potential of the panels because 'there is no other existing structure for police-public consultation which has the capability of delivering the level of involvement for local people'. However, he advised that the whole concept of community liaison be reviewed, because of many of the problems identified above, and a permanent community liaison unit be created to service the panels:

> Specifically, help is needed to increase the confidence of panel members; help them understand their role, functions, powers and potential; enable them to carry out basic research on police/community issues within their own areas; assist them to understand local police strategies and their place in defining local police priorities; clarify the panels' aims and objectives (Community liaison officer, March 1985).

If this development was to be achieved, the proposed unit would have to work with 'community groups of all kinds to publicize and popularize the work and potential of the panels' and provide structured links to the police committee. Thus, in response to the difficulties he had encountered, Linbert Spencer was proposing a process of further formalization. A professional community liaison unit was to be given the role of assisting the liaison panels by carrying out research and enabling them to articulate their needs. How the professional community liaison unit tackled the ongoing problems of community representation and participation will be addressed later in this book. Before that, it is necessary to analyze why and how Manchester City Council decided to create alternative structures of community representation and participation through their police monitoring initiative.

5 City Council and police monitoring

In the May 1984 local government elections the left-wing of the Labour Party, after an arduous and bitter struggle with the right of the party, finally won control of Manchester City Council. This was a dramatic change because the 'old guard':

> in charge of the Town Hall virtually uninterrupted for decades, regarded the city party as a machine to be wheeled out at election time to rubber stamp the status quo (*Manchester Evening News,* 15 May 1984).

The leading local newspaper informed its readers that the new leader of the council was 'so left-wing he made Red Ken Livingstone appear moderate', and that a coup d'etat had taken place:

> Manchester Town Hall was firmly in the grip of Labour's hard left today. Councillor Graham Stringer, new left-wing leader of the now controlling Labour group, said their radical no-cuts confrontation-seeking manifesto would now become the policy of the city council (16 May 1984).

The left was indeed determined that the radical socialist manifesto presented to the electorate at the May elections would be implemented. This time there was to be no compromise with either the right of the party or the opposition parties on the council:

> The manifesto is firmly based on the belief that councils in Labour strongholds like Manchester should act, not only as a platform for resistance to the Tory government, but as a real socialist alternative

that can show that socialism works in practice. For that reason Labour's manifesto sets its aims high - to begin to build a city of PEACE, EQUALITY and DEMOCRACY, a SOCIALIST CITY (*Red Banner,* June 1984).

Labour promised to: make the council more accountable to local communities by decentralizing services to neighbourhood offices and setting up a central participation unit; open Town Hall proceedings to the public; turn the city into a nuclear free zone; create and defend jobs; and actively oppose all forms of discrimination based on a person's sexuality, race or physical ability. Thus, it mirrored, to a large degree, the basic concerns of new urban left administrations elected in other parts of Britain in this time period. They all demonstrated:

> a concern for issues hitherto absent from or marginal to conventional local government, such as...women's rights, and racial equality; a disdain for many of the traditional ways of conducting local authority business; a view of local government as an arena both for combatting the policies of a Conservative government and for displaying by example the potential of grass roots socialism; and, perhaps more fundamentally, a commitment to notions of mass politics based upon strategies of decentralization and/or political mobilization at local level (Gyford, 1985, p. 18).

As Wainwright (1987) has pointed out, in exile from mainstream politics in Manchester, councillors on the left consciously worked with 'the community' to build an alternative power base and construct a popular policy agenda. The renegade left consulted with tenants' groups, public sector unions, community centres, black, womens' and gay groups in the formulation of its radical manifesto. This meant that the interests of the marginalized found representation on the formal political agenda in Manchester when the left came to power.

The decision to implement all commitments meant fulfilling one of the most controversial proposals in the manifesto: to make the Greater Manchester Police genuinely accountable:

> We do not believe that community liaison panels will assist local people in having a greater say in the operations of police activity. In order to campaign for real accountability of the police to the communities they serve, we will set up a police monitoring group. We will also consider setting up a committee to establish guidelines for council policy towards and cooperation with the police (Party

Manifesto, 1984).

The people of Manchester were subsequently reminded of the democratic history of municipal policing by the new leader of the council:

> The police forces were set up by municipal corporations to help their own communities. The forerunners of the Greater Manchester Police, paid for and controlled locally, largely met the needs of different sections of the city's community. That is not to say a 'golden age' of policing ever existed. The police simply got closer to meeting the needs of the community than today's unaccountable police forces. Later, when the chief constable sat at a desk in the Town Hall, local politicians on the watch committee ran the police on behalf of Manchester. If they got it wrong, people could vote them out (Stringer, 1987, p.5).

Had the right of the party retained power in Manchester, this controversial electoral commitment would have been shelved. A significant number of 'traditional' Labour councillors were opposed to this particular policy, arguing that the council should be working with the police to formulate policies that would reduce the incidence and fear of crime. This opposition was to have important implications for the long term success or failure of the new initiatives.

From commitment to committee

The Manchester Labour Party's electoral mandate to press for full democratic control over policing meant that the city was destined to become the first place in Britain with both a statutory police committee and a formal police monitoring committee, both supposedly representing 'the community' on policing issues, and both controlled by the Labour Party. Although the Labour-controlled committees agreed not to criticize each other in public, they did view each other with considerable disdain.

Representatives from the City Council and the police committee met in May and September 1985 to discuss their differences. The police committee argued that Manchester was constitutionally different to London, and that the police monitoring committee had no statutory powers to call the chief constable to account for the manner in which Manchester was policed, or to effect the policing of particular neighbourhoods. The police committee had that vital power. Committee delegates also argued that there was 'a crying need to do something about policing in Manchester' and that liaison panels - a local

Labour Party initiative - could extend police accountability because if local support for them was forthcoming and adequate resources were allocated to them, the police would have to 'ignore demands at their peril'. The committee, it was pointed out, had respected the wishes of Manchester City Council in the interests of unity, but under the Police and Criminal Evidence Act, there was a legal duty to establish consultative arrangements, and 'if necessary [the committee] will go ahead WITHOUT the participation of the City Council' (Minutes of meeting, 6 September 1985).

However, the City Council representatives disagreed, stating that the electorally mandated monitoring initiative would be more effective than the police committee, because it could use its local authority powers to influence policing practices and crime problems in Manchester in three very direct ways. First, its proposed police monitoring committee would work with other council departments (planning, housing, direct works, recreation, social services) and local people to formulate city wide community safety strategies. In doing so, the monitoring committee would be able to demonstrate that there was an effective alternative to police-driven multi-agency approaches. Second, the committee would counter all attempts by Greater Manchester Police to use council departments as accomplices in policing operations that had nothing to do with conventional crime control. And finally, a full-time research unit would be established and its monitoring and evaluative work would produce fine-grained pictures of the policing in Manchester. These pictures would be used to challenge the chief constable's depiction of the city's policing problems. Liaison panels were rejected on the grounds that:

> there is a commitment to articulating the concerns of sections of the Manchester community, particularly black people. The City Council's view is that its role is to assist groups in the community to make 'informed' demands, hence a team of research and development staff have been established...there is little convincing evidence to persuade the Manchester City Council police monitoring committee to alter its scepticism about liaison panels... The City Council feels therefore that its energies should be channelled into articulating the needs of its many communities and to campaigning for alternatives to the present system (Minutes of meeting, 6 September 1985).

In November there were further exchanges about both the liaison panels and the implications of the imminent demise of the police committee. A joint working party was established in an attempt to resolve the differences and to provide a forum for communication between the two Labour groups. The police committee's representatives were anxious about the consequences of Manchester City Council's stance on the new joint boards, especially its demand for no opposition representation. They made it clear that if the community relations unit was to survive abolition, Manchester would have to change its attitude and consider working with sympathetic opposition members on certain issues.

It was also agreed that the working party should sketch a report on the achievements of the police committee, and what principles and practices needed to be preserved to ensure that the accountability campaign recommenced. However, on the issue of situating liaison panels in Manchester no consensus was reached.

After much internal discussion and a series of visits to meet with the Greater London Council's police committee and those of Lambeth, Camden, Hackney and Southwark, a full council committee, a working party and a permanent research and development unit, were established. Advisors and co-optees were appointed to Manchester's new 'watch committee' to provide the expertise and local knowledge on policing issues that the councillors did not possess. In doing so, the committee was attempting to reach those sections of the community who were in conflict with the police. In contrast, the Conservative and Liberal opposition were denied access to the decision-making processes. Such a hard line was taken by the Labour group because of the opposition parties' public pledge to vote, at the first opportunity, for the abolition of the police monitoring committee. These breaks with Town Hall tradition generated endless and bitter arguments at the monthly meetings, with opposition councillors protesting that Labour was behaving in a completely undemocratic manner.

Deliberations on community representation and participation

The promise that the monitoring committee would create alternatives to the unrepresentative liaison panels ensured, from the outset, that it would be embroiled in the problematic issues of community, participation and representation. Labour councillors argued that the city wide network of monitoring groups they were proposing would be very different from the liaison panels because they would represent the different needs of 'the community', defined as those who were vulnerable to the practices and policies of an unaccountable police force in Manchester. This vulnerable community was made up of those subject to lack of effective police response to racist attacks; those being criminalized by racist, brutal and intimidatory police officers and those suffering from the consequences of the incapacity of the Greater Manchester Police to prevent and detect crime.

Thus, the deliberations about the setting up of monitoring groups were underpinned by very different notions of community, representation and participation to those articulated by the police committee and the community liaison officer. The police monitoring committee acknowledged that there were certain groups within the community whose interests needed to be prioritized in terms of the policing to which they were subject. This was the reason why Labour councillors believed that monitoring groups would be genuinely popular.

During the initial meetings of the police monitoring committee and research unit, further differences between the monitoring groups and liaison panels were articulated:

1. Liaison panels were deemed to be part of an attempt to create a much larger overarching policing system which had a nationally set agenda, whereas monitoring groups were to be part of a decentralized police service which would correspond to the needs of the community.

2. Liaison panels were part of an information gathering exercise which was geared towards furthering political control, whereas monitoring groups would, through their local knowledge and information, would set the agenda for local policing needs.

3. Liaison panels were part of a sophisticated multi-agency policing strategy geared towards increasing surveillance, whereas monitoring groups would empower local people to challenge policing practices and hold officers to account.

4. Liaison panels were geared towards calming down and educating community expectations, whereas monitoring groups would encourage people to enter into an open debate on their policing needs.

5. Liaison panels represented the policing needs of the authoritarian state, whereas the monitoring groups represented the community demand for a democratically accountable police service.

As far as the police monitoring committee was concerned, authentic community policing would only be possible when decentralized policing arrangements were introduced and when the community was in a position to decide what type of policing it wanted. There could be no community policing until policing was under direct community control.

It was left to the committee's working party, made up of members of the Labour Party, the monitoring committee and interested others, to formulate policies on how to proceed with the establishment of monitoring groups. The initial meetings generated a wide-ranging debate about how to bring about community involvement in policing issues. There was a genuine belief that monitoring groups could be established quickly. Those attending the first meeting in June 1984 discussed the practical difficulties of realizing 'a real input from the community'. Concern was expressed about whether communities existed, whether they could be created where they did not, and whether, if they did exist, they should be the cornerstone for Labour Party policy, given the possibility that their members might hold reactionary rather than progressive views:

> We have a problem where the police are needed but not wanted. The police are not the answer. We as a council must build up our communities; then the incidence of vandalism will be reduced and the communities will be able to look after themselves.
>
> Communities in Manchester are non-communities, they do not have collective strength.
>
> The council must do something about it. For example, how much money goes into these areas, on what basis. We must help to create the conditions for developing strong communities because the problems of policing lie within the strength of those communities.
>
> I know from my constituency that the difficulty with all this is that they are not a liberal community. Their view of policing and needs might be very different to what you propose.

During late 1984 and early 1985, the discussion continued, with questions being raised, in the light of the establishment of liaison panels throughout the rest of Greater Manchester, about genuine community consultation, the relevance and possible role of existing community groups and the validity of existing community representatives and groups.

In April and May 1985, the issue of setting up monitoring groups was discussed in considerable detail. It was stressed that if the initiative were to be successful, there would have to be: real grass roots participation, the possibility of exerting influence, and effective council support. It was agreed that diversity and flexibility would be central. Some groups would emerge out of already existing community groups, some would be geographically based whilst others would be issue based. However, there were tensions because although the dangers of the council imposing unwanted structures upon the community were acknowledged, certain Labour Party members tended to view the proposed monitoring groups, like the other council initiatives, as a means for harnessing support for the party and the council. It is within this context that the idea emerged that, ideally, the new monitoring groups should be premised on the existing Labour Party ward structure.

It was also confirmed that monitoring groups should not be funded or staffed by the council because it was important that they retain their autonomy. If it were deemed necessary, the committee should transfer monitoring group applications to other council committees for funding as required. Direct support from the committee would be limited to helping with accommodation, telephone bills and publicity needs. What should be given was support from the research and development unit rather than money. In order to stimulate public debate on policing and mobilize communities, it was agreed that the research unit should orchestrate a high profile city-wide campaign, hold public meetings and produce an informative magazine or newspaper on policing issues. It was also agreed that any group or locality wanting to set up a monitoring group should be vetted. This latter point came up at the working party meeting in May 1985 when a request from a residents' association in North Manchester was discussed. After investigation, it was discovered that this association was extremely right wing in its views.

Mobilizing the community

A considerable amount of the new police monitoring research unit's time was devoted to monitoring and collating information on: complaint patterns; policing strategies and crime statistics; all contact between council departments and the police; local and national civil liberties issues; and public order policing developments.

The unit, from the outset, found itself having to react constantly to the unfolding policing crisis in the city (Wright, 1985). And it should always be remembered that for sections of the left, 1985 was 'the year of living dangerously', when Britain was cloaked by the shadow of authoritarian policing (Scraton, 1987, pp. 161-8). In Manchester, the monitoring unit took the chief constable's statement about 'basic crime as such, theft, burglary, even violent crime' not being the predominant police concern as its overarching anti-left realist starting point. This departure point was of great significance because it meant that tracking, detailing and highlighting political and coercive policing developments in Manchester would be a primary focus for the monitoring unit, rather than 'mundane' petty criminality.

No sooner had the new unit become operational than the 'Battle of Brittan' happened in March 1985. Given the nature of the policing tactics used, the allegations of police brutality and the incapacity of the police committee to institute an independent investigation, the police monitoring committee established its own highly controversial inquiry in May 1985 (Platts-Mills,

1985). The unit was stretched by having to service this inquiry and by responding to developments resulting from the incident. It had to provide, for example, prolonged support for Sarah Hollis and Steven Shaw, two of the students at the centre of the inquiry who claimed that they were being systematically victimized by Greater Manchester police officers (Walker, 1986). The unit also took a lead position in the unfolding Stalker Affair (to be discussed in chapters seven and eight). In both cases, the unit was remarkably successful in ensuring that its version of events influenced public debate. It was clearly capable of functioning as an effective monitoring organization in its own right.

However, the unit was also politically mandated to work with communities to establish police monitoring groups. There were two very active and highly politicized issue based monitoring groups - Youth and Allied Workers' Police Monitoring Group and the Gay Men's Police Monitoring Group (formed in 1984) - already in existence and there was little difficulty in making contact with them or ensuring that certain of their concerns were taken on board by the monitoring committee. For example, at the behest of youth workers, a police and youth sub-committee was established to compliment the work of Greater Manchester Council's working party on police involvement in youth work. The monitoring committee also produced a 'Bust Card' for gay men and agreed to support gay men who were being harassed by the police. It also supported public meetings held by both monitoring groups.

However, attempting to create community or neighbourhood based monitoring groups was much more difficult. The reality was that the unit did not have the resources or requisite knowledge base to carry out its own high profile monitoring work and engage in low level community development work throughout the city. It was hoped that prototype neighbourhood monitoring groups might emerge from residents' petitions on policing and crime, which had been submitted to the council in late 1984 and early 1985. If this happened, it would also deter the police committee from attempting to establish liaison panels in the city. The nature and outcome of the subsequent meetings provide an insight into the 'Pandora's box' opened up by the promise to organize neighbourhood monitoring groups in Manchester.

Thornton Road

In April 1985, in the semi-final of the FA Cup, Liverpool FC played Manchester United at the 'neutral' ground of Manchester City. Afterwards, the police lost control of the crowd, and running battles between rival sets of fans ensued, with one street in particular suffering considerable damage. A panel of three representatives from the police, the deputy chair of the police monitoring committee, the chair of the police committee, a senior representative of Manchester City and the local Labour councillor met with 150 furious residents to discuss the incident.

At this very heated public meeting, the criticism was directed mainly towards Manchester City. Many of those present complained about the life long tribulations of living so close to a large football ground, and the fact that the club refused to take any responsibility for its unruly supporters. Residents were also concerned about who was going to compensate them for the damage they had suffered.

The police representatives deflected attention from themselves, by saying that it would be unfair to hold them responsible for society's ills. When one member of the audience asked why, if there were enough officers to man a police band, there were not enough to protect Thornton Road during a highly charged football match, he was jeered by the audience. The police monitoring committee representative argued that residents should be worried by the apparent lack of a coherent policing policy to protect their property and should push to make the police answerable in the future. The chair of the police committee argued that a liaison panel should be set up to deal with such police-community problems. However, those present at the meeting were not interested in taking police officers to task. All attempts to focus on the policing issues raised by the disorder were finally undermined when the Manchester City FC representative stated that what happened outside the ground was of no concern to the club. The meeting exploded. In this atmosphere there was no possibility of the police representatives being challenged over how and why they had lost control of the situation.

This meeting did not produce either a monitoring group or a liaison panel. On the contrary, the meeting mandated the police to adopt harder measures to deal with football supporters in the city. The Saturday following this meeting, supporters of Manchester City, for the first time, faced riot clad officers, police dogs, riot vans, intensive police cordoning and body searches on their way to the ground. No-one from the monitoring committee or the police committee was present to witness the police response to the residents' complaints.

The research unit was not unduly concerned that a monitoring group had not emerged. It is certainly questionable whether such a structure would have been 'progressive' in nature. It would have been composed of middle-aged, white pro-police residents, and would have been monitoring Manchester City rather than local policing. It was noticeable, for example, that black residents who had endured years of racial abuse from visiting supporters to the ground, and little police protection, were not present at this meeting.

Longsight

The police committee also convened a public meeting in Longsight in April 1985, in response to residents' complaints about the number of burglaries in the area. Representatives of the police, the police committee and the monitoring committee were present, as well as Gerald Kaufmann, the then Shadow Home Secretary and local MP. The police committee believed that the meeting would generate the first liaison panel in Manchester, whilst the monitoring committee hoped that a monitoring group would emerge. Those few residents who bothered to attend complained bitterly about hooliganism and burglary, and the ineffective police response. One resident said that when he reported a burglary, police officers laughed in his face. The police representatives stated that they could not meet all demands, and had to make choices about how to respond with such resources as were available. Another elderly resident claimed that when he reported a break-in, he was sworn at by the police officer and had the telephone put down on him. The police representatives replied that he could not understand why members of the public did not use the official complaints' system when such incidents occured.

When discussion turned to the disappointing attendance at the meeting compared to the number of people who had signed the original petition, the councillors were reminded that the meeting had been advertised for 'the people of Longsight', but that it was difficult for people to relate to such a large area. Residents argued for more localized meetings, and it was pointed out that the petition was not actually from the people of Longsight, but from one particular estate where, in the past, up to seventy people had attended residents meetings.

Gabrielle Cox, in response, explained the philosophy underpinning community liaison. She defended the decision to have an area based meeting as opposed to specific neighbourhoods, arguing that 'there are occasions when a wider area is needed to balance the communities'. She went on to argue specifically for the setting up of a liaison panel, claiming that such a structure would allow people to have small meetings where they could identify and discuss local issues, and then they could attend the broader community-wide panel meetings to discuss their concerns.

The representatives from the monitoring committee attempted to demonstrate the limitations of such an approach, by asking questions about the implications of the coal dispute for the policing of the area and the role of Special Branch in Manchester. The police representatives refused to answer on the grounds that they were operational matters and not really relevant to local policing issues. The monitoring committee took hope from the fact that no enthusiasm had been shown for the setting up of a liaison panel, and that the police, in refusing to answer their questions, had shown that they were not prepared to enter into serious dialogue. As far as the monitoring committee was concerned:

> the Longsight episode had a profound impact on determining Council policy on contact between the police and the community and the futility of the liaison panel approach (Police monitoring committee report, no. 6).

Although it is certainly true that the police committee had failed in its efforts to promote a liaison panel, there was little evidence to suggest that the meeting would have supported a monitoring group. What residents wanted was a positive response from the police. However, there was no indication from the police representatives that this would be forthcoming either.

Benchill

The other petition awaiting the unit presented even more of a dilemma for the police monitoring committee. In January 1985, a petition was signed by 130 residents of the Benchill area of Manchester, stating that they had been were being terrorized by gangs of youths and demanding that the council and police do something. A public meeting took place in July 1985 to enable residents to set up a monitoring group. This was the first meeting sponsored solely by the monitoring committee and there was no police or police committee presence.

The intention was, through organizing different workshops, to have a more detailed discussion of different community concerns: women and policing, youth and policing and old people and policing. However, the reality was dramatically different and illustrated the difficulties of attempting to facilitate full community participation. Very few young people turned up to the meeting because they thought it was a police organized meeting, and the old people did not attend because of the lack of adequate transport. Therefore, the idea of breaking the meeting up into specific workshops had to be abandoned, and a very heated free-for-all discussion took place about the inadequacy of council services and the lack of a police presence at the meeting. There was also a general air of cynicism about what exactly the police monitoring committee could do about local crime problems. As a consequence, the meeting did not produce a monitoring group.

Discussion

The police monitoring committee started from the premise that the police should accept the right of the community and its elected representatives to have a real say about how police resources were allocated, because it was the community that had to live with the fallout from these decisions. In doing so, the committee was raising fundamental questions about community, representation and participation. The stress was on creating structures that would facilitate the participation of the under/non-represented communities. It was emphasized that there should be voluntary and active participation with community groups setting their own agendas. In theory, the police monitoring committee took on the role of neutralizing power imbalances by silencing the political opposition, making sure that right wing community groups did not get access to resources and blocking all attempts to set up liaison panels in Manchester. Furthermore, through establishing a research and development unit, the committee was also signalling its determination to challenge the chief constable's monopolization of knowledge and information about how Manchester was policed. And there is little doubt that the unit, from its inception, impacted dramatically on public debate and internal council thinking about the policing of the city.

However, the committee encountered real problems in its attempts to hold the police to account and establish neighbourhood-based monitoring groups. First, the City Council had no control over this particular public service. Therefore, there was little that it could do to assuage community concerns and demands. It did not even possess any powers to ask the chief constable for reports on the policing of the city. Second, despite awareness of the difficulties of imposing structures on communities, the initiative remained 'top-down' in origin, located within heavily bureaucratic and hierarchical Labour Party and council structures. Finally, there was the assumption that the different under/non-represented groups and interests conceptualized their problems in the same manner as the police monitoring committee, and therefore would react favourably to the idea of monitoring groups. In the case of youth and community workers and gay men this was the case - both groups clearly felt that forming monitoring groups would help them in their disputes with the police.

But it quickly became clear that other communities did not necessarily think in these terms. What emerged from the meetings held in Manchester during the first half of 1985 was that there was no desire amongst those present to watch the police in the way envisaged by the monitoring committee. There was, for example little interest in discussing wider police controversies such as the policing of the miners' strike, the 'Battle of Brittan' or the speeches and actions of the chief constable. Instead, local people were demanding that local police officers and council departments take concurrent action against escalating crime, hooliganism and insecurity. And because the City Council had not developed any crime prevention strategies, its representatives could not offer any constructive suggestions. Thus, the meetings demonstrated that the council was extremely vulnerable on the crime question.

What also became apparent, despite the rhetoric of community policing, was the shocking gap that existed between senior police officers' understanding of local crime problems and the 'lived realities' of local residents in certain areas. In this sense, the monitoring committee had stumbled on a real source of community discontent in certain neighbourhoods. There was a clear need for some type of highly localized fora (as opposed to liaison panels) where residents could meet police officers to discuss local crime problems, police priorities and the quality of service being provided. The meetings also posed questions about the usefulness of 'open' public meetings as a forum for rational discussion. During the meetings there was a tendency for the majority viewpoint to be articulated. Anyone offering an alternative perspective was likely to be howled down. As the police monitoring committee and the police committee found out, in unstructured public meetings it is difficult to move the discussion on from specific to more general issues.

It should also be noted that the first meetings involved traditional Labour-voting white constituencies. No similar petitions were forthcoming from black neighbourhoods during this period, despite ongoing campaigns relating to the policing of their areas. The police monitoring committee found real difficulties, for example, in responding to the Jacki Berkeley incident and no monitoring committee campaign was forthcoming. This stood in stark contrast to the role the committee played in the 'Battle of Britain'. This reflected the council's more general difficulty of fulfilling the manifesto commitment to be more responsive to ethnic minority concerns. For example, the council chose to locate 'race' as one of the concerns of the equal opportunities' committee rather than establishing a separate 'race committee'. This decision produced allegations that the council was lumping together 'race' with sexual orientation, disability and gender and Labour councillors were informed that there were 'two kinds of racists in our society; those who hate "Blacks" and those who know what is good for "Blacks"...[and] the council is in danger of falling into the second category' (*City Life*, 23 August 1985).

The feedback from the first forays into the community and the first attempts to set up neighbourhood-based monitoring groups resulted in a considerable rethink of the overall community development strategy. As will be seen in Chapter Eight, the political controversy generated by the police monitoring committee's other high profile campaigning work also impacted dramatically on its work in this area.

6 Losing the fight for police accountability

As the 1980s progressed, a panoply of legislative measures was used by successive Conservative governments to bring high spending Labour-controlled local authorities under control. Proposals were introduced to regulate revenue and capital expenditure (thus enhancing fiscal accountability) and QUANGOs were appointed to bypass unmanageable and unpredictable local political processes. The Conservatives pushed forward with the attempted marketization of local government services in order to enhance efficiency and effectiveness and to increase consumer choice. A concerted effort was also made to assist private capital access public land and development contracts. This constituted a direct and wide-ranging attack on new urban left administrations 'wedded to the idea of the state as an instrument of social justice and determined to resist pressures to dismantle the welfare state system' (Horton, 1990, p.174).

The increasing subordination of local government was taken to its logical conclusion when, in July 1985, the local government bill became law, abolishing the Labour-dominated Greater London Council and the other metropolitan county councils from April 1986. As critics pointed out, it was the first time that an entire layer of government, controlled by an opposition political party, had been eliminated by a central government (Flynn and Leach, 1984; Harris, 1986; Butcher, Law, Leach and Mullard, 1990). There had been no Royal Commission or public inquiry and there was, 'little justification for abolition in either financial or administrative terms, but the government was determined to destroy the power base of what it described as the "loony left" '(Johnson, 1990, p. 74). As a result, the main duties and powers of 'the mets', including the powers of the police committees, were transferred to a system of statutory joint boards.

Restructuring the police committees

The legislative changes had an immediate and significant impact on the campaigns for police accountability. As part of the restructuring, new police authorities were established to discharge the obligations of the 1964 Police Act for the districts previously encompassed by the old committees. Strict central government guidelines were laid down concerning the composition and powers of the new boards. To the consternation of the government's opponents, the act changed the form of political representation previously governing the committees. The joint boards were to be made up of representatives of the constituent district councils reflecting, as far as possible, the party balance of power. This meant that in future councillors were much more likely to represent the parochial interests of their own councils rather than being concerned about county-wide issues. Furthermore, there was every possibility, given that the joint boards would be composed of new elected members, that the knowledge base painstakingly built up by the old police committees would be lost. Continuity would lie with the magistrates because the nature of their representation remained the same. This, in turn, meant that the political complexion of all but one of the new joint boards would be dependent on the magistrates' voting patterns since they held the balance of power.

Boards were to raise their finance through a precept on the constituent councils whilst also being subject to the financial control laid down in the 1984 Rates Act for three years. The Home Secretary was given potential control over the day-to-day running of the joint boards by being given a say in decisions concerning staffing and the allocation of resources. He was also allotted the power to restructure joint boards by allowing district councils to become separate police authorities and amalgamating different police areas. Thus, this act gave central government unprecedented formal control over police authorities and, as Loveday as argued, it was expecting the authorities 'to shoulder the responsibility of improving the efficiency and effectiveness of their forces'(1987, p. 282).

Soon after the passing of the bill the Home Office directed the metropolitan district councils to begin the process of selecting nominees and to start making financial, budgetary and staffing decisions from October 1985. The intention was that the new joint board would shadow the old police committee in the countdown to abolition. However, it was not a smooth transition because many Labour-controlled district councils initially refused to participate in the new arrangements or assume their new responsibilities.

Other complex developments in the politics of law and order negatively affected the accountability campaigns. First, 'community' based crime prevention emerged as a significant component of the Conservative government's law and order agenda. Second, certain police forces, in response to intense pressure, began to re-conceptualize their relationship with 'the community' and to embark on organizational re-structuring. Third, the Labour Party leadership committed itself publicly to becoming the party of law and order. This involved taking crime seriously and constructing a community-wide 'coalition against crime'. Fourth, and intimately allied to the Labour Party's re-positioning, was the ongoing ideological onslaught on the radical campaigns for police accountability by the left realists.

The overall result was the formation of a discourse on what Johnson (1992) has described as the 'co-production of public safety' which prioritized preventing crime, tackling the fear of crime and meeting the needs of crime victims. This formidable discourse had immediate and serious consequences for the accountability campaigns because it was consciously appropriating, re-working and re-inscribing the concepts of community, representation and participation. In doing so, it was effectively displacing and de-centring demands for the democratic governance of the police.

Community participation: the 'united front' against crime

Active citizenship

The Conservative government continued to prioritize social order. The police were allocated substantial resources and patronage; the court system was augmented; a significant prison-building programme was embarked upon and legislation covering all aspects of the workings of the criminal justice system was introduced (Savage, 1989; Pilger 1990). The emphasis on law and order meant that the government continued to give unqualified support to controversial public order policing. Despite the serious constitutional issues thrown up by the year long policing of the miners' strike, there was no public inquiry. Nor were there any into the serious disturbances which engulfed Handsworth (Birmingham), Brixton, Liverpool 8 and Broadwater Farm (London) in the autumn of 1985. As far as Conservative ministers, police representatives and sections of the British media were concerned there was nothing to explain: the striking miners had chosen to break the law and the disturbances were orchestrated by murderous drug dealers and 'travelling agitators'. At the 1985 Conservative Party conference, the Home Secretary announced the strengthening of public order legislation and the upgrading of the riot capabilities of the police. This, in essence, constituted the political response to the various conflicts. Little attention was paid to those who protested that the 'pacification' programme being carried out by the police was seriously eroding civil liberties in Britain.

Nevertheless, the government did have to confront the political consequences of prioritizing the crime issue. Although spending had increased in real terms by thirty per cent, it had little effect on a dramatically increasing crime rate. As Savage (1989) noted, the Conservative's conspicuous expenditure had not prevented crime, deterred criminals, protected people, eradicated fears or helped victims or reformed offenders. Criticism of the Conservatives' law and order policies was fuelled by the publication of a national crime survey which, for the first time, attempted to provide an 'accurate' picture of the extent and nature of crime in Britain (Hough and Mayhew, 1983). This survey demonstrated that although crime was much more prevalent than indicated by official statistics, it was of a petty nature. The survey also emphasized that the fear of crime was out of proportion to the risk of being a victim of crime. It concluded that more expenditure on law and order was not the most effective answer to such fears:

> For many sorts of crimes, people themselves might take effective preventive action, either acting individually or together with others. The police could do more to promote preventive action of this kind while the trend towards putting more officers back on the beat may have the desirable effect of reducing fear of crime (Hough and Mayhew, 1983, p. 34).

Such conclusions stimulated debate about the effectiveness of the police in controlling crime (Hope and Shaw, 1988; Maguire and Pointing, 1988; Walklate, 1989).

The response of the government was the unveiling of a 'totalizing' community-wide policing strategy. This had two main thrusts. First, as Tuck (1991) has noted, 'a new community emphasis' emerged within Home Office thinking. 'The community', as Stan Cohen had argued in 1979, would, rather than the police or indeed the state, have to shoulder frontline responsibilities for social control and the prevention of crime:

> For just at the historical moment when every commonplace critique of "technological", "postindustrial" or "mass" society mournes the irreplaceable loss of community, so a new mode of deviancy control is advocated which depends on the same lost community being present (1979, p. 609).

The respectable law-abiding citizenry was to be mobilized to participate in the situational and social fight against crime and to help police their own neighbourhoods:

> At the very centre of our ideas on how to control crime should be the

energy and initiative of the active citizen. His or her contribution must be mobilized and should be the core of the radical rethinking we need on prevention and control of crime (John Patten, Minister of State, Home Office, 1988).

As a consequence, the concepts of 'community' and 'participation' were decoupled from demands for police accountability and re-defined within a crime prevention discourse, in which 'the community' of active citizens, ideally, worked in partnership with the police. The proper role of 'the community' in policing matters was participation in neighbourhood watch schemes, crime prevention panels, victim support schemes and the Special Constabulary. 'The community', in effect, would be realized and mobilized by neighbours networking with each other, as a civic duty, to define and take responsibility for policing the boundaries of their locale. In this context, there was also renewed support for the police-community consultation arrangements, even though there was considerable evidence (even excluding events in Handsworth, Brixton, Liverpool 8 and Broadwater Farm) to show that, as in Greater Manchester, there were serious problems over both which sections of the public were participating in the committees and the actual worth of the committees (Morgan and Maggs, 1984; 1985).

Second, to complement the voluntary efforts of the community and the private individual, a professional multi-agency approach to crime prevention was championed, to harness the efforts of criminal justice and local and central government departments and produce a receptive climate for the police to work in locally. In 1984, a 'landmark' inter-departmental circular on crime prevention was published, which stressed that crime prevention was not solely a police matter, and that inter-agency linking was crucial if crime were to be curbed in a cost effective manner (Bottoms, 1990). This was followed by the revitalization of the Home Office standing conference on crime prevention and the setting up, at the Prime Minister's behest, of a ministerial group to co-ordinate and intensify the government's crime prevention strategies in 1986. The Home Office subsequently sponsored Safer Cities and Crime Concern initiatives in 1988-89 (Windlesham, 1993).

These initiatives posed a dilemma for radical local authorities. At a time when their powers and resources were being severely curtailed, the crime prevention proposals held out the promise of both an enhanced role for local authorities and extra central government funding. However, in order to broaden their crime prevention responsibilities and access funding, local authorities would have to enter, as the subordinate partner, into local working partnerships with non-elected bodies and to recognize the role that the private sector could play in increasing public safety and delivering effective crime prevention measures.

It is no coincidence that this 'mixed economy' approach began to unfold at a moment when the Conservatives were attempting to redefine radically the relationship between the state, its institutions and the citizenry. This policy shift complemented the government's overarching attempt to resurrect disciplinary and moral codes which emphasized individual responsibility and self-regulation.

Moreover, it overlapped with the government's ideological crusade to curb public expenditure. In the long term, community self-policing and public-private crime management strategies would offer considerably more 'value for money' than continuing to allocate unlimited resources to an inefficient and ineffective publicly funded policing system. It was becoming clear that while the Conservative government was determined to frustrate all demands for enhanced local democratic accountability, it was willing to countenance central fiscal accountability. In 1983, for example, the Home Office, in response to the government's Financial Management Initiative, released 'Manpower, Effectiveness and Efficiency in the Police Service' (circular 114), which stated 'the constraints on public expenditure at both central and local government levels make it impossible to continue with the sort of expansion which has occurred in recent years'. The message for senior police officers was that they must become more proficient in the management of the resources allocated to them (Morgan, 1986). The full, and ironic, implications of the Conservative's slowly unfolding demand for police 'efficiency, effectiveness and economy' will be discussed later in this book.

Contractual police-community relations

Public concern about increasing crime rates, the manifest failure of the police to curb crime, and the alienation of increasing sections of the public as a result of controversial police campaigns against the 'enemies within', forced an organizational response. Sir Kenneth Newman, the commissioner of the Metropolitan Police (1982-7) attempted to counter the barrage of criticism and ongoing demands for democratic accountability by demonstrating that the force was capable of reforming itself and responding to community demands. Newman realized that in certain neighbourhoods the breakdown of police-public relations was so complete that they were in danger of becoming 'no go areas'. The response was the unveiling, from 1983, of a post-Scarman strategy that signalled the force's intention to fight for the 'hearts and minds' of the community by 'broadening the search for consensus', and to re-establish the authority and legitimacy of the police on the streets of London (Kettle and Shirley, 1983; Wright, 1985; Gordon, 1987). Newman's strategy and philosophy overlapped, in certain respects, with the government's approach to the problem of crime and also provided additional direction for the provincial forces.

The commissioner supported Scarman's community consultative arrangements as fora where the assent of legitimate community representatives for crime-fighting initiatives could be mobilized by the police, and where the education of the community about the realistic role the police could play in crime control could take place. The basis of Newman's plan was the establishment of a contractual relationship between the police and the community. This 'notional contract' was:

> an extension of the concept of 'policing by consent' but [it took] the argument forward from a passive endorsement of policing to an active involvement in a participative venture (Newman, 1983, p. 9).

He also argued, for similar reasons to those of James Anderton, that interagency policing strategies should be implemented, under the aegis of the police, to deal with the problems of difficult urban areas where 'community', consent and legitimacy did not exist. In these 'symbolic locations' where the nefarious 'underclass' dwelt:

> It is not sufficient to think only in terms of crime control. We need to lift the problems to a higher level of generality, encompassed by the expression 'social control', in a benign sense, in order to provide a unifying concept within which the activities of the police and other agencies can be co-ordinated (quoted in Rose, 1992, p. 36).

Newman was, in effect, conceding that there were limits to the policing that could be carried out in such areas by the police, and that every effort had to be made to share the responsibility for policing with other statutory agencies.

To deliver such a policing strategy, especially in the aftermath of Smith and Gray's (1983) study of the Metropolitan Police which highlighted serious managerial deficiencies at all organizational levels, Newman had to reform the force so that it could move beyond a 'crisis management' mode of functioning. Plans with specified objectives and guidelines were produced and attempts were made both to streamline the management structure and decentralize the decision-making process. Community bobbies were given a key role in forging a new relationship between the force and the community, and in order to put more officers back on the beat, civilianization of those tasks not requiring the skills and powers of police officers took place. There were attempts to develop styles of policing that could take account of the characteristics of particular neighbourhoods and the prioritization, through 'policing by objectives' programmes, of particular crimes that were of local concern.

To complement the role of the community in taking responsibility for its own welfare, the public order capabilities of the force were enhanced through the acquisition of new equipment, the upgrading of training and the re-thinking of the policies needed to deal with London's 'symbolic locations'. In January 1987 it was announced that the Special Patrol Groups were being replaced by Territorial Support Groups.

Thus, there was a concerted effort to redefine the role of the police in the fight against crime, involving the creation of new channels of information and communication with the community and other statutory agencies. As far as Newman was concerned, if his reform strategy were successful, force effectiveness would be improved in three key ways. First, the problem created for the police organization by rising crime rates would be 'solved' through redesignated it as a shared community problem. Second, by working with the community in various consultative committees and implementing internal reforms, the police could show that effective accountability was not dependent on enhancing the role of elected representatives. And third, the maintenance of public tranquillity could be realized through the creation of a more efficient riot control force, which would have the legitimacy of the community. Newman believed that the restoration of public order was a precondition for successful policing. Through this strategy, the fabled 'social contract' between the police and the community could be re-established. Such a 'contract', inevitably, also defined who were of the community and who were not. Scotland Yard's reform strategies underwent further revision after the policing disaster in Broadwater Farm in 1985 (LSPU, 1987; Rose, 1992).

The attempted restructuring of the Metropolitan Police was continued by Newman's successor, Sir Peter Imbert, who, in response to ongoing public disquiet, and perhaps more significantly murmurs of discontent from government ministers, brought in a management consultancy firm to investigate 'what the organization stands for, how it does things and how it is perceived' (Wolff Olins, 1988, p. 1). As a consequence, the 'Plus Programme' was launched in April 1989. It constituted the prototype 'mission statement' for British policing and promised the community the necessary structural and cultural reform to create a quality police service for the 1990s. The gradual re-conceptualization of policing as a service (as opposed to a force), which needed to be responsive to customers, was to have a considerable impact on debates about police accountability in the 1990s.

Partnership approaches to crime prevention

The highly damaging 'loony left' campaign, instigated by influential sections of the media and critics outside and inside the party impacted dramatically upon Labour's law and order stance as the 1980s proceeded. Under Neil Kinnock's leadership and a series of major policy reviews, a concerted effort was made to modernize the party and to reestablish links with those sections of the working class alienated by the 'loony left' policies of certain radical municipal socialist authorities (Thatchell, 1983; Wainwright, 1987; Negrine 1989). The party leadership, in a damage limitation exercise, distanced itself from all controversial issues and policies, and during the 1987 election campaign virtually jettisoned the interests of the dispossessed:

> the leadership cast its vote unflinchingly for the 'traditional' image, in search of the 'traditional Labour voter'. Again, everybody understood that this, too, was a code. It is a code for 'back to the respectable, moderate, trade unionist, male-dominated working class'...It signalled the distance of Labour from all those 'fringe issues' and a commitment to rooting Labour political loyalties exclusively through an identification with the traditional culture of the left (Hall, 1988, p. 263).

During this period the 'new model' Labour Party was pressed by its opponents on its Achilles' heel - law and order. Considerable pressure was exerted upon the party during the miners strike to condemn picket line violence and later to expel Bernie Grant, leader of Haringey Council, for his 'anti-police' statements after Broadwater Farm erupted (Rose, 1992). At the Conservative Party conference, Margaret Thatcher's keynote speech denounced the Labour Party's 'anti-police' stance. Mrs Thatcher accused Labour of undermining the rule of law by harassing and obstructing the police, and she promised that her government would 'oppose politicians national or local who want to interfere with the operational independence of the police' (*Guardian*, 12 October 1985). In November 1985, the Police Federation renewed its demand for Labour to deal with those members who were anti-police (*Police Review*, 29 November 1985). In January 1986 the Home Secretary made another attack on police authorities who were in conflict with their chief constables, stating that 'they help to create an atmosphere in which crime can thrive and responsible citizenship is condemned' (*Police Review*, 31 January 1986).

This was followed in March 1986 by a Conservative statement accusing certain Labour politicians of spreading malicious anti-police propaganda (*Manchester Evening News*, 1 March 1986). In December 1986, another government minister, Norman Tebbit, released a dossier listing the extremist policies of local councils such as Manchester claiming that they, rather than Labour's national leadership, represented the true face of the Labour party.

It was in this political moment that the Labour leadership began to highlight publicly its unqualified support for the police, its zero tolerance of crime and criminal actions, and to distance itself from those members of the party and radical pressure groups campaigning for police accountability. Fortunately, for the party leadership, left realism was available to justify intellectually the jettisoning of a radical police reform agenda (Keith and Murji, 1990).

Because of the focus on the politics of policing and the processes of criminalization, there was a tendency among more radical police critics to view 'crime' as a racially inscribed concept and the fear of crime as exaggerated and to distance themselves from crime prevention initiatives because of the authoritarian dangers 'inherent' in multi-agency policing. They also maintained that the police were structurally incapable of responding to the needs of the community because their real role was to protect an authoritarian social order. Events such as the policing of the miners strike, Wapping, the 'Battle of Brittan', Handsworth, Brixton and Broadwater Farm did nothing to change this template.

However, as was detailed in the opening chapter of this book, left realists argued that such an abstentionist position on crime and policing was a monumental political miscalculation because crime left victims and suffering in its wake. It impinged on the fundamental right to live without the fear of being robbed or assaulted and impacted differentially on women and inner city working class communities. Despite protests to the contrary, their analysis bore a remarkable resemblance to that of right of centre American criminologists in the 1970s:

> We must get our priorities clear: violent and predatory crime are what matter most...This is not only because these crimes harm particular individuals and represent the citizens' prime fears. It is also because they threaten our cities and destroy our sense of community (Morris and Hawkins, 1977, p. 8-14).

For these types of reasons, the British left realists argued, there was a pressing political need for Labour councils to devise 'a unified crime control plan' which would impact positively on neighbourhood problems (Jones, MacLean and Young, 1986; Kinsey, Lea and Young, 1986). This would involve Labour councils supporting Newman's multi-agency philosophy and neighbourhood watch schemes and supporting Scarman's consultative committees because:

> they represent a public arena where anxieties, doubts as well as strategies can be aired and where the sense of public alienation with policing and the problem of crime control in general can, to an extent, be assuaged (Jones, MacLean and Young, 1986, p. 216)

The realists had in effect accepted Scarman and the Home Office's squaring of the circle. Such a forceful revisionism, backed up by 'sophisticated' crime surveys and a soaring crime rate, challenged fundamentally those on the left who argued that democratic accountability of the police (rather than crime control) was the real issue that should concern democratic socialists.

Official Labour Party statements promulgated realist 'theory', promising that a future Labour government would give full support to the police, respect the operational independence of chief officers, and advance policies to bring about community support for the police in the fight against crime (*Police Review*, 29 November 1985; 25 April 1986). In May 1986, Neil Kinnock denounced those in his party involved in 'police bashing' (*Guardian*, 16 May 1986). Other Labour members asserted that it was the moral duty of the party to do something about crime rather than nihilistically attacking the police. In June 1986, the shadow Home Secretary, Gerald Kaufmann, stated that a crime wave was engulfing Britain as a result of the government's refusal to provide adequate numbers of police officers. In the same month, Sir Kenneth Newman was able to state that the policies of both Labour and the Conservatives on law and order were virtually indistinguishable (Sim and Gilroy, 1987).

Just how sensitive the Labour leadership was to the charge of being anti-police can be gauged by its response to the leaking of its 1987 local election manifesto proposal to place the police under local democratic supervision, and the comment by the Home Secretary that the proposal was 'lunacy'. Instead of attempting to defend the manifesto commitment, it was rewritten in a more neutral form (*Times*, 4 February 1987). However, this did not stop the Home Secretary asking the leadership to denounce publicly those Labour local authorities, such as Manchester, which were attempting to 'undermine and discourage the police' and to reject proposals to give police authorities more powers:

> I can imagine no step more dangerous for policing in Britain than to entrust the main decisions on the policing of our cities to the enemies of the police (*Guardian*, 21 March 1987).

Government ministers also argued that the refusal of certain Labour councils to participate in Scarman's consultative arrangements was proof that demands for democratic accountability were the thin end of the wedge: the real objective of Labour's extremists was to subject the police to direct political control (*Independent*, 27 May 1987).

During the 1987 election, the electorate was promised that tackling crime would be a top priority for the next Labour government. The left realist inspired 'Protecting Our People' stressed that local authorities and the community, working in partnership with better resourced police officers, would constitute a co-ordinated multi-faceted approach to fighting crime. In its critique of the Conservative's failure to defeat crime, the document harked back to the golden days of social democracy when the respectable law-abiding community and the police were at one. It was emphasized that unity against crime and criminals would be the basis for both re-establishing the legitimacy of the police and re-building working class communities that had been devastated by Thatcherism. Within these proposals, the position of the police was enhanced in relation to statutory and voluntary agencies.

There was an electoral commitment to give more powers to police authorities and to abolish magistrate representation. However, issues of police accountability were reworked within a wider instrumentalist crime control agenda. A democratic framework for decisions about policing was viewed as being a functional necessity for effective crime control. Within this new Labour agenda, there was no role for 'loony left' police monitoring initiatives. Instead, the party committed itself to working within the existing consultative arrangements and sometime in the future turning them into 'community police councils'. Consequently, as Reiner (1989) has noted, during the 1987 election, on policing issues at least, 'inter-party conflict was muted by a "new realism" which seemed to infect all parties'. It could be argued that if the conflict was muted, it was because the Labour Party had opted for the constitutional status quo on policing issues and decided to contest law and order on a terrain fashioned by the Conservatives:

> In effect, the Labour Party is no longer addressed primarily to challenging police power per se but rather to re-ordering police priorities away from public order and towards crime prevention and control. The difficulty with this approach, on a political level, is that it moves some way towards accepting the Tory agenda of 'law and order' and places Labour spokesmen in open competition with their opponents in bidding up public anxieties about crime, with all the racist overtones that entails (Bridges, 1986, p. 80).

Thus, within the Labour Party's criminal justice proposals, the interests of those who were living in fear of crime, concerned about preventing crime and victims (or potential victims) of crime were stressed. Within this agenda, there was little space for the representation of the interests of those who were the victims of discriminatory policing practices. After the 1987 electoral defeat these processes of prioritization and marginalization intensified.

Representing the community: victim support

For all participants in the law and order debate, the ultimate intention of individual and community participation in crime prevention and corporatist policing strategies was to diminish the risk of becoming a victim of crime and to make the criminal justice system victim - as opposed to offender - centred. It was in this context that the 'victim' became the key signifier in criminal justice debates with her/his rights being represented by the National Association of Victim Support Schemes (NAVSS) - an organization with no recognizable roots in any particular community. As Rock (1990) has noted, the NAVSS deliberately worked with a narrow conception of 'suitable victims' - victims of burglary, robbery, 'muggings' - in order to prove itself to be deserving of official patronage and media support. At no time, for example, did it publicly criticize the policies or practices of the criminal justice agencies. Instead, NAVSS worked closely with the police, seeking the endorsement of chief constables and guaranteeing police representation on its management committees. It also cultivated, with the co-operation of the media, a particular representation of crime victims deserving of public sympathy. Not surprisingly, given its political agenda, it distanced itself from more radical groups who had been working with and championing the rights and needs of victims of sexual and racial violence as well as victims of police malpractice.

At a time when they were frantically trying to re-establish their legitimacy, the police realized the value of giving patronage to such a conservative 'community' organization which, through the manipulation of public fears, campaigned for the rights of particular crime victims rather than concerning itself, for example, with miscarriages of justice and police accountability. NVASS could play a crucial role along with Neighbourhood Watch, Safer Cities and Crime Concern, in mobilizing community support for the police in the fight against crime and prove to be a useful ally on Scarman's consultation committees. As Rock has noted:

> It professed to represent the community just at the time when the police were searching for the respectable community with which they could form an alliance (Rock, 1990, p. 250).

Thus, it had an invaluable role to play in the police's ideological struggle to isolate and marginalize vociferous anti-police community groups. The victims' movement created the space for the police to respond positively to two categories of crime victims - victims of domestic violence and racial violence - whose interests had been 'represented' and articulated by the monitoring groups and rape crisis centres. In both cases, the police were vulnerable to the accusation that they effectively re-victimized victims because of the nature of their response: general lack of interest; delayed responses; reluctance to investigate; refusal to prosecute; unwillingness to afford adequate protection and in certain instances outright hostility to complainants. Their critics were able to draw a stark contrast between the lack of police resources devoted to these categories of serious crime and the resources devoted to policing victimless crimes and harassing certain communities. In the case of racial attacks, the real sting in the critics' tail was the accumulated, and in many instances, indisputable evidence that the most systematic racially motivated attacks were carried out by police officers.

Rather than acknowledging the validity of any of the criticisms and entering into dialogue with radical groups, the police used NAVSS to reclaim the agenda. Instead of working with radical rape crisis centres, for example, certain forces began to set up their own specialist units and medical examination suites to 'manage' rape victims. They also encouraged inter-agency responses and local victim support schemes to work with victims of sexual violence and even trained volunteers to handle rape referrals (Hanmer, Radford and Stanko, 1989).

The same was true of victims of racial attacks. Between 1983 and 1987, the police, with encouragement from the Home Office, began to formulate a multi-agency response to their critics (Hesse, 1992). In 1987, the Metropolitan Police announced that it was launching a campaign against the 'moral and social evil' of racially motivated attacks. The campaign specifically focused on Newham and Ealing where local monitoring groups had been strident in their condemnation of the police response. And, as in the case of domestic violence, NAVSS was officially encouraged to move into this new area of victim work.

Not surprisingly, given its stance and the patronage it received from the police, NVASS was also welcomed by the Home Office. It too had found a respectable 'voluntary' organization that it could work with and upon which it could bestow the official mantle of 'authentic' community representative:

> It was supposed by the Home Office that victims' support would play the part of the community in the notional contract offered by the new policing strategy...It was to be an allegory, a representation of the community (Rock, 1990, p. 406-10).

Thus, key state agencies had succeeded in finding and fostering a community organization which could be used to reclaim problematic victims and be trusted to 'speak for' the police against their critics. In so doing, they were able to define the demands emanating from radical groups as unrepresentative of the community. Thus, there is considerable evidence to support Viano's (1987) view that 'the victims' movement agenda was co-opted by conservative political groupings to further justify crime control'.

Conclusion

By the late 1980s, the confrontation between the Conservative government and 'radical' local Labour administrations had been 'resolved'. The nature of this 'resolution' for those campaigning for democratically-based police accountability was profound. As part of the extensive re-ordering of central-local state relationships, police committees were finally abolished and new forms of political representation and tighter central control imposed. The Conservatives were determined that there would be no repeat, in the new police authority settings, of the conflict that had characterized the early 1980s. In reality, if the government had its way, future debates about police accountability would take place within a very different conceptual framework and be informed by a very different set of managerialist discourses. Moreover, every effort was made to marginalize 'loony left' local administrations in order to force them to abandon their radical policy positions on controversial or minority issues, such as their support for police monitoring projects and resistance to consultation committees.

Radical campaigners for democratic accountability were also confronted by a broad based discourse on crime and multi-agency crime prevention which reclaimed and reworked the concepts of 'community', 'representation' and 'participation'. In this time period, as has been recounted, concerted efforts were made to mobilize the law-abiding community to participate in the fight against crime and the criminal underclass. Funding and patronage was also given to a variety of proxy 'community' organizations which could mobilize and represent the interests of the victims of crime. This powerful 'mobilization of bias' exposed the vulnerability of Labour-controlled local authorities on the vexed question of rising crime rates and how to respond to them politically.

There was another important reason why community safety became a local authority priority in this period. By the late 1980s it had become clear that desperately needed central and inner city regeneration would not be realized through re-industrialization or economic investment by the state. The continuing hegemony of neo-liberal economic approaches at both the nation state and global levels ensured that this would not happen. Instead, a broad consensual view began to emerge in Labour-controlled localities that the future of their cities lay in attempting to create a new urban economy premised upon financial and retail services, cultural consumption, gentrification and leisure. 'The city' would have to be re-imagined, re-packaged and re-sold to potential investors and consumers as an exciting and profitable place. Reassuring people that the city was a safe and non-threatening place to spend time and money was deemed to be crucial to this regeneration strategy. Thus, improved public safety and manifest social order, as quality of life issues, became intimately linked to the future well-being of Britain's cities. This led to an acceptance among many local authorities that they had a crucial role to play in the regulation, surveillance and policing of civic space and the devising of social policies to tackle vagrancy, truancy, homelessness, drug dealing and disorder. And, this in turn, provided a crucial overlap of interest with central government's safer cities initiatives.

These multiple pressure points, especially in the context of the realities imposed by the re-election of the Conservative Party in 1987, forced radical local authorities to respond to the community's fear of crime by reconsidering their opposition to consultation committees, neighbourhood watch schemes and situational and social crime prevention partnerships. This overall shift in emphasis meant that the interests of the:

> truly marginalized, those whose voice was apparently 'shrill' and biased... those badly treated in police custody, those denied elementary rights, the urban black and female population, the gay and lesbian, the travellers, those with even slight criminal records and even a large section of the unemployed... were...pushed out of sight and their policing needs dispensed with (Walker, 1986, p. 35).

The next two chapters will analyse the specific repercussions of the national shifts for the local accountability campaigns of the Greater Manchester police committee and Manchester City Council's police monitoring committee.

7 Police authority and community liaison

Several problems faced the Labour group in the countdown to abolition of Greater Manchester police committee. First, it had to persevere with its efforts to hold the chief constable to account in a context where the latter, either on his own or in conjunction with the opposition, could destabilize committee business by simply resorting to delaying tactics. Second, there was the distinct possibility that the magistrates, Conservatives and the chief constable would be in control of the new police authority. If this transpired it was likely that the community liaison panels and the Labour group's other initiatives would not be augmented. Third, if Labour did in fact manage to gain control of the new police authority, Manchester City Council, because it had been allocated the largest representation, could become the lead authority. It was clear that Manchester's uncompromising stance on policing would alienate the magistrates, the political opposition and more significantly delegates from other more traditional Labour councils. The only beneficiary from such Labour disunity would be James Anderton. Furthermore, given that the police monitoring committee was totally opposed to the liaison panels, there was every possibility that its representatives on the new police authority would not mourn their passing. Thus, it is not surprising that in the transitional period between the passing of the Local Government Act and the setting up of the joint boards, the conflicts within the police committee and disputes about the new police authority intensified.

The demise of the police committee

On 7 June 1985, James Anderton went on the offensive against his police committee. Instead of being present at the monthly meeting, he attended a conference of chief police officers where he outlined the contours of the crisis in British policing. He attacked the Home Office for interfering with the core of traditional police work through its support for the privatization of certain policing functions. He condemned the government for failing to provide adequate resources and, referring to the 1984 Police and Criminal Evidence Act and the setting up of a Crown Prosecution Service, for implementing changes that would seriously hinder the police in the fight against crime. Finally, he claimed that attempts by certain police committees and 'unscrupulous' politicians to 'interfere' with policing strategies and tactics constituted an attempt to 'prostitute' the British police. Hence, he believed that the time had come to jettison 'sentimental attachments to local accountability and management':

> You cannot police a community by police committees. Unless I am very much mistaken, the majority of the public would prefer policing at the discretion of their chief constable rather than policing with the consent of the police authorities (Anderton, 1985).

Gabrielle Cox condemned the suggestion that a crisis was being precipitated by police committees which attempted to carry out their statutory duties. She said that the real threat to policing by consent was posed by those who refused to accept the outcome of the democratic process and added that the time had come for the community to make up its mind whether it wanted democratic policing or policing on the dictate of one individual. Subsequently, the chief constable was asked to acknowledge, in writing, the lawful powers of scrutiny given to the police committee under the existing constitutional arrangements. Anderton, in turn, stated that he had no intention of signing such a document as it would be both 'inappropriate' and 'legally irregular' under the 1964 Police Act.

During the August 1985 committee meeting, the chief constable refused to expand upon his comments, saying that he had discussed the question in the context of a 'private' ACPO meeting. The chair condemned the manner in which he had publicly denigrated his police committee:

> I would say to the people of Greater Manchester that the trend of his speech is that the police should not be accountable to democratic structures. Come abolition the semblance of accountability which currently exists will be gone. We are moving down the road to the tyranny of the chief constable. There is a substantial minority of people, especially those who have contact with the police, who are not happy with them. I'm not going to demand anything from the chief constable - that's like spitting in the wind. We've seen what happens [reference to Merseyside] when the relationship between the police and

local representatives breaks down - they are investigated by Special Branch for inciting public disorder.

A motion was passed, despite the furious opposition of the magistrates and Conservatives, stating that the chief constable's speech showed contempt for the police committee and the structures of democracy. Anderton responded by seeking legal advice on the resolution.

Three other issues further inflamed relations between the chief constable and Labour members of the committee as abolition approached. First, Anderton submitted a report on the policing of the Home Secretary's visit to Manchester University which contained less information than reports he had circulated to MPs. As far as the Labour members were concerned, the chief constable was making it clear that MPs had more rights to information on the policing of Greater Manchester than his own police committee. This was a particularly inflammatory course of action because rumours were circulating that certain Greater Manchester police officers were systematically intimidating students who had been involved in the demonstration. Second, the chief constable decided to repeal the committee's access to completed complaints' files on the grounds that certain members had criticized the handling of investigations. This decision arose out of a difference of opinion concerning a case emanating from the 1981 disturbances. Finally, the chief constable announced that he had acquired 500 plastic bullets and four special guns for the force. This deed constituted a final breaking point in relations between James Anderton and Labour members of the committee.

The chief constable was criticized for not consulting the police committee before purchasing such controversial weaponry, and Labour members requested that the bullets and guns be returned to their manufacturer. Deadlock was reached when committee members demanded, during the November meeting, that Anderton furnish a report justifying the need for such weapons as well as providing a demonstration for committee members. He refused on the grounds that such demands were an infringement on his operational independence. As far as Gabrielle Cox was concerned, the guns and bullets were the police committee's property and the chief constable, in deliberately ignoring its resolution, was declaring himself to be above the law and disregarding the constitutional powers of the committee.

Anderton used the police casualties suffered during the disturbances in London and Birmingham to justify his decision to purchase the weapons:

> We have two choices in the police force - either we stay where we are and die, or we ignominiously cut and run. As long as it is in my power, I have no intention of leaving my officers unprotected...I shall never abandon the citizens of Greater Manchester to the mercy of

rioters, rapists, looters and criminals (*Times*, 2 November 1985).

The acquisition of plastic bullets was consistent with his overall public order policing philosophy, discussed earlier in this book. He was not prepared to rely on 'defensive formations' which, he believed, led to heavy police casualties. If plastic bullets gave his force a proactive 'edge' in such situations, then they should be readily available. When Labour members responded by arguing that there was no evidence of such weaponry aiding in the policing of public order situations, Anderton replied tersely: 'What proof do you want me to bring you? A dozen dead policemen?'

On 4 November 1985, the chief constable addressed a meeting of the Greater Manchester Police Federation, telling his officers that he had no intention of returning the plastic bullets, and that the reason why he had not informed the police committee of his decision was because he knew what the reaction would be. Anderton then launched another full-scale attack on the police committee, claiming that it was a disruptive influence and that he would be grateful when the new police authority took over. He once more questioned the value of the sub-committee structure, the numerous meetings, the incessant and unreasonable demands for hundreds of reports and the mass of bureaucratic resolutions:

> Much of what has passed for police committee business has been a total sham and of limited value either to the police force or the public we try to serve (*Manchester Evening News*, 5 November 1985).

By this time Anderton was also complaining to fellow chief constables that the sub-committee structure was being abused by the police committee (Oliver, 1987, p. 231). The chief constable also alleged that the full committee meetings were nothing more than 'a convenient stage for the presentation of anti-government and anti-police propaganda', and indicated that there was no possibility of his further co-operation with the committee:

> When, as in Greater Manchester, a police force resents as deeply as I know we do, the stances sometimes taken and public statements made in the name of its police committee, there can be no sensible or lasting basis for trust and confidence between the force and its committee (*Guardian*, 6 November 1985).

Legal advice was sought by both parties over the ownership of the plastic bullets. The crisis deepened when it was legally established that the weaponry was the committee's property and it had the right, therefore, to dispose of it. At the next committee meeting, the chief constable informed members that since the dispute centred on the question of ownership, he had cancelled the order and had instead secured equipment on 'permanent loan' from the Metropolitan Police, with the approval of the Home Office and the Constabulary Inspectorate (*Police Review*, 13 December 1985). The chair responded that such a decision effectively sabotaged the whole tripartite structure of police accountability. The Home Secretary's support for the chief constable indicated that he 'was prepared to impose plastic bullets on a community when its elected representatives have made it clear they do not want them'.

The chief constable, in response to being asked whether he recognized the statutory right of the police committee to make the final decision about the purchase of plastic bullets, refused to be drawn, saying that where the committee could show its decisions to be 'firmly and lawfully based', he had a duty to comply. The issue was finally resolved when representatives of Greater Manchester and the three other metropolitan police committees which refused to sanction the acquisition of such weaponry, were informed by the Home Secretary at a meeting on 5 December 1985 that if they persisted with their opposition, their chief constables would be entitled to procure it from a central Home Office store. After this position was confirmed in a 1986 circular, Northumbria's police committee sought a judicial review. However, it was unsuccessful, with the Appeal Court upholding the Home Secretary's decision by reference to the provisions of the 1964 Police Act. This outcome was further proof, if any were needed, that the police committees had no real power to call their chief constables to account, and that the latter could depend, if any dispute arose concerning the tripartite structure, on the unquestioning support of the Home Office (Ewing and Gearty, 1990).

In December 1985, the committee, in an unprecedented move, decided, despite the vociferous opposition of the magistrate and Conservative members, to appoint Stanley Bailey, chief constable of Northumbria Police, to investigate whether James Anderton's behaviour brought the Greater Manchester Police into disrepute. This inquiry was completed and discussed by the new police authority in December 1986, with Bailey warning members that they should not set themselves up as complainant and adjudicator in the case, because the principle of 'natural justice' would be contravened. However, fortunately for the chief constable, the issue was 'lost' amid legal wrangling and the fog of rumour and speculation that descended in the wake of the Stalker Affair.

At the final police committee meeting in March 1986, because James Anderton could not attend, it was left to deputy chief constable John Stalker to respond to the committee's recommendation that, in the aftermath of the Holloway Road incident, identification numbers should be clearly stamped on police vehicles. Stalker stated that irrespective of what the police committee advocated, it would be up to the chief constable to make a final decision on this matter.

Gabrielle Cox also reported on the last five years of the police committee's business. Her statement was a damning indictment of the existing system of police governance. She identified a series of issues which, for her, clearly illustrated the impossibility (for police committees) of holding chief police officers to account. First, there was the issue of establishment levels, raised most explicitly by the coal dispute:

> We cannot believe that a matter of this importance should simply be presented to the police committee as a fait accompli, and we fail to see how the public can have confidence in a process of reallocation of resources from which elected members are excluded. We wish to see an end to the system where a chief constable is able to reduce an area's establishment without recourse to public consultation and debate (Cox, 1986, p. 7).

Second, there was the question of how force objectives and priorities were determined. This again was done without reference to the wishes of elected representatives or the community:

> This means that the direction of expensive resources happens not as the result of a collaborative process between police and community, but simply by virtue of a statement handed down internally to members of the force. In our view this is a symptom of a deep underlying unwillingness to accept that effective policing is not imposed but has to be done in partnership with the community. It is arguable that autocracy, far from representing strength, demonstrates a fear of genuine debate and criticism (p. 9).

Third, there was the matter of the complaints' procedures. Gabrielle Cox said that the setting up of a specific sub-committee to scrutinise the manner in which complaints from members of the public are dealt with by the force had 'deepened rather than ameliorated' the committee's concern about the adequacy and impartiality of the system. And the chair also made clear that the chief constable's refusal to allow committee members to see completed files was not acceptable:

> We do not believe public confidence will be enhanced by a system which responds to criticism by shutting down the system to scrutiny by the police committee (p. 10).

Overall, as a result of working on the sub-committees and talking privately to particular senior officers, including the deputy chief constable, certain members of the Labour group felt there was good reason to be seriously concerned about the irrational decision making processes and authoritarian managerial structures of the force.

The fourth issue identified in this 'end of term' report was the lack of committee involvement in the selection of senior officers. Because the force chose its own candidates and the Home Office had the ultimate power of approval, the police committee had little say in appointment matters. This meant that senior officers could be appointed who were not favoured by the committee. The final matter commented upon by Gabrielle Cox was the implementation of public order policing policies which the committee fundamentally disapproved:

> We are angry that the chief constable chose to buy plastic bullets without any consultation, that he would not accept our decision to dispose of them, and that the Home Secretary subsequently used a legal stratagem to frustrate the wishes of the police committee - the only representatives of the people in policing matters in Greater Manchester (p. 16).

The chair concluded by saying that a frequent criticism of the police committees was that they did not use the powers given to them under the 1964 Police Act, and this, rather than a lack of powers, was the reason why chief police officers had been able to exercise their autonomy. However, as far as she was concerned, the Greater Manchester police committee had attempted to exercise their powers to the full but:

> found the act to be vague, unworkable and the source of conflict rather than enlightenment. It is this fundamental legislative flaw at the heart of the police system which requires urgent attention if we are to maintain a consensual rather than a coercive system of policing (p. 16).

She finished by saying that if policing by consent were to be achieved, the police would have to recognize that the community and its elected representatives had the right to be involved in the setting and assessment of priorities, the devising and monitoring of policies, and decisions about the acceptability, or otherwise, of specific strategies. Not to be outdone, the magistrates responded to this 'inflammatory' speech by tabling a motion of no confidence in the chair.

During the last months of the old police committee, a shadow police authority was formed under the chairmanship of a Conservative councillor and a magistrate. The police committee did offer to advise the new authority on procedural matters. However, all offers were rebuffed.

The new police authority

Constituted formally on 1 April 1986, the new police authority consisted of thirty elected members and fifteen magistrates. From the outset, because the latter held the balance of power, it was evident that there would be a struggle for political control of the joint board. At the first meeting, a Conservative councillor acted as chair and a magistrate as vice chair. Once it was confirmed that Salford City Council, and significantly not Manchester, for a variety of complex political reasons, would be the lead district, Norman Briggs a right-wing Labour councillor was elected as chair, with the magistrate remaining as vice chair. However, although representatives from Manchester's police monitoring committee had been unsuccessful in their initial efforts to dominate the new authority, they believed that they could do so eventually by taking every opportunity to question the chief constable about the policing of Manchester.

The Stalker Affair

A glorious opportunity presented itself in May 1986 when it was sensationally disclosed that John Stalker, the deputy chief constable and stalwart defender of the force against its myriad critics, had been removed as head of an inquiry into a 'shoot-to-kill' policy in Ulster, and suspended from duty pending investigation of alleged disciplinary offences. The resulting Police Complaints' Authority inquiry, conducted by Colin Sampson, the chief constable of West Yorkshire (who also took over responsibility for the Ulster inquiry), centred on allegations that the deputy chief constable had associated, in a manner likely to bring discredit to the force, with 'known' members of Manchester's 'criminal' fraternity, including Kevin Taylor, a businessman and leading member of the local Conservative Party. Accordingly, the new police authority found itself embroiled in an unprecedented and absolutely chaotic turn of events, even by the controversial standards of the Greater Manchester Police and its chief constable (Doherty, 1986; Taylor, 1987; Stalker, 1988; Murphy, 1991; Taylor, 1991).

Although the appointment of an investigating officer could only be made by the police authority, private negotiations took place between the chief constable, the chair and clerk of the authority, instead of the matter being tabled for discussion at a properly constituted meeting. The high-handed manner in which these decisions were taken infuriated many members of the authority. As a consequence of the chair taking unilateral action, authority members had not been consulted and this begged the question of whether the proper procedures had been followed. In principle, it should have been the police authority, not the chair working in collusion with the chief constable, that made the final decisions about Stalker's suspension and the appointment of an investigating officer. Moreover, there were serious misgivings about Norman Brigg's refusal to inform members about the exact nature of the allegations against Stalker, particularly when rumours circulated that certain Home Office officials and senior members of the Royal Ulster Constabulary were 'in' on the decision to suspend him.

Certain members were convinced that the chief constable had cynically involved the new and inexperienced authority chair (and therefore the authority) in an officially sanctioned smear campaign designed to wreck Stalker's Ulster inquiries. The state of internal disagreement and the confusion caused by ruthless and persistent media questioning about: why Stalker had been suspended; who was really behind the suspension; and the criminal associations of senior Greater Manchester Police officers, led the new authority to hold its meetings in private during this period. Its members also embarked on renewed discussions with the chief constable and the Home Office over the handling of virtually every aspect of the Stalker affair. Left-wing members also resolved that the chief constable would, at some stage, be held to account for his actions, particularly when rumours began to circulate alleging that his 'lifestyle' would not emerge untainted from the same degree of scrutiny to which Stalker had been subjected.

The inevitable outcome in May 1986 was the rejection by all sections of the authority of Sampson's 1,000 page report, which called for Stalker to face a tribunal to answer ten charges of discreditable conduct. Because members viewed the report's allegations as trivial, John Stalker was immediately reinstated with a warning that in future he should be more circumspect in his personal associations.

Ironically, one of the few genuine majority decisions taken by the authority resulted in renewed conflict because the gaze then turned to the chief constable's role in the affair. Certain left-wing authority members, most notably Tony McArdell and Ken Strath, manoeuvred for the setting up of a formal inquiry into Anderton's handling of the initial allegations against John Stalker and media allegations that he had associated with known criminals, misused his official police car and seriously damaged force morale.

However, this campaign suffered a serious set back when Tony McCardell, the left's candidate, failed to win the election in September 1986 for the vacant post of authority chair. Stephen Murphy, the new moderate chair, took a more conciliatory line and it was agreed, despite the fact that Kevin Taylor's lawyers were attempting to bring an action against the chief constable and other senior officers for conspiracy to pervert the course of justice, that Anderton would not be questioned any further about the Stalker Affair or allegations of professional misconduct. This was rationalized publicly in terms of the police authority wanting rapprochement with the chief constable.

Instead, the authority called, with little effect, for the setting up of a full judicial inquiry into the Stalker Affair. This new 'friendship' also led to the left being foiled, once and for all, in its attempt to ask the chief constable fourteen specific questions about his role in the Stalker affair.

The moral state of the nation

In December 1986, two issues rocked the fragile calm. John Stalker announced his retirement, claiming that he had been 'frozen out' since returning to duty and that the re-opening, in November, of the Moors Murders' inquiry, without consulting him, constituted the final insult. Furthermore, on 11 December, the chief constable made his infamous comment, in the middle of a speech about police handling of Aids and hepatitis, about certain categories of 'people swirling about in a human cesspit of their own making' (*Times*, 12 December 1986). Although there was outrage among police authority members about the latest twist to the Stalker saga, it was 'the Aids speech' that dominated the headlines.

The left demanded that Anderton resign immediately. What infuriated them was the chief constable having the audacity to pronounce on moral matters at a time when he and his force stood accused of 'crimes' ranging from rape, vigilantism, serious corruption and collusion with criminals to conspiracy to frame their own deputy chief constable. Even the conciliatory police authority chair raised questions about Anderton's professional judgement in making such controversial remarks so soon after the Stalker affair. He stated that since the old committee had been abolished, every effort had been made to check the conflict that had existed previously:

> Yet in a matter of minutes, Mr Anderton seems to have demolished all the bridges which have so painstakingly been built between the police and the authority during the past few months (*Manchester Evening News*, 16 December 1986).

Another intense argument followed between the Labour group and the magistrates and opposition during the full authority meeting of 19 December. A four point motion was passed stating that: the chief constable should retract his speech; the authority disassociated itself from the homophobic views of the chief constable; moves be instigated to discipline the chief constable and that the authority backed the Aids awareness campaign (*Times*, 20 December 1986). The chief constable argued that he had been deliberately misrepresented and stated that he would not be silenced and would not retract his comments.

The conflict escalated when the national media began to reproduce local rumours that the Stalker Affair and the chief constable's recent public pronouncements had impacted on force morale, leading to declining confidence in Anderton's leadership among senior officers. The result was the demand by local Labour MPs that an independent inquiry be set up under S32 of the 1964 Police Act, into the operation of the force and the announcement by the police authority that it was thinking of establishing a confidential 'grievance hot line' for those officers concerned about force morale. However, after further negotiations the announcement was made on 3 January 1987 that the chief constable and the police authority had drawn up yet another compact to work together.

However, in January 1987 James Anderton returned to the state of the nation's morality in interviews on radio, television and in the press. Representatives of the authority met immediately with the Home Office and the constabulary inspectorate to make it clear that if the chief constable did not refrain from such statements, they would petition for his resignation. As the result of two further meetings at the Home Office, a compromise, known as 'the tripartite agreement', was reached on 27 January 1987, whereby the chief constable and the chair of the authority agreed to meet regularly to discuss matters of common interest as it 'was important to prevent a repetition of the controversies which had arisen during the first nine months of the authority's existence'. However, the chief constable made it clear that the settlement did not mean that he had been muzzled:

> I think the chairman would agree that I have not been gagged and that I am free to speak at my discretion. I shall consider in the future when I wish to speak upon any issue germane to the policing of Greater Manchester whether or not it would be in everyone's best interest and prudent to discuss my intentions with other persons (*Times*, 28 January 1987).

And, despite the widespread media view that he should resign, Anderton must have taken comfort from the indirect public statements of support he received from both the Prime Minister and the Home Secretary (*Guardian*, 24 January 1987).

At a police authority meeting on 30 January 1987, a motion was passed, despite the opposition of the magistrates and Conservatives, asking the Home Office to discipline the chief constable if, in future, he breached his promise not to cause any further controversy. Further conflict was muted as a result of the chief constable becoming the President of ACPO for the year, and the right of the Labour Party consolidating its control of the authority. In May the left's efforts to discipline Anderton for his Aids speech were finally abandoned when the authority clerk concluded that there was no evidence that the chief constable had committed any disciplinary offence. Instead, Anderton was given the all-clear to spend £150,000 on upgrading the force's anti-riot capabilities. The left was also foiled in its attempt to censure the chief constable over the 'Battle of Brittan' when Steven Murphy accepted assurances that public order tactics had been revised to ensure that demonstrations were policed differently in future.

In September 1987, in his last major speech as ACPO President, Anderton called for the castration of rapists. The police authority defended the chief constable's right to make the statement, whilst complaining of media inaccuracy. However, in December the media reported the chief constable's views on the desirability of flogging criminals until they begged for mercy, and the criminalization of homosexual practices. The police authority responded by seeking legal advice on whether Anderton's remarks violated previous agreements, thus constituting a disciplinary offence. In January 1988, a special disciplinary committee was set up to look at the chief constable's speeches.

In principle, several courses of action were open to the authority. First, under Section 5 of the 1964 Police Act he could be called upon to retire in the interests of the efficiency of the force. Second, proceedings could be initiated under the 1985 regulations, governing the discipline of senior officers. And finally, the authority could seek a High Court declaration and injunction relating to his breaking of the January 1987 tripartite agreement. But, at the February meeting, after seeking legal advice and taking into account the advice of the Home Office, members decided to take no further action. Instead, both the authority and chief constable accepted the terms of a letter from the Home Office recording the chief constable's assurance that he would in future abide by 'the tripartite agreement'. It stated that

> There is a responsibility, in the interests of the police service and of the force in question, for a chief constable not to jeopardize, knowingly and necessarily, the reputation and efficient functioning of a force by purposely making public statements or comments calculated or reasonably likely to provoke or produce controversy (*Police Review*, 26 February 1988).

Nonetheless, the letter also reiterated that the chief constable remained free to make public statements about his professional duties and responsibilities, and that the prior consent of the police authority was not required on such matters. Thus, despite the fact that he had manifestly, and some would say deliberately, breached prior agreements, the autonomy of the chief constable was reaffirmed by the Home Office.

After this, the Greater Manchester police authority and the chief constable disappeared from the public gaze. A sense of new realism and consensus characterized the proceedings of the police authority as, for reasons discussed in the next chapter, Manchester's influence subsided. This new realism led to a re-writing and re-presenting of history. For example, glossy annual reports stated that the conflict was the result of 'a carry over of attitudes from the old police committee'. The chair of the authority noted in one of these reports that the only reason he and the chief constable now visited the Home Office was to complain about the detrimental impact that centrally imposed resource constraints were having on the fight against crime.

However, there is no indication that the chief constable ever changed his views. In March 1991, the newly knighted James Anderton announced his retirement. He told the assembled media that he had no professional regrets. He would have liked to have ended his career as commissioner of the Metropolitan Police but because of his controversial actions that was not to be. He also conceded that he had hoped to be able to 'so powerfully influence society and the community in the matter of rightful conduct that they would turn away from crime and disorder and wilful behaviour'. However, as far as he was concerned, he had failed and there was now a 'great sea of wrongdoing' (*Times*, 15 March 1991).

In his last annual report Sir James Anderton restated his fundamental belief that every effort should be made to prevent the police becoming 'central government pawns or local government lackeys':

> it is imperative that nothing should alter the present position whereby the impartial direction and control of a police force is uniquely vested in the independent office of chief constable (1991, p. vii).

He also argued that good police-community relations would be secured:

> not by the existence of politically-based police authorities, but by the integrity of the police officers we recruit, the standard of training they receive, the quality of service they deliver, the accountable autonomy of chief constables and their freedom from political direction and interference (1991, p. viii).

Thus, the chief constable survived a decade of attempts to call him to democratic account for his statements and actions. Such was the autonomy of chief police officers in the 1980s that, in James Anderton's dealings with both the police committee and police authority, he successfully avoided having to: provide meaningful reports and information; abide by agreements; consider fiscal restrictions; take heed of the views of elected representatives on operational dilemmas; or countenance, publicly at least, that any of his officers (apart from John Stalker) was capable of wrong doing or that in certain areas the edifice of police legitimacy and authority had virtually collapsed. It was this flaunting of the mechanisms of formal accountability that finally produced the sustained political campaign to have him removed from office. However, it also failed.

What now has to be also analyzed is what happened to the community liaison initiative during this period of conflict and resolution.

New directions in police-community liaison

In the countdown to abolition, the Conservative opposition and magistrates continued to question the value and purpose of the community liaison initiative. Disagreement centred, in particular, on Linbert Spencer's recommendation that a professional unit be established to support, service and develop the panels. At the April 1985 committee meeting, the Conservative's argued against such a unit on grounds of finance, stating that the committee had no right to bequeath such an expensive and unnecessary initiative to the new police authority.

They also tabled questions about who the proposed unit would be accountable to, pointing out that it would be independent of the chief constable and the force structure. The fear was expressed, in the light of what Manchester's police monitoring committee was doing, that the unit and strengthened panels might actively resist the police. Consequently, the Conservatives and magistrates demanded that the proposal be sent to the Home Office for approval.

It became apparent that the chief constable was also decidedly unhappy with the proposition. He argued that the original Home Office idea was that consultative arrangements should be inexpensive and non-bureaucratic. However, the police committee was proposing a costly and elaborate development of community liaison and this would place an unacceptably heavy burden on his officers. Consequently, he asked for a deferment on any decision until a managerial study had been carried out to determine whether such a unit was justified. He also requested that the force inspectorate and the Home Office be consulted before any final decision was made.

In June 1985, during an argument about the chief constable's refusal to discuss force reorganization plans with the committee, there was further argument about the future of community liaison. The Labour members argued that changes to local policing arrangements should only take place after proper consultation with the committee and panel members. Labour councillors maintained that if confidence in the police was to be restored it would have to be recognized that local communities had the right to be involved in formulating policies about how they were policed. However, such a suggestion horrified the Conservatives:

> Supposing the community liaison panels say 'we do not agree with the chief constable - we want the most for our patch'. Where does this leave the chief constable?

They emphasized that if such a scenario developed, the panels would be interfering with the operational autonomy of the chief constable. As far as the magistrates were concerned this was totally unacceptable and unrealistic:

> the community liaison panels should not have any say in the deployment of police officers. To give them the idea they have a such a right is frustrating because they do not.

Although the chief constable did not enter into this particular debate, in the same month he publicly questioned the usefulness of formal consultation arrangements in eliciting community involvement. He also argued that such arenas were 'wide open to political abuse':

> I became very concerned when I learned that certain persons meeting privately in my area had spoken of the panels as providing a structure to use 'political clout', and as 'power bases in the community' against the kinds of pro-police policies a Tory controlled joint board would produce (*Police Review*, 14 June 1985).

The Labour group pressed ahead with the proposed unit as quickly as possible to preclude any blocking action the chief constable might be planning, and to signal to Manchester City Council that the committee was determined to further its liaison initiative.

Unresolved issues of community representation and participation

The remit of the community relations unit, which became operational in June 1985, differed significantly to that of the community liaison officer. The overall function changed from finding a means 'to improve relationships between police and community, initially in the area of Moss Side' to working 'with community liaison panels and other community groups to promote the community relations policies of the police committee and develop structures which increase the accountability of the police to local communities'. The community liaison officer had tried, however unsuccessfully, through his complaints work, to include the interests of those for whom the police were the problem. However, the new unit concentrated on crime prevention and educating the public about policing. Such a focus meant there was the real possibility that the interests and concerns of Moss Side would no longer be prioritized on the agenda of the unit.

However, whilst the crime control work of the unit expanded considerably, it still had to address the problems associated with attempting to ensure that all sections of the community were adequately represented and participating in the liaison panels.

One of the first decisions was to produce a panel newsletter - *Community Liaison* ('Police and People Working Together') in order to: give the panels a higher public profile; strengthen the links between the various panels; create a means of communication between the panels and the community and counteract the anti-community liaison position being presented by the police monitoring unit's *PoliceWatch* magazine (see next chapter). It reported on the work of the panels and new policing and crime prevention initiatives. There was little coverage of controversial policing issues such as the 'Battle of Brittan' or the Stalker Affair. Any critical comments focused on the anti-community liaison stance of Manchester City Council.

When the new police authority took over, it established a working party to examine the future function and structure of the twenty-one community liaison panels. Its deliberations (which took into account the guidance provided by Home Office Circular No 2/1985 and feedback from panel members) prompted 'a radical course of enhancing and improving [the] consultation arrangements', with the authority stressing the 'need to involve even more people in the debate' (*Community Liaison*, No 3, 1986). The reality was that the highly structured and formalized liaison panels were continuing to generate the over representation and participation of certain sections of 'the community' as well as little general public interest. In 1987, with the agreement of the chief constable, a new policy statement called *New Directions* was released, restating that:

> regular liaison between the police and the community not only leads to a better understanding, but has concrete results in reducing the fear of crime, promoting community safety and giving the community a real voice in policing their neighbourhood (Greater Manchester police authority, 1987, p. 1).

The community relations unit was given the key role of restructuring the format of the meetings and panel business in an attempt to generate wider and more meaningful public participation because, as the Home Office circular had stressed:

> If a group is to have the confidence of the local community as the focus for local consultations on policing matters, it is essential that its membership should be as representative as possible of that community...[and] attract the fullest public support and appropriate community participation (Home Office, 1985, para 7).

New Directions forcefully reminded the liaison panels that they did not represent the community but were representative of it. In order to ensure maximum participation and active discussion, panels were advised to adopt a flexible 'open forum' approach. There would be no restrictions on the total number of people wishing to become panel members. Membership would be open to anybody living within the sub-division, as well as representatives from the local council, police, business and statutory and voluntary organizations. Everyone present at a given meeting would have voting rights, and minority views were to be acknowledged and recorded. Annual meetings would elect a panel chair, vice chair and press officer.

The panels were urged to find a real local role for themselves by being dynamic, campaigning and 'nomadic'. They were urged to hold meetings in all parts of the sub-division, in different types of venue and at different times so that all sections of the community would have the opportunity to attend and to ensure that the interests and priorities of no one area dominated. Furthermore, panel members were encouraged to meet with other community groups and, where necessary, institute local 'surgeries' to identify neighbourhood problems and possible solutions. The message was clear: if 'the community' would not come to the panels then they would have to go to different sections and parts of the community.

In terms of the panels' business, there was a promise that sub-divisional commanders would provide regular reports to enhance panel members' understanding of local police policies. The unit would also provide additional information on issues of concern. At the end of the formal business, the public would be able to ask questions, so long as they did not infringe upon operational aspects or relate to individual complaints which were under investigation.

The crucial question to be assessed is how the police authority and community relations unit's new strategy impacted on the specific problems identified by the community liaison officer, namely (a) establishing panels across the whole of Manchester (b) setting up a panel in Moss Side and (c) ensuring that all sections of 'the community', especially ethnic minorities, women and young people, joined in the work of the existing panels.

Manchester City Council

In March 1985 the position of Manchester City Council was discussed publicly for the first time during a full police committee meeting, when opposition councillors demanded to know why a liaison panel had not been set up in the city, given that this was where the real police-community and crime problems were. Labour councillors argued that panels could not be set up in areas where they were not wanted, and conceded that community support for the idea had not been forthcoming, especially in Moss Side. It was also pointed out that there was a serious geographical problem with Manchester because sub-divisional boundaries did not correspond to 'recognizable' or 'natural' communities.

The chief constable also censured the committees' refusal to set up liaison panels in Manchester:

> I find it strange that in areas where panels would conceivably perform a helpful function none, at present, exist, whereas police committees are being pressed to formulate panels where nobody at all sees a need (*Police Review*, 14 June 1985).

He claimed that the 'Manchester problem' could have been avoided if the Home Office had entrust chief constables, rather than police committees, with the duty to organize consultation/liaison arrangements. As it stood, he argued that if the police committee were serious about setting up liaison panels in Manchester, it would have to bypass the council. In July 1985, when the chief constable reported that the sub-divisional boundaries in the city were being reviewed, thus removing one of the problems, the police committee decided to situate panels in Wythenshaw and Longsight as part of a phased programme of establishing panels in Manchester.

Thus, as was discussed in chapter five, the police committee persevered with its exertions to create liaison panels in the city. In addition to the meetings previously reviewed, in March 1986, at a meeting of local voluntary and statutory agencies, it was agreed to establish two panels in Wythenshawe. At the meeting, Gabrielle Cox said that she hoped that the exercise would be repeated throughout the rest of Manchester. However, it failed to elicit an enthusiastic response from local people, and it was not until late 1988 and early 1989, after the police monitoring committee had been abolished and the influence of Manchester's representatives on the new police authority had declined (see chapter eight), that the next attempts were made to introduce liaison panels. What is significant is that, unlike elsewhere in Greater Manchester, the structures that were proposed were diverse and flexible. They were not based on the city's sub-divisional boundaries, covered much smaller geographical areas and stressed openness, informality and participation instead of representation. It is questionable whether under the Home Office guidelines, certain of the Manchester 'fora', could be defined as consultative committees.

Moss Side

The efforts to 'sell' community liaison in Moss Side were repeatedly hindered by issues arising from the policing of the area. There was ongoing disquiet about the activities of the multi-agency community liaison panel established by Linbert Spencer. It was finally abandoned at the end of 1986 when, as a result of allegations that the police were engaged in undercover intelligence gathering activities in Moss Side, Manchester City Council prohibited its representatives from attending meetings. Moreover, the outcome of the Jacki Berkeley case confirmed the arguments of those groups opposed to having anything to do with the Greater Manchester Police. In March 1985, she was found guilty of all the charges brought against her, including that of wasting police time, and was given suspended prison sentences of various lengths. This once more brought allegations of a cover up and demands that a public inquiry be set up into the policing of Moss Side (*Race Today*, May, 1985; *Guardian*, 15 March 1985). The profound dissatisfaction with the outcome of the case was one of the reasons for the large attendance at a meeting on the policing of black communities held in the area in May 1986 which, among other things, reaffirmed local opposition to the community liaison initiative.

In 1986, the case of Viraj Mendis took firm roots in Moss Side. After his final appeal against deportation for being an illegal immigrant was rejected, he took sanctuary, with the support of the local clergy, in a local church. In 1987, an alliance of local groups organized a high profile campaign, including well attended public meetings and demonstrations, to prevent the Home Office attempting to remove Mendis, against his will, from the church. Given the history of local resistance to immigration related policing actions, the Viraj Mendis case, if not handled delicately, was always going to have a detrimental effect on police-community relations in Moss Side.

Whilst the case was still progressing towards an inevitable conclusion, Moss Side was rocked by the rape and murder of a black woman, Elsa Hannaway, allegedly by a black man, in October 1987. For possibly the first time in over a decade, widespread co-operation was forthcoming with the police describing the response to their appeals for information as 'overwhelming'. However, the police-community alliance was short-lived. The police were accused of cynically using the murder investigation as an excuse to: conduct indiscriminate violent raids in Moss Side in a manner not seen since 1981; question every black male with dreadlocks; and put pressure on people to become police informants. The resentment and allegations resulted in further public meetings, and the formation of Action for Black Justice. The refusal of senior police officers to take the allegations seriously resulted in another impasse in police-community relations and the rebuilding of the wall of silence (*New Society*, 13 May 1988).

In the same time period, the first wave of 'drug related' shootings took place in the area as well as the first media reports claiming that Moss Side was the drug centre of the north of England. This destabilized police-community relations further because of complaints about the role of the police, both in responding erratically to the drug problem (containment, non-enforcement, indiscriminate raids, the attempted cultivation of informers), and colluding with the media in the pernicious criminalization of black youth, and the labelling of Moss Side as a lawless 'outsider' community. Furthermore, as a consequence of the police handling of the Elsie Hannaway murder investigation, all possibility of obtaining information from law-abiding sources dried up.

It was in this context that the community relations unit attempted to launch a liaison panel in E division north. Approximately eighty people turned up to a meeting convened by the police authority in July 1988. During a heated discussion, the authority was told that even if the community liaison structure had worked elsewhere in Greater Manchester this did not mean that it was be suitable for Moss Side. Authority representatives were told that the area already had its own organizations and leaders and was capable of representing its own interests. It was agreed to delay the setting up of a panel and instead to set up a working party to have talks about talks.

This working party met for the first time in September 1988 to discuss the 'best sort of arrangements for the police authority to obtain the views of the people in the E north sub-division about policing the area and improving police/community relations'. It was stressed that whatever arrangements were established would have to enjoy the full confidence of local people and could not be imposed upon the community. Consequently, it was agreed that because of the different communities encompassed by the sub-division, there should be a number of open membership local fora which would report to a parent panel.

Prior to the next meeting in December (which was supposed to finalize the proposed consultation structure), members of the community relations unit canvassed local organizations, voluntary groups and local councillors. Members of the working party were also asked to identify and talk to key individuals in their areas and to construct 'a list of people you feel represent your area and who could offer advice or would have criticisms about the proposed scheme'.

However, this delicate negotiation process was derailed in January 1989 when approximately fifty police officers made a dramatic SAS style raid on the Ascension Church in order to deport Viraj Mendis to Sri Lanka. This caused an immediate outcry because the police had not only carried out the wishes of the Home Office, but in doing so had violated the sanctity and sanctuary of a church. Hence, a policing action had been decided upon that was opposed in the locality. For key groups and individuals this was additional proof that it was not possible to enter into useful dialogue with the police. Local anger was fuelled further by the rumour that a local community police officer had been involved in the organization of the raid. It was agreed, after discussions between the community relations unit and local community representatives, to postpone subsequent meetings until the situation calmed down. However, this did not happen because in the same time period the area was rocked by numerous shooting incidents. Hence, the sensitive policing circumstances of Moss Side frustrated all efforts to set up a community liaison panel.

Ethnic minorities

Serious problems also persisted with attempts to bring about ethnic minority participation in the panels in other parts of Greater Manchester. The Press Officer for the Bury North liaison panel, for example, stated that although it had a trusting and supportive relationship with its police officers, 'there are sections of the community, especially the black community, who would not totally share this view' (*Community Liaison*, No 8, 1988). In an attempt to promote greater ethnic participation, two of the panels adopted anti-discrimination statements 'as a first step to increasing the awareness of issues important to black and Asian members so that racist comments and attitudes can be examined and changes made' (*Community Liaison*, No 3, 1987).

North Trafford, in acknowledgement of the fact that ethnic minority communities were not adequately involved in the consultation process, set up, in December 1989, a separate ethnic communities sub-group 'where their concerns could be heard by the police and the Greater Manchester police authority'. Representatives from the minority communities in this area argued that such a sub-group was needed because the structure of the panel meetings was 'too formal and intimidating', thus precluding the space necessary to raise their specific concerns. Consequently, it was highly unlikely that they would ever attend panel meetings. The community relations unit fully supported such a forum, arguing that it represented one of the few opportunities for consultation with this particular community.

Efforts were also made to encourage participation through ensuring that the business of the panels was directly relevant to ethnic minorities. For example, racial harassment was one of the issues championed by the community relations unit, and Manchester Council for Community Relations was encouraged to work in conjunction with the police to formulate a policy statement. At 'Forum 1988', one of the key sessions focused on police responses to racial harassment. The police officer in charge of the session also detailed moves to improve police-community relations by recruiting more members of ethnic minorities and educating officers in 'social skills' which would them to understand and respect other cultures. However, the unit also had to confront the uncomfortable reality that in certain areas, there was the distinct possibility that the prioritization of minority concerns would have alienated other sections of the community.

Young people

The importance of securing the participation of young people was re-emphasized during 'Forum 1985'. It was recognized that they were the section of the community most likely to be in conflict with the police and also the main source of local disturbances and criminality. The community relations unit recognized that there was a distinction between ensuring representation, and the 'varying degrees of commitment the young people will have to participation', and emphasized that:

> there are many and varied ways of involving young people in the debate with regard to policing - if not panels themselves. It is up to the panels to see what input they want from young people (*Community Liaison*, No 2, 1986).

It was argued that if the liaison panels were interested solely in youth representation, this could be achieved by adjusting panel proceedings. However, increased participation would only be realized if panel members took a more active role in meeting young people in their communities. Consequently, during 1986-1987 eight of the panels set up working parties and tried a variety of approaches in an attempt to persuade young people to attend meetings. Salford South, for example, set up a working party 'to liaise with the City of Salford to see what could be done to support police work with young people' (*Community Liaison*, No 2, 1986). The panel subsequently carried out a survey of young people in two schools on attitudes to the police and youth provision in the area. However, they subsequently reported that they found the whole exercise frustrating because of the negative response.

Certain panels evolved a strategy based upon the idea that if young people would not attend liaison panel meetings, then the panels should go out to meet with them. Consequently, panel representatives arranged meetings at local youth clubs, community centres and colleges, using questionnaires to find out young people's views on policing. The Swinton and Walkden panel, for example, went to a local youth centre. As a consequence, a youth committee was formed to represent the young people affiliated to the centre and a representative was chosen from this committee to attend the meetings of the liaison panel:

> It is to be hoped that this representative is accorded the same respect as other members of the panel - and that they in turn, ensure that they do speak on behalf of the young people they represent (*Community Liaison*, No 2, 1986).

Trafford and Salford North liaison panels made the most systematic attempts to resolve the problem through an 'educative approach'. In January 1988, thirty-five young people and eleven youth workers from Trafford went to a rural retreat 'to learn about decision making and participation' (*Community Liaison*, No 8, 1988). The weekend consisted of young people discussing, the nature of decision-making, relations with statutory agencies and the nature of community resources. There was also discussion, with the councillors present, about the role of councillors in the local community.

Salford North held a weekend for young people from two local youth clubs premised upon the notion that 'it is essential that the views of young people are heard with regard to their community and its policing'. In order for young people to participate in the liaison panel, it was asserted that they needed knowledge about the law, the duties of the police, the rights and responsibilities of citizens and the ways in which communities operate.

Initial meetings, at the two youth centres, focused on legal rights, the responsibilities of young people and 'discussion about the work of the police and an understanding of reasonable attitudes towards them' (*Community Liaison*, No 11, 1989). Youth workers then issued invitations to the seventeen young people who were present at the first meeting to attend a weekend conference to discuss how a community develops, the diversity of needs within it, the causes and consequences of crime and the role of the council in their lives. A further meeting with police officers discussed policing, crime and crime prevention. Finally, the young people appointed a representative to attend liaison panel meetings on a regular basis.

Another strategy involved attempting to create school based youth forums in order to improve consultation between young people and the police and reducing juvenile criminality. Efforts were also made through involving local youth workers 'to develop their own facilities, thus keeping them off the streets and also to give them the skills to improve the image of young people within the community'. The youth fora were also intended to link into the work of the liaison panels.

Women

It became apparent to the community relations unit that the concerns of women were not being raised during full liaison panel meetings. This was because women were still, for a variety of practical reasons, considerably under-represented on certain panels and because of a hesitancy by women to raise sensitive 'private' issues in public. Thus, concerted efforts were made to prioritize domestic violence; child sexual abuse; and women's treatment by the criminal justice system within the work of the police authority and the liaison panels.

At a general level, the new police authority publicly committed itself to campaigning for greater protection for women and a complete re-orientation of the criminal justice system to recognize women's needs:

> In a very changing world women are taking full part in activities. At the same time the world is decreasing for them because of the fear on the street, in public transport, even taxis (*Community Liaison*, No 10, 1989).

Specific events and separate fora were also established so that women's issues could be adequately addressed. Liaison panels were encouraged, through staging 'Women Alone' exhibitions, to promote awareness of personal safety and strategies which would reduce the risk of becoming a victim. The exhibitions consisted of self-defence displays and self-protection tips, as well as demonstrations of crime prevention equipment. 'Forum 1988' had a specific workshop on 'Women - their safety and concern' which focused on crime prevention, victim support services and criminal injuries compensation.

A multi-agency group on violence against women in the home was set up in one part of Manchester in 1990 after it became apparent that the relevant agencies were not picking up the scale of the problem and were not responding in a manner that inspired confidence among local women. The focus of this group was to ensure that all statutory and voluntary bodies were working to provide a co-ordinated response to this problem. In the same time period, women members of the police authority established a working party on women's issues to ensure that domestic violence became a force priority in

1991, and participated in the redrafting of force policy on this particular matter. From August 1991, offenders were to be arrested wherever possible and domestic violence officers were appointed to each division so that victims could be provided with a better level of service.

The establishment, in late 1986, of St. Mary's Sexual Assault Referral Centre was to be the ultimate proof that the police and police authority was taking the needs of female victims of crime seriously. This multi-agency approach, involving police surgeons, doctors, psychiatrists, gynaecologists and venerologists, was justified on the grounds that 'public opinion, both as represented by voluntary organizations and by individuals, was often highly critical of existing arrangements'. The centre was located within a local hospital, and financed by the police authority and the Department of the Environment.

Discussion

During the last months of the operation of the old police committee, all attempts by Labour councillors to engage the chief constable in dialogue failed, most noticeably on the issue of his unauthorized acquisition of plastic bullets. Despite the remarkable and strenuous efforts of councillors to press Anderton to account for his extremist statements and actions, constitutional and political considerations severely limited the scope for effective action. It was clear to those campaigning for democratic accountability in Greater Manchester that the only way to resolve this dispute was to dismiss the chief constable. The police committee was abolished instead.

Ironically, the first year of the new police authority witnessed an intensification of the conflict over the policing of Manchester. However, through Anderton's continued assertion of his autonomy, the unwavering support of the Home Office, and the ideological divisions within the police authority, the extraordinary campaign for police accountability finally exhausted itself.

Prior to its abolition, the police committee, despite considerable opposition, set up a community relations unit to strengthen its community liaison initiative. The new unit discarded the 'representative' work of the community liaison officer and eventually closed the community liaison office in Moss Side. Thus, the concerns of black people - the reasons why the initiative was set up in the first place - were no longer a specific priority. Furthermore, reflecting national developments documented in the previous chapter, crime prevention, not police accountability, became the essential concern for the unit.

For the most part, the police authority's formulaic 'representative model' continued to facilitate the interests of those sections of the community who wanted to co-operate with the police in preventing crime. However, even this base-line constituency was not unproblematical. It was not clear that, if left to its own devices, this constituency would have continued to participate because there was little that the panels could do to impact positively upon local crime and environmental problems - the power to do that lay elsewhere. The problem was compounded by the fact that there were many other 'community' groupings also concerned with crime prevention issues, most obviously neighbourhood watch and crime prevention panels. This meant that the panels had real difficulties in finding a genuine grass roots role for themselves. This lack of a role also meant that without the considerable infrastructural support provided by the police authority and the police, many of these liaison panels would have collapsed. The bottom line was that they were not a bona fide 'community' demand and not representative of 'the community'.

It was these unspoken realities that led the community relations unit (and indeed the Home Office) to realize that if progress was to be made it would have to make strenuous efforts to open, widen and deepen the liaison initiative by involving all parts of Greater Manchester and addressing the interests of ethnic minorities, women and young people.

Repeated attempts were made to coax Moss Side to take part in some form of liaison structure. To this end, the unit made it clear that any forum that was established did not have to operate like those elsewhere in Greater Manchester. But every time some progress was made, controversial police actions resulted in community representatives retreating from the negotiation process because such actions raised fresh questions about whether community liaison was capable of resolving the deep-rooted problem of the policing of Moss Side.

Of great significance was the fact that very flexible and open liaison arrangements were eventually used in Manchester. A localized 'open forum' structure, stressing participation rather than community representation, was used in three areas in an attempt to initiate the community liaison process. Elsewhere in Greater Manchester, as a result of a major rethink, panels were encouraged to address ongoing problems of community under/non-representation by transforming themselves into less rigid, less formal and more local entities. However, problems remained. What is notable, for example, about the initiatives to involve young people, is how little progress was made. Formal meetings were not attended whilst report from informal ones were likely to note that 'the meeting was too large and rowdy to be productive. By the end of the meeting little had been achieved' (Community Liaison, No 8, 1988). What some of the panels had to confront, as a result of their meetings with young people, was the issue of poor police-youth relations. When the Ashton panel had a meeting in a local college, there were no police representatives present:

It may well be that it was a good thing; several young people needed to be assured that there were no police in the hall before entering, and members speculated that they may not have been so forthcoming if they thought that policemen were there and perhaps noting who said what (*Community Liaison*, No 2, 1986).

Thus, the exercises tended to result in the incorporation of the few young people who were willing to talk with the police and who were prepared to acknowledge and discuss the problems that young people caused the community. The obvious question is how representative were these young people, especially in certain areas of Salford where there was deep seated loathing of the local police among young men.

There were similar problems with the efforts to enhance female participation. In line with national developments, the safety interests of women were made a priority and they could be accommodated within the remit of the liaison panels. However, the unit did not address the divisions of interest that could exist between women. Consequently, the interests of radical women's groups working in the area of women's safety were in danger of being marginalized and excluded. Thus, during Forum 1989, although there were supposed to be representatives present from all women's organizations and groups, Rape Crisis and Women's Aid were not present. Instead, the conservative Women's National Commission was able to present an analysis of women's concerns which emphasized the importance of the family. It was also a traditional women's organization that led the session on women's safety.

Such a process of exclusion also transpired when the police authority decided to provide financial support for a rape examination centre. As Foley (1991) has convincingly argued, this development, in effect, was a declaration of war on the local Rape Crisis Centre which had providing a service since the early 1980s. Representatives of the new Sexual Assault Referral Centre constantly compared their 'professional', 'full-time', 'objective', 'multi-agency', 'clinical service' with the 'unprofessional', 'voluntary',' non-medical', 'politically extreme' 'practices' of the Rape Crisis Centre. Concerted efforts were made, therefore, to exclude and silence Rape Crisis because of its radical discourse on sexual abuse.

As the preceding analysis has indicated, the tensions between inclusion and marginalization seem to be the almost inevitable consequence of setting up, in a top-down fashion, 'representative' institutional arrangements within tightly defined parameters. The problem with allowing all sections of the community equal rights of representation is that it can lead to, for a variety of reasons, the systematic non-participation of powerless groups and marginal interests. And of course it should not be forgotten that the community liaison initiative was originally established as a response not to the problem of crime but to the fact that politically and economically powerless and racially disadvantaged sections of the community were in open conflict with the police in Moss Side.

8 City Council and community safety

The police monitoring committee declared that it would refuse to have anything to do with the new police authority because it was part of the Conservative government's strategy to nullify democratically mandated political opponents and finally remove policing from the realm of local governance. However, in private, careful consideration was given to whether abolition could enhance the monitoring initiative. One of the major difficulties which had plagued the committee since its inception was that, unlike the pre-1964 borough watch committee, it was not in a position to confront the chief constable over the policing of Manchester. In fact, Greater Manchester Police ignored the majority of letters and requests from the committee. However, the composition of the new police authority meant that representatives from the monitoring committee would gain direct access to the chief constable. There was also the distinct possibility that Manchester City Council, because it had the most representatives and a fully operational research and development unit, would take responsibility for the servicing of the new authority. This would mean that the monitoring committee would be able to keep the liaison panels out of the city and, more significantly, challenge the organizational edifice of the Greater Manchester Police. Thus, the proposed changes could, in theory, allow the monitoring committee's campaign for police accountability to advance on two fronts.

Controversy and reaction

In the countdown to abolition and immediately after the new police authority took over, the police monitoring committee moved centre stage in the struggle for police accountability in Manchester. Documenting and highlighting the corruption, incompetence and maladministration of the Greater Manchester

Police remained at the forefront of the committee's work. And it made extremely belligerent pronouncements about: the 'Battle of Brittan'; the 'Justice for Steven Shaw Campaign'; police powers and citizens' rights; plastic bullets; police misconduct; freemasonry in the police; police racism; police sexism; council contact with the police; police in schools; and the effectiveness of the new police authority.

The monitoring unit, to the consternation of its critics, produced its own confidential form for registering complaints against the police, published a 'know your rights' package, distributed information on suing the police, and issued 'wanted' posters for the police officers who allegedly carried out an attack on Steven Shaw. It also played the crucial role of providing detailed briefing papers for the City Council's representatives on the new police authority and, it is alleged, leaked sensitive authority documents to the media.

Neither did the monitoring committee's line on the Stalker Affair win it any friends. Although the monitoring committee, and its representatives on the police authority, proclaimed that Stalker had been set up by a top level conspiracy, it did not see the deputy chief constable as a saint or folk hero. The evidence unearthed by the various investigations demonstrated the:

> arrogance of senior police officers who...attend money-raising functions for the Conservative Party. And attend them in an official capacity with absolute impunity. This kind of 'acceptable' behaviour demonstrates the transparency of the claim that the police are politically neutral. Can anyone imagine any deputy chief constable anywhere attending a fund-raising function for the disqualified Lambeth councillors? (Stringer, 1987, p. 5).

And, as was detailed in the previous chapter, it was obvious that certain members of the monitoring committee were using Stalker to 'nail' the chief constable once and for all. To compound the controversy, in February 1986, the first issue of *PoliceWatch* was published and delivered to every household in the city. Unlike the Greater London Council's esoteric and doom-laden policing publications, *PoliceWatch* was intended to be populist, provocative and glossy in order 'to draw a wider community into policing matters and the policing debate' and to 'contribute much to improving the community's knowledge and understanding of policing issues'. In order to do so, it would: explain the political rationale and policies of the police monitoring committee; enhance the public's knowledge about local and national developments in policing; counter the disinformation on policing and crime issues propagated by the *Manchester Evening News* and the powerful press office of Greater Manchester Police; agitate for change; and provide a means for community groups and individuals to disseminate their views on policing to a wider public:

> Your experiences of how you are policed and your thoughts on how it can be improved are of interest to us and the police monitoring committee and *PoliceWatch* bulletin can be your voice (*PoliceWatch*, No 1, 1986).

Policewatch had an uncompromisingly aggressive presentational format with headlines such as: PUBLIC ORDER: OUT OF ORDER?; WE ONLY COMPLAIN ABOUT THEM BECAUSE YOU DO; PLASTIC BULLETS: THE GRIM REALITY; STALKER SILENCED; ARE POLICE PRIORITIES YOUR PRIORITIES?; HAD AN ARRESTING EXPERIENCE?; KEEPING P.A.C.E. WITH THE LAW; CAUSES FOR COMPLAINT? Its inflammatory proselytizing ignited a firestorm of debate. The paper was immediately denounced by the political opposition in Manchester, Conservative MPs, and the national Labour leadership. The magazine was condemned in the House of Commons as a 'scurrilous and divisive document', a 'blatant misuse of ratepayers' money for subversive campaigning' and an example of the 'vicious anti-police propaganda spewed out by various hard left controlled authorities' (*Manchester Evening News*, 25 February 1986; 1 March 1986).

Gerald Kaufman, the Shadow Home Secretary and a Manchester MP, informed a fringe meeting of the Police Federation in May 1986 that the magazine was a 'scandalous, scurrilous, unbalanced and untruthful publication' and that the views expressed in it were 'in no way representative of the Labour leadership' (quoted in Walker, 1986, p. 203).

Manchester's position on community liaison also came under scrutiny in the Home Affairs Committee's 1986 investigation into racial attacks and harassment. In John Stalker's evidence to the committee, he agreed with the proposal that consultative/liaison committees should take a key role within multi-agency approaches to this particular problem. However, he informed committee members that in Manchester this would not be possible because the police did not enjoy the goodwill or support of the City Council. In its summing up, the committee recommended that the Home Secretary seek an explanation as to why certain councils were flaunting Home Office guidelines on consultative arrangements. It also warned those councils that a multi-agency approach was essential to tackling racial violence and that refusing to co-operate with the police was an act of 'political self-indulgence from which the sufferers will be the ethnic minorities'.

Hence, because of the high profile stance of the committee and the campaign by its representatives on the new police authority to have the chief constable sacked (already detailed in chapter seven), Manchester City Council was being identified nationally as a 'loony left' administration. For sections of the local Labour Party, such labelling increased their already considerable misgivings about the extremist 'posturing' and 'antics' of the monitoring committee. Questions were also being asked about why Manchester was spending scarce resources on police monitoring when the council's interests were now directly represented on the Labour-controlled police authority. Moreover, certain senior council officers and core service departments wanted a return to the days of close and respectable relations with senior police officers.

Concern was heightened further when, in the run up to the May 1986 elections, the opposition parties decided to make police monitoring an electoral issue. The Conservatives described the establishment of the monitoring unit and *PoliceWatch* as 'madness on the rates', whilst Liberals denounced Labour for refusing to support liaison panels and for setting up a structure that engaged in 'destructive criticism' of the police. Opposition candidates presented the case for spending scarce council resources on helping the victims of crime instead of slandering the police, and pledged to persevere with their campaign for the abolition of the police monitoring committee.

Because of the apprehension (it is claimed that) a decision was taken by the council leadership to suspend the distribution of *PoliceWatch* until after the elections. Instead, all households received a user-friendly 'A-Z' of the council's services. Moreover, the party manifesto made little mention of the work of the police monitoring committee, choosing instead to focus upon crime, policing and the inner city. And when residents finally received *PoliceWatch,* they were able to read about the council's commitment to taking practical steps to help them 'feel safer in their homes and on the streets':

> It is recognized by all of us that the breakup of our old close-knit communities together with high unemployment and levels of deprivation will doubtless lead to crime and also fear of crime. It follows that a recreation of that spirit which once existed in Manchester will do something to decrease crime (No 2, 1986).

Certain Labour candidates attempted to distance themselves completely from the stance and work of the police monitoring committee, providing the electorate with examples of how they were working with local police officers in the fight against crime. In Levenshulme, for example, the candidate emphasized that campaigning for crime prevention, more bobbies on the beat and more resources for the police, would be one of his main concerns. In Moston, the Labour Party stressed that they were 'not extremists' and that they 'supported the police in their attempts to establish better community relations'. In Beswick, the candidate stated that he opposed those who were attempting to undermine the police through constant criticism, and that he backed the police in the fight against crime. The Labour nominee in Lightbowne gave his complete support to neighbourhood watch, community liaison panels, community policing and multi-agency efforts to fight crime.

The fact that the Labour Party strengthened its hold over the council in these elections was proof for some party members that a cautious approach on crime and policing issues had succeeded. It also meant, just as significantly, that several Labour candidates who were opposed to the whole initiative had been elected.

Neighbourhood Watch

The police monitoring committee's stance on neighbourhood watch schemes generated further political destabilization. In December 1986, the committee reiterated its opposition to such schemes on the grounds that they were unaccountable, would encourage 'snoopers' and informers and exacerbate people's fear of crime, rather than tackling Manchester's crime problem. Consequently, it refused to consider applications from several residents' associations for funding to erect 'Homewatch' signs. Committee and unit members were suspicious of the motives of those who were upfronting the issue and believed that they could be part of a police set-up. The *Manchester Evening News*, as part of its continuing campaign against the 'Marxist extremists' in control of the Town Hall, led the inevitable counter-attack, claiming that 'Labour councillors [had] stunned community leaders by condemning popular Home Watch groups as information gathering exercises'. The paper subsequently stressed that such illogical and irresponsible actions were besmirching the good name of Manchester.

The political fallout was so serious that a council-wide damage limitation exercise was immediately embarked upon. It was agreed that the council should, as a matter of priority, upgrade its (virtually non-existent) crime prevention work at all levels (Police monitoring committee, Reports Nos 102-6). Every major service department was asked to identify resources and approaches that could be earmarked for crime prevention work. A community safety working party was established, and the policy and resources committee agreed to the appointment of a community safety officer. The police monitoring unit was also directed to organize a series of workshops on community safety for relevant officers of the council, and to produce a community safety booklet for residents.

The speed with which the police monitoring committee moved to respond to the internal political manoeuvring, and to embrace the new political realities posed by the issue of crime prevention, is demonstrated by its response to the decision to appoint a community safety officer. A paper of February 1987 justified locating the post within the monitoring unit because:

> The committee has consistently expressed its view that the local authority is in a position to influence crime and fear of crime, particularly through a community based strategy which does not marginalize these issues from others, such as appropriate policing and service provision. Whilst recognizing that solutions lie primarily in major structural changes, the committee has accepted that it is possible to create a safer community - noting also that the ultimate success of such an initiative is dependent on adequate resources for investment in services, facilities and the fabric of neighbourhoods (Police monitoring committee, Report, No 123).

This tentative but significant redefinition of the unit's work was accompanied by endeavours to justify the council's position on 'Homewatch'. Tony McCardell, the chair of the monitoring committee, maintained that neighbourhood watch schemes were cosmetic, displacing crime rather than tackling the root causes of crime. What was needed, before any solutions were embraced, was an open debate about the nature and extent of the city's crime problems. Manchester residents were also told that:

> Our wish is to be involved with a proper community safety policy. We do have an alternative to HomeWatch - and it is a sign of the times that we do have to call it an alternative - that is, reverting to more bobbies on the beat...A better use of resources, with more officers on the beat and fewer in riot vans, might allow the police to solve more break-ins and halt the ever increasing crime rate (*PoliceWatch*, No 5, 1986).

Graham Stringer, the leader of the council, also assured the people of Manchester that the council was not anti-police, but conceded that it faced a dilemma on this particular issue. On the one hand, it had serious and valid reservations about neighbourhood watch schemes because they were no substitute for persuading the police to provide an effective and sensitive service, and research suggested that they diverted scarce police resources from 'the less articulate and less organized sections of the community'. On the other, it faced legitimate 'demands from local community groups to help them make their areas free from such crimes as burglary and assaults and from the fear which such crimes create' (*PoliceWatch*, No 6, 1987).

The council had decided, therefore, not to hinder residents who wished to set up 'Homewatch' schemes. But, perhaps more significantly, Stringer also unveiled an alternative community safety imitative to prove that 'Manchester City Council [was] committed to supporting groups of residents who want to protect themselves, their communities and their homes from crime'. In future, council grants would be made available to enable residents to set up their own neighbourhood safety schemes. Council departments would also work with local communities and other statutory agencies to: improve locks, doors and windows on housing estates; introduce more effective caretaking, security systems and park warden schemes; redesign landscapes to produce a safer public environment; and improve street lighting and the lighting of council property. Manchester City Council, like other radical local authorities around the country, was, in effect, having to realize that as a property owner and landlord, it was a victim of crime on a massive scale. Of equal significance was the fact that it was also in a position, as the major service provider, to take practical steps to improve matters.

Community consultation and participation

At the same time as the council's response to the neighbourhood watch debacle was working itself out, the police monitoring committee was considering two reports which would also have a bearing on the future direction of its work. The council's policy and resources committee, which had been monitoring the work of the council, passed a resolution in July 1986 requesting all committees and departments to consider its report on 'Consultation and Participation', and spell out what action was being taken to decentralize and co-ordinate service provision and to involve residents in decisions relating to the management of their homes and environments.

The second report took the form of a highly critical internal review of the activities of the monitoring unit (Walker, 1986). It acknowledged the quality of the high profile campaigning and support work being carried out. However, it was very concerned that, even in comparison with some of the London police monitoring initiatives, the Manchester unit seemed to have few meaningful links with either core service departments or the public. He reminded the unit that one of the reasons why police monitoring committees had few friends inside local government structures was because they were challenging, in the name of democratic accountability, one of the most powerful state agencies. The reality was that most senior officers and politicians wanted good relations with the police and this made monitoring committees extremely vulnerable. Such vulnerability was heightened if these committees did not have secure moorings outside the Town Hall. And Walker believed that this was the case in Manchester.

He believed that part of the reason lay in the fact that the initiative had constructed an abstract conceptual model of police monitoring. Consequently, little time that had been given to thinking about what police monitoring groups were, where they came from or what purpose they served. He told the unit that there was no ready-made formula that could be used to establish monitoring groups. Their very essence was their spontaneity, diversity, autonomy from state institutions and they certainly could not be imposed as a political imperative. The report argued that if any progress was to be achieved on this front, the unit would have to develop a much sharper and deeper community focus in order to establish the relevance of democratized policing practices to local people and the council. 'The community' rather than the council chamber would have to become the real site of police accountability.

Abstract and academic type theorizing should be cut to a minimum, as should ideological attacks on political policing, because they found 'no reflection in the lives of ordinary people'. There was no combat-ready oppositional consciousness to be tapped into. The unit's development workers would have to go out into different neighbourhoods and forge meaningful alliances by working closely with local people over a period of years, to identify distinct needs and the tenor and nature of territorial police work. Such deep and protracted developmental work would be able to uncover the complex histories and conflicts that existed between the police and different communities, and disaggregate policing patterns so that different local practices and priorities became visible:

> they should not consider themselves as primarily setting up monitoring groups, but should consider this as a second stage to their work as and when their field work shows a clear indication of real community will and need...in the first instance they should be the monitoring group (Walker, 1986, p. 75).

The report also realized that the political problem of crime would have to be confronted positively. It stressed that the unit could puncture the dominant interface between policing and crime by developing democratically constituted 'security and welfare' policies, which demonstrated the inadequacy of the crime prevention programmes being promoted by the police:

> It is of vital importance that the council bases its programme not on police propaganda but on the feelings of any community affected or threatened by crime...women and black people have the greatest fear of violent attack or harassment, yet these groups are given next to no protection from the police (Walker, 1986, p. 59).

The document advocated that the unit should audit police performance and investigate and monitor the problems of security and fear of crime in different parts of Manchester by commissioning its own local crime surveys. It stressed that if the monitoring committee did not challenge the hegemony of the police on the ground by demonstrating that they had effective community safety alternatives, elements of the council would be quite willing to embrace Home Office driven undemocratic crime prevention and multi-agency policing 'partnerships'. And this would make the council accountable to the police rather than vice versa. Walker's reading of the situation in Manchester made it clear that an immense amount of detailed, thorough and long-term grass roots work would have to be engaged in to demonstrate the practical benefits of democratically constituted and directed local policing arrangements.

The main thrust of both reports was that the monitoring unit should prioritize proactive community development work. Such recommendations had serious implications because the unit had effectively withdrawn from such work because of: the experience of the meetings narrated in chapter five; the feedback from the existing monitoring groups which stated that they preferred to retain their autonomy; and the conspicuous failure of police authority efforts to establish community liaison panels in the city. As a result, it was decided to play a reactive role. The committee would provide support for any group that asked for assistance and would facilitate single issue meetings because they were 'one of the best ways of making the police accountable to Manchester people' (*PoliceWatch*, No 5, 1986). Thus, the unit's community contact work took the form of assisting groups to organize meetings, such as the 'Black Communities and Inner City Policing' conference, Youth and Allied Workers' Police Monitoring Group training days, Women and Policing meetings, 'Battle of Brittan' and Stalker Affair meetings and some of the Gay Men's Police Monitoring Group's meetings (Police monitoring committee, Reports Nos 44, 61, 68, 73, 81, 94).

However, now the unit was being urged to go back out and work in very diverse neighbourhoods. An 'Area based Monitoring And Consultation Initiative', which would uncover what Mancunians thought about crime, security and policing, was ratified by the monitoring committee in March 1987 (Police monitoring committee, Report No 137). By July of that year, the mass of the initial consultative work had been completed. It focused on identifying and making contact with 'relevant and appropriate groups', defined as local neighbourhood and voluntary organizations such as tenant and resident associations, and youth and community groups. Nineteen groups were identified in north Manchester, sixteen in south Manchester and seventeen in central Manchester, and letters were sent to them (as well as to tenants and residents) entitled 'Policing and A Safer Community: Obtaining Your Views':

> As you are probably aware, the City Council has for some time taken

the view that the promotion of policing of a nature, style and quality which meets the needs of the residents of Manchester is clearly in their interests. In order to respond to these concerns, the City Council set up a committee, police monitoring. It seeks to achieve the promotion and support of effective policing policies by consulting with residents on policing activities, crime prevention and making communities safer.

As part of this process the council has decided to begin a systematic consultation process with groups in the community, whether they be tenant or issue based (Police monitoring committee, Report No 137).

It was hoped that the community groups and organizations would be the foundation for the consultation process. In addition, small area based crime surveys were conducted on the Nell Lane Estate, Chorlton (south Manchester), Mossbrook Court, Collyhurst (north Manchester) and Hulme (central Manchester) (Police monitoring committee, Report no 137). Eventually, in these areas meetings took place between local police officers, councillors, the police monitoring committee and residents to discuss local problems. A bewildering and often contradictory set of demands and issues emerged from these meetings. However, one thing that they shared in common with the previous meetings discussed in chapter five was a belief that all the statutory agencies, including the police and the council, had been ignoring their needs for years.

Such fora were also used to bolster the monitoring committee's continued opposition to liaison panels, which, through the high profile work of the police authority's community relations unit, were increasingly encroaching upon Manchester. In this context, it was even suggested by the police monitoring committee that their very localized resident's arenas could act as the official consultative committees in Manchester:

> We believe that there is a far more effective system than that favoured by the Greater Manchester Police. We want the public to meet head-on with not only the police but also with people from the Town Hall, to tackle issues of criming in a realistic manner. By bringing together police, councillors, housing and planning officials, and community development workers, who have on-the-ground real liaison with the residents, questions on community safety can be approached by bodies who may be able to do something about it. Unfortunately these forums will still not make the police truly accountable - only a change in legislation can do this. But at least they will allow the public a chance of saying what they want (*PoliceWatch*, No 9, 1987).

Monitoring committee representatives also began to make overtures to the police in a manner which would have been inconceivable in 1984:

> Let us hope that the police can put aside any prejudices that they have against the police monitoring unit and work fully with the city council in a realistic attempt to tackle crime in our city (ibid).

And local police officers in certain parts of Manchester began to reciprocate, by acknowledging that for certain communities smaller meetings would be a realistic way of tackling local issues. They also recognized that the co-operation of local council departments, rather than community liaison and neighbourhood watch schemes, was the key to impacting positively on neighbourhood problems.

Women, policing and the fear of crime

Issues around women, crime and policing also acted as a powerful incentive for the deepening of the council's community safety work. At the same time as the police monitoring committee was established, so were several other initiatives, including the equal opportunities committee.

Its steering group on women's issues established a women and violence working party and held women only public meetings on this issue in different parts of the city during 1986. The women who attended articulated their concerns about: using public transport; assaults on female children; safety on estates; the importance of refuges for women; racial harassment; adequate and secure housing provision; and sexual harassment at work. Problems of policing were also discussed during these meetings, with some women wanting to see a more assertive police response, whilst others, principally black women, said that they would not feel safe with an increased police presence in their neighbourhoods. However, within the context of overall fear of sexual violence, policing was just one concern, and not necessarily the major one. It was not just the police who were the problem, but men. These issues were deliberated by the equal opportunities committee in January 1987 and a report, 'The Safety of Women in Planning the Environment', was produced.

During the same time period, the monitoring committee also established a women and policing working party. The committee hoped that its deliberations would be able to promote a city-wide debate about how police priorities impacted on women's lives:

> The police monitoring unit is pledged to campaigning for an accountable police force, one that meets the needs of the community

it is supposed to serve. Women as part of that community must have their voices heard to ensure that their needs, their wishes and their priorities are reflected in police practice and in police policy. Women must feel safe to go about their everyday lives without constantly fearing for their safety (*PoliceWatch*, No 3, 1986).

The working party held meetings for women in September and October 1987 and included workshops on policing and: domestic violence; sexual offences; children's rights; public order situations; prostitution; kerb crawling; black women; mental health and lesbians (Police monitoring committee, Report No 172). The working party also recommended that the monitoring committee appoint an officer to work solely on women's issues.

A contentious self-report survey of women was launched in October 1986 'to enable women to give their views and discuss their experience of policing in Manchester'. This survey was intended to assess the full frequency of crimes against women, their fear of crime and the precise nature and pattern of the police response. The survey findings, based on 2,000 questionnaires, were also intended to form the basis for the campaign to compel the police to take the needs of women seriously.

The final report highlighted: women's realistic perception of risk and vulnerability; their widespread experience of crime, abuse and harassment; (irrespective of social background); how the very rational fear of becoming a crime victim regulated and controlled their lives. In relation to reporting incidents to the police, the survey found that, for a variety of reasons, there was significant under-reporting of violent crime. For example, a staggering seventy-three per cent of rape victims did not report the incident. Many of those women who did contact the police complained about the unsatisfactory and often inappropriate treatment they had received, and this raised 'very serious doubts about many issues of policing, particularly in terms of priorities, training, supervision, monitoring and accountability' (*PoliceWatch*, No 9, 1987). Consequently, the report recommended that the police should intervene in a positive manner and use whatever means are necessary to arrest and charge assailants.

However, it was not just the inadequate response of the police that constituted a problem for women in Manchester. It was apparent that every council department and committee was responsible for formulating and implementing policies that had a detrimental impact on the safety of women. Therefore, the committee report emanating from the survey advocated the adoption of a strategy which included the improvement of public transport, the lighting of public spaces, secure housing provision and safeguarding the funding needs of Taboo, Rape Crisis and Women's Aid (Police monitoring committee, Report No 164). Significantly, because the monitoring committee and council were perceived to be 'white' institutions, it also recommended that the council fund, as a matter of urgency, a separate survey to examine 'black women's experiences and that this is done by, and in consultation with, black women, in a manner which is relevant and useful to them. Any recommendations or campaigns which result from this survey must take this on board' (Police monitoring unit, 1987, p. 3).

The point of overlap between the work of the police monitoring committee's working party and the work of the equal opportunities women's steering group can be found in the latter's November 1987 report, 'Planning a Safer Environment for Women'. This was an important policy document because it utilized the findings of national crime surveys, the Merseyside and Islington surveys (Hough and Mayhew, 1983; 1985; Kinsey, 1984; Jones, McLean, Young, 1986), Home Office crime prevention statements and the monitoring committee's 'Women and Violence Survey Report' to argue that:

> crimes against women are often qualitatively different from those against men, in that they have a sexual element. Situations or environments which are not necessarily threatening or unsafe for men, may be so for women. Male designers and planners may not therefore identify certain elements in the environment as facilitating crimes against women (Manchester City Council, 1987, p. 3).

The report stated that the police alone could not provide a comprehensive or adequate response to the problems faced by women. It was stressed that whilst real modifications in the level of violence against women could only be achieved by societal change and the redistribution of power, design-related changes had the potential to improve security by reducing the opportunities for crimes to take place. This comprehensive report listed a variety of environmental factors that could be realistically modified in order to promote greater safety, and concluded by saying that:

> Although this report has concentrated on the safety of the environment for women it is obvious that, by improving the environment for women, the proposals will be of advantage to children and men particularly elderly or disabled men. The result will be a city where people of both sexes, of all ages and races, can live in greater safety and enjoyment (Manchester City Council, 1987, p. 19).

The report did not consider in any great detail policing issues because it did not see the police as being part of the solution to the problems that women faced. But neither did it see them as being part of the problem that certain women faced. For example, there was no reference to the fears of black women. The solutions focused upon multi-agency coordination to create a safer environment for women. This meant that the police still had a role to play in these security conscious environments. This work on women and violence during 1987 augmented the council's increasing prioritization of community safety.

Community safety and women's safety also had a pivotal role to play during the 1987 local elections. As with the 1986 elections, concerns were expressed within the Labour Party that some of the council's controversial policies would be electorally damaging. The opposition parties continued to denounce the police monitoring committee and *PoliceWatch*. The Conservative candidates stressed their complete support for the police, whilst the Alliance promised to persist with their campaign for the introduction of community liaison panels. The latter also pointed out that Labour had been forced to reverse its position on 'Homewatch', and that, sooner or later, it would have to do the same in relation to community liaison panels.

Labour candidates in their election literature emphasized the party's concern with crime prevention, community safety measures and women's safety. Except in this context, no mention was made of police accountability or the police monitoring committee. As part of the campaign, a leaflet was produced narrating the main priorities of the party. A section on 'Action against Male Violence' highlighted Labour's commitment to making Manchester a safer place for women.

Labour suffered set-backs in these elections and lost nine seats. The implications for the police monitoring initiative were significant. First, there were nine more councillors committed to voting for its abolition at the first opportunity. Second, it confirmed the fears of those sections of the Labour Party who had been concerned with the electoral consequences of the monitoring committee's antagonistic actions. In any inquest, there was every possibility that the monitoring committee would be identified as an electoral liability along with the council's other minority 'loony left' activities.

From police monitoring to community safety

These two factors took on real significance in December 1987 when the council had to formulate a response to central government limitations on local government spending. Prior to this, Manchester City Council, like several other Labour-controlled authorities, had survived by a variety of creative 'accounting' measures and by eventually reneging on its 1984 manifesto promises not to set a rate. However, the outcome of the 1987 general election 'forced the defiant Labour councils to their knees' (Wolmar, 1988). Manchester was compelled to confront a fiscal crisis of monumental proportions.

On 11 December 1987, the council's policy committee agreed to a £6.5 million package of cuts in services. This caused a public outcry, and a council meeting to discuss how and where the cuts would be implemented was disrupted by demonstrators demanding that the Labour Party adhere to its 'no cuts' manifesto. Because of the uproar, a further meeting took place on 17 December, with twenty-eight members of the Labour Party siding with the opposition to defeat the proposed spread of cuts. The opposition then successfully proposed an alternative inventory of specific cuts. This included the abolition of the police monitoring committee.

This meeting also witnessed the council having to call upon the police to deal with demonstrators. Ironically, all the work of the police monitoring committee on public order policing and police-council contact was ignored when it came to dealing with the demonstrators. Headlines such as: 'MODS WANT SWIFT AXE TO POLICE TEAM'; 'POLICE UNIT PLEDGE AS THE AXE LOOMS'; and 'AXE POISED OVER POLICE WATCHDOG', heralded the imminent demise of arguably the most controversial police monitoring initiative in Britain. Opposition councillors threatened to take court action if the decision was not implemented immediately, whilst the right of the Labour Party insisted that police monitoring unit staff be reallocated and the police monitoring committee disbanded as soon as possible. A council meeting on 28 January 1988 conceded to a package of cuts that included the disestablishment of the police monitoring committee and *PoliceWatch*.

In March 1988, the council's policy and resources committee agreed 'that with immediate effect, recognizing the devastating effect which crime and fear of crime has on the lives of Manchester residents, the focus for the council's policies on policing and community safety should be the development of practically based policies aimed at supporting community based initiatives' (Policy and resources committee, 17 June 1988).

In order to formulate a response, a community safety section (incorporating some of the police monitoring unit posts) was established to develop the concept of crime prevention from its narrow associations with the police and 'bars and bolts', to the wider issue of the strategic role of the local authority in the production of a safer environment. It was argued that whilst the physical security of estates and residences was useful, it would not enhance people's personal safety or sense of security in their homes or neighbourhoods. Community safety in Manchester would focus upon the interdependence of types of crime prevention, the social structure of particular communities, the social causes of crime and the social distribution of risk. The intention was to challenge the dominant idea of crime prevention that had:

> an inbuilt bias towards individualized personal property protection

measures known as 'target hardening'. Such a narrow approach fails to meet important needs as it is not possible to 'target harden' women against rape or 'design out' heroin pushing. It particularly fails to recognize the experience of large numbers of women who suffer assault and injury in their homes as well as a result of domestic violence and whose situation no amount of improved street lighting or fencing will alter. Community safety must recognize that the effectiveness of a policy or approach is influenced by both the relations between offenders and victims and the relations between social groups - as defined by class, race, sex and age within a locality (Policy and resources committee, 17 June 1988).

The council would assist the 'development of communities' and community-based initiatives by working with communities to: improve general security and safety; provide specific community safety improvements for those citizens known to be particularly vulnerable; and formulate policies which would avoid fuelling the fear of crime and placing restrictions on the activities and lives of vulnerable groups. In order to achieve this:

> The council's developing community safety policy should start from the concerns of the residents, and have as a basic premise the need for the local authority and other agencies, such as the police, to concentrate their resources on those offenses thought by residents to be most problematic (ibid).

Essentially what was being proposed was a council co-ordinated multi-agency approach. The crucial departure from previous policy was the recognition of the role, however limited, that the police, as a local service provider, had to play. Thus, it was suggested that the community safety section would liaise with crime prevention officers of the Greater Manchester Police and utilize relevant police and Home Office literature on the issue.

This 'future directions' report also argued that because of lack of staff and resources, the community safety strategy could not be implemented on a city-wide basis. It was therefore agreed to concentrate efforts on a 'show case' pilot project in the predominantly white working class Monsall area of Harpurhey because it was: a recognizably 'bonded' neighbourhood; perceived as a problem area and suffered from a range of problems that were suitable for social intervention. The community safety team had found a recognizable community with which to work. In November 1988, after consulting national Labour Party, Safe Neighbourhoods and Home Office crime prevention literature, the community safety strategy was unveiled. The aims were to provide support for crime victims and reduce opportunities for crime, fear of crime and the numbers of entrants into the criminal justice system. In order to stimulate a community response to crime and fear of crime and promote 'a neighbourhood centred mode of life', the council in 1989-90 began surveying the area, working with local residents and linking up with all the relevant statutory agencies, including the police, and local voluntary groups such as victim support and neighbourhood watch schemes.

All references to monitoring the behaviour of the police and opposing liaison panels were absent from these proposals. Indeed, there was scant mention of the police, because it was assumed that there was little they could do on their own about the crime problems of the area. The debates had thus virtually come full circle, from a critique of policing and multi-agency approaches and the dangers of such approaches to the utilization of a multi-agency crime prevention approach. In fact, the conceptualization of the problem and the approach work fitted in well with the principles laid out in the various Home Office circulars. £250,000 capital funding, for improving the physical environment of Monsall, was obtained from the Department of Environment's urban programme in 1990. What we witness, therefore, is the coming together of left realist approaches and Home Office proposals on community crime control, and much of that had to do with the emergence of 'community safety' and 'women and crime' as potent and inescapable political issues, both in Manchester and nationally.

Discussion

This chapter has documented the political debate and antagonisms generated by the police monitoring initiative and the dramatic and complex reorientation that took place between 1985 and 1989. This shift in focus resulted from a series of inter-related pressures that bore down upon the police monitoring committee. First, its controversial statements on policing, both locally and nationally, made it politically vulnerable within a council which was itself exposed. Manchester was repeatedly singled out by government spokespersons, and indeed by certain members of the national and local Labour Party, as a prime example of 'loony leftism'. The City Council's policies on racial issues, for example, provoked considerable hostility. An inquiry, in 1986, into the killing by a white pupil of Ahmed Iqbal Ullal, a pupil at Burnage High School, criticized teachers and the council for implementing anti-racist policies which seemingly privileged the needs of black pupils and antagonized, unnecessarily, white parents. The national media used these findings to argue that Manchester's anti-racist strategy was directly responsible for the death of the pupil. It was in this moment that the council began to retreat from race issues and, some would argue, prioritize, by default, white working-class concerns.

The revival of a bi-partisan discourse on the need for multi-agency crime prevention provided the second source of pressure. The police monitoring committee's political vulnerability was intensified by its pronouncements on the Greater Manchester Police and its opposition to neighbourhood watch, community liaison panels and multi-agency policing. The pressure to do something practical about crime increased once the monitoring committee took on board increasing local and national concern about women's safety and fear of crime. The third pressure point emerged from council demands that all departments should become involved in unified co-ordinated community work. Such a course of action was also advocated by an internal report that argued that the monitoring unit, as a matter of urgency, should rethink its strategy for working with local communities. All of these demands forced the monitoring unit back into different neighbourhoods where it found that police monitoring groups and the political accountability of the police were not the issues that concerned key sections of the electorate in Manchester. They wanted an effective response to local crime related problems and were not interested in hearing that their (irrational) fear of crime was being used to justify an authoritarian clampdown.

As a result, the radical and politically perilous campaign for changes in the governance of the Greater Manchester Police was replaced by politically beneficial and realizable multi-agency community safety initiatives. Consequently, certain 'majority' public interests and demands were prioritized, most notably, and understandably, the crime related concerns and fears of women and other residents. However, at one and the same time, the marginalization of the interests of those 'minority' groups in the city subject to questionable policing practices occurred. Even in terms of the community safety initiative, it could be argued, given the escalating levels of crime, poverty and deprivation in the area, that Moss Side was the part of Manchester most deserving of the council's attention. But, for a variety of political reasons, the people of Moss Side were effectively left on their own to cope with the serious crime related problems they faced.

9 Unsettled accounts

> Everything has already been imagined before: what is difficult is to imagine again (Goethe).

This book has addressed the question of whether it is possible to realize democratic community representation and participation in policing matters? To do so, it has ranged across a variety of issues, themes, initiatives, places and times. In the process, it has hopefully reminded the reader of just how intense protracted and wide-ranging the campaigns for democratic police accountability were in certain parts of Britain in the 1980s. It is now necessary to reflect on the key issues raised in previous chapters.

Chapter one reviewed the turbulent historical moment within which radical campaigns for democratic accountability were 're-birthed' as a political project in the 1970s and early 1980s. In the post-war period, policing came increasingly to reflect the interests of one group - the police. This public bureaucracy's internal rationales and logics defined the type and nature of service delivered to different social groups. Its employees were virtually the sole determinants of people's policing needs. However, in specific locations the exercise of coercive and discriminatory policing practices began to generate myriad resistances by 'the policed', and these eventually coalesced into highly localized political demands that the police should be brought under control. Since organizational and legal supervisory checks were manifestly failing to impact upon such policing practices, it was argued that the imposition of strong democratic regulation was necessary. The 1981 riots placed the issue of police accountability on the national political agenda because they established that consensual policing was a myth. The conspiracy of silence about the true nature of police-public relations in certain areas of the country had been finally broken. The riots and the Scarman report triggered an intense dispute on the left about how best to establish meaningful community representation and participation on policing issues.

I argued that the ideological thematics underpinning the different leftist positions should have been addressed in a more thorough manner because they constituted the theoretical and empirical terrain on which radical discourses and initiatives would have to confront the authoritarian state in the 1980s.

The next chapter analyzed the complex theoretical issues and problems which were embedded in the demand for community representation and participation. I concluded the chapter by asking whether it would be possible to imagine participatory democratic arrangements and processes that:

a. Are flexible and spontaneous.
b. Recognize plurality, fragmentation, difference, heterogeneity, antagonism and conflict of interests.
c. Produce a democratically constituted (and ongoing) deliberation about 'real' needs and concerns.
d. Are empowered to bring about manifestly relevant and meaningful transformations.

It was argued that if this was not strived for, any radical democraticization project would be flawed, and there would be every possibility that the marginalized and the dissenting will not participate or be adequately represented.

The following three chapters analyzed how the national debates about police accountability played themselves out in the local setting of Manchester. Chapter three narrated how those groups campaigning about abuses of power and racial injustices perpetrated by police officers, especially in Moss Side, finally had their concerns publicly acknowledged as a result of the 1981 county council elections of that year. The ensuing heated political debates, proposals and counter-proposals resulted in two distinctive models of police accountability being unveiled. One model was primarily concerned with furthering community representation, while the other advocated a participatory approach.

Chapter four discussed how a revitalized police committee attempted to establish the right to be able to debate and influence the way policing was exercised, the values, choices and decisions underpinning it and the objectives being pursued in different parts of Greater Manchester. However, James Anderton made it clear that he would resist all attempts by the police committee to undermine his 'divine' autonomy. The outcomes of the resultant disputes indicated that the chief constable could depend on the legal principle of operational independence and his organizational responsibilities for the direction and control of the force to frustrate and curtail the committee's attempts to enhance its role. What was confirmed beyond doubt was that the police committee was not an equal partner in the tripartite agreement. It had no means of controlling the policing of Greater Manchester and had limited means of redress in any dispute with the chief constable.

The chapter then chronicled the problems encountered by the community liaison officer in his attempt to articulate the policing interests of black people and to establish liaison panels to facilitate community representation, especially in Moss Side. In this locale, his claimed 'representative' status was rejected, from the outset, by key sections of 'the community' he was supposedly representing. They argued that Moss Side did not need another consensus-seeking emissary. In addition, all efforts to establish a community liaison panel were actively resisted by local groups, who argued that such consultative panels were ill-conceived, superficial and totally unacceptable because they had no powers to resolve the conflicts over the policing of the area. These groups demanded measures to bring about the effective control of the local police. Perhaps this steadfast politically framed opposition to the panels could have been overcome if widespread public support or council backing for the initiative had materialized. However, this was not the case.

Instead, liaison panels were established in other parts of Greater Manchester. However, even within these uncontentious entities, a multitude of problems, relating primarily to adequate community representation and participation, surfaced immediately. The characteristic homogenized features of the model appealed to white, middle-aged males who viewed themselves as respectable community representatives and who wanted to assist the police. Important sections of the community - ethnic minorities, women and young people - were excluded (or were excluding themselves) from the liaison process. And despite the efforts of the community liaison officer to rectify the gendered and racialized absences, at no point were the interests of those in dispute with the police represented within the liaison panels.

Chapter five then considered how the rejection of the police committee's undemocratically constituted and powerless liaison initiative eventually produced a police monitoring model which was championed by the local state in the form of Manchester City Council. The monitoring initiative attempted to foreground and articulate the interests of those for whom the police were the problem, by opening up a much more localized debate about policing in the city. In essence, the monitoring committee argued that root and branch reform of policing was needed, and that only full local democratic control this would bring this about. However, it faced several problems. First, the council had no control over this particular local service and there was little that it could do to assuage public concerns and demands. Second, it was politically committed to establishing city-wide monitoring groups to realize active community participation on policing issues, but public meetings held in various neighbourhoods indicated that there was no particular desire to 'watch' the police. Residents wanted local police officers and the council to act against escalating crime, hooliganism and insecurity. The reality was that the monitoring model was not appropriate for those residents and neighbourhoods whose primary concern was crime rather than the police.

Chapter six returned to the national scene and detailed how, from the mid-1980s onwards, a series of complex reconfigurations politically decentred the police accountability campaigns. First, the Conservative government, as part of its ongoing assault on the powers and autonomy of local authorities, abolished the metropolitan police committees, and it became clear that future debates about police accountability would be framed by a very different set of discourses. Second, a hegemonic discourse on crime prevention emerged to reclaim and rework the concepts of 'community', 'representation' and 'participation'. The state made an overall attempt to re-establish the legitimacy of the criminal justice system by politically centring the interests of victims of crime. At the same moment, the political meaning of escalating crime rates for left-run local authorities deepened. Of crucial significance was the fact that it was becoming apparent that multi-agency approaches and proactive policing were crucial if women (and children) were to be protected from violent physical and sexual abuse. Local authorities were forced to realize that abstentionism on the crime question was not a political option. They had to take the problem of crime seriously and began to reconsider (i) their opposition to consultation committees, neighbourhood watch schemes and crime prevention partnerships and (ii) support for police monitoring. The outcome was that the interests of the victims of crime were prioritized and the interests of 'the policed' were marginalized.

The next two chapters considered the specific repercussions of the national shifts for the local accountability campaigns in Manchester. As chapter seven indicated, through the chief constable's continued assertion of his autonomy, the unwavering support of the Home Office, and political considerations, the extraordinary campaign for police accountability finally exhausted itself. This was despite the crises unleashed by the Stalker Affair and the chief constable's highly controversial statements on political, social and moral matters. By the end of the decade, the politically 'calmed' police authority had opted for a consensual working partnership with the chief constable at any price.

The chapter also detailed the strenuous efforts to widen and deepen the consultative process. Repeated attempts were made to persuade community representatives in Moss Side to take part in some type of liaison structure. However, controversial police actions provided fresh proof of the inherent limitations and potential of the community liaison model for Moss Side. Instead, local groups continued with their own protests and campaigns about the unsatisfactory policing of the area.

Flexible and open liaison arrangements which stressed public participation rather than community representation were eventually used elsewhere in Manchester. In the rest of Greater Manchester, panels were encouraged to address ongoing problems of the under-representation of ethnic minorities, women and young people by transforming themselves into less rigid, less formal and more locally relevant entities. However, problems remained, especially in relation to young people and ethnic minorities, and even though the safety interests of women were made a priority, the voices of radical groups who had campaigned in the area of women's safety were to a considerable degree, sidelined.

Thus, the liaison initiative continued to facilitate the interests of those sections of the community who wanted to assist the police in preventing crime. The problem with this was that it lead to the systematic non-representation and non-participation of those groups for whom the police were, in any way, a problem.

Chapter eight documented the profound transformation that took place in the work of Manchester City Council's police monitoring initiative in the late 1980s. During 1986-87 the monitoring committee and research unit continued with its attempt to place the interests of the policed on the local political agenda for the first time. The unit generated an alternative picture of the policing of the city, and its high profile campaigning and monitoring work ensured that the 'Battle of Brittan' and the Stalker Affair received national attention. The committee was also able to provide practical support to independent monitoring groups. Furthermore, its well briefed representatives on the new police authority were at the forefront of the intense campaign to force the chief constable to resign. Indeed, it could also be argued that it was Manchester's aggressive attitude that ensured that Labour quickly gained control of the new police authority.

However, the nature of the monitoring initiative's offensive against the Greater Manchester Police and its controversial stances on neighbourhood watch, community liaison panels and multi-agency policing generated intense conflict and made it politically vulnerable. The pressure to take crime seriously mounted once the monitoring committee realized that women's fears and experience of crime, and an effective response to local crime related problems, were issues that concerned key sections of the electorate across the city. These were 'community' wide concerns as opposed to the 'minority' concern of police accountability. The limitations of and contradictions embedded in the police monitoring strategy were cruelly exposed in this politically charged climate, and community safety rather than police accountability became a council priority. The reality was that a political consensus could be forged out of controlling crime whereas campaigning for police accountability only generated division, conflict and controversy. Consequently, the political marginalization of the interests of those groups in the city which were governed and disciplined through coercive policing practices occurred.

So what are the lessons that can be learnt from this case-study? It has raised a multiplicity of general questions about (i) the adequacy of the existing constitutional principles of police governance and (ii) the practical import of the police being immune from the processes of democratic control. It has also attempted to illustrate the very real complexities and difficulties of establishing effective and meaningful forms of local democratic representation and participation in policing matters. And in relation to this last point, I would argue that we have to take the following 'realities' seriously.

First, there is no logical justification for policing to stand outside of democratic control. In a democratic polity the fundamental constitutional principle underpinning police accountability should not be that 'reasonable people can make anything work'. This very principle guarantees that the problematic policing of certain groups in and areas of Manchester in the 1980s will never be adequately accounted for. It also means that no-one will ever be held personally to account for such policing practices and policies.

Second, there is no such thing as 'the community' and it has to be realized that very different types of arrangements need to be negotiated, locally, for different areas and groups. Third, no overarching top-down model of community representation is as adequate as that afforded by direct participation. Attempts to impose formulaic and tightly framed (and by definition reductionist) models are doomed to failure because they cannot possible be mapped on to the diversity of interests and complexity of differences within a given locale. Civic spaces must be created that allow for meaningful participation in decision-making. Fourth, powerless initiatives, no matter how well-meaning, are incapable of resolving real conflict and antagonism. The reality is that such conflicts cannot be talked away. As Chantal Mouffe has argued:

> instead of shying away from the component of violence and hostility inherent in social relations, the task is to think how to create the conditions under which those aggressive forces can be defused and diverted and a pluralist democratic order made possible (1993: 153).

Fifth, local 'concordances' can only be worked towards through self-definition, self-articulation and on-going debate. Finally, political authorities and representatives, in areas where there has been a serious breakdown in meaningful relations between the police and the policed, have to recognize that their needs are obviously different and have to be dealt with separately. Those wishing to stabilize those relations must (i) acknowledge that conflict and antagonism not consensus and accord are the starting points (ii) hear the complaints and concerns being articulated about the police and (iii) recognize that for any semblance of trust to be established there will have to be transparent changes in local policing practices and philosophies, and in certain areas, even in personnel.

And this takes us back to the starting point of this book, because in order to ensure that this happens, there must be the transition to democratically constituted pluralistic policing arrangements. Stan Cohen (1987) has argued that to be realistic about reforming the criminal justice system, one must be unrealistic. This must be the starting point with the police. To be realistic about any aspect of policing, one must indeed be unrealistic. We must stop trying to 'square the circle' and begin to imagine policing without modernist conceptions of 'the police'. To be for the full democratization of policing, one must be philosophically anti-'the police', whether it be the authoritarian or social democratic state variant. The aim must be to replace the inflexible practices, procedures and ideologies of a discredited and malfunctioning state bureaucracy with an alternative vision of policing as a set of highly localized political and social settlements constructed out of (but firmly embedded in) a multitude of different and often conflicting interests. Policing must become a realm of socialized deliberation and choices. It is this complex and ambitious set of demands and needs that forms the case for the radical democratization of policing arrangements and procedures.

What are the possibilities for such a radical democratic imaginary 'becoming'?

Options for change?

In the late 1980s, many police officers seemed to believe that the defeat of the left's campaign for democratic accountability, their semi-military suppression of the 'enemies within' and the re-election of a Conservative government would result in a golden age of stability and consolidation in policing matters.

However, this golden age never materialized because whilst the issue of democratic accountability had been resolved, an intriguing question was lurking off-stage. Would the police escape the scrutiny of the disciplines of the 'evaluative state'? And within this overall question, an even sharper one awaited an answer. Would a neo-conservative government, obsessed with controlling public expenditure and rolling back the state, continue to allocate scarce resources to an expensive public policing bureaucracy, when research had established that the private citizenry was the key to controlling crime?

Ironically, no sooner had a formal political consensus on policing been re-established than renewed debate about the future formation and purpose of the police emerged. A succession of statements and recommendations were made by senior officers and Conservative politicians, indicating that a radical restructuring and re-presentation of policing would take place in the course of the 1990s.

National developments

Nationalization

In autumn 1988 a debate commenced concerning the desirability of nationalizing/regionalizing certain police functions. Sir John Wheeler, the chairman of the all-party House of Commons Home Affairs Committee, declared that the forty-three police forces in England and Wales should be merged to create between five and ten regional forces because, as they stood, they were 'insufficiently business like'. The report of the Home Affairs Committee reiterated Wheeler's criticisms, stating that it was necessary to create some form of national police force, if the 'glaring deficiencies, incompetent use of resources and blinding incompetence' of the management of the present system were to be overcome (*Independent*, 26 July 1990). ACPO also addressed this issue, stating that individual forces should set their local aims and objectives within the context of a nationally agreed statement of common police purpose (ACPO, 1990, p. 6). The stress would be on ensuring national standards in an organization traditionally marked by regional diversity.

To keep pace with these national developments, moves were made to consolidate the position of ACPO. A new constitution was introduced to enable the association to formulate common policy on policing issues, and to standardize the practices of the various forces. According to David Owen, the then ACPO president, such corporate steps were necessary in order to ensure that ACPO remained 'an organization of potent influence and a fulcrum for the development of the police service' (*Guardian*, 22 February 1991).

Localization

Proposals were also unveiled for the introduction of very localized and even de-amalgamated community policing arrangements. The Audit Commission, in its deliberations on the future shape of policing, was not primarily interested in the debates about nationalization/regionalization. The Commission focused on the substructure of the police system and advocated the devolution of routine policing to self-contained locally based command units (Davies, 1990). It recognized that the majority of crime would remain local in origin, and that a departure from local policing could 'undermine that very relationship which is a crucial part of the contract of co-operation between the police and the public'(*Guardian*, 13 July 1989). Sir Peter Imbert also supported the idea of devolved territorially based policing where commanders in charge of local areas would be relatively autonomous (*Police*, 1990, p. 43).

Thus, support was forthcoming for a move away from the old centralist 'command' model of policing to 'soft' organizational configurations, benefitting from economies of scale and characterized by considerable flexibility and diversity. As Sir John Woodcock of Her Majesty's Inspectorate argued:

> The service needs to be thrown open to the consumer, its structures redesigned to allow the public more fully to assist in the setting of priorities. The police service needs to admit the limits of its power. In a single ugly phrase, the service needs to deprofessionalize (1991, p. 174).

Privatization

The question of the privatization of certain policing functions also emerged. The government continued to encourage the self-help (or Do-it-Yourself) policing model. The 'active citizenry'(through neighbourhood watch schemes), 'active' local companies (through providing funding for particular crime prevention projects) and local social services (through multi-agency strategies) were allocated a pivotal position in the fight against crime. Considerable efforts have also been made to revitalize the volunteer Special Constabulary - 'active citizens' in uniform. The government has also been ambiguous in its attitude towards the growth of the private security industry, which is not surprising given its commitment to encouraging the private sector to compete with the public sector. It became apparent that there was the distinct possibility that in the course of the 1990s 'non-core' police functions would be contracted out through private tendering arrangements, and that private security firms might be patrolling in particular neighbourhoods.

Reconceptualizing policing

Despite the support for 'hiving off' certain police tasks, chief police officers are loathe, for well-founded ideological reasons, to jettison their local policing functions. Indeed, as has been documented in the previous section, the police force is attempting to restructure in order to deliver both national police functions and local ones. However, it has been recognized that it will be necessary to rework both the objectives and culture of the organization if the restructuring is to succeed.

As a consequence of the 1988 Wolff Olins report, the 'Plus Programme' was launched by the Metropolitan Police in April 1989. This programme was intended to be the prototype 'mission statement' for policing in the 1990s. Internally, there would be more flexible and responsive management through streamlining the traditional command hierarchy. Considerable emphasis was being placed on open management, meaningful consultation with all ranks of officers and changing both the managerial and 'canteen' cultures of the organization. It was hoped that these changes, in conjunction with equal opportunities and 'generational renewal', would 'deliver' a very different type of police organization and police officer. Externally, a new relationship was to be forged with the community. The 'Plus Programme' stressed the idea of providing a professional quality service to customers. The vocabulary of the market place has entered policing and this is dictating a rethinking of the police as a *service* concerned with consumer satisfaction, rather than as a *force* primarily preoccupied with law enforcement (see also ACPO, 1990). This would be achieved through implementing a philosophy of 'reassurance' policing, which would be characterized by a visible police presence on the streets, and compassion, courtesy and respect for customer rights. Thus, 'quality of service' was to be the official cornerstone of policing in the 1990s.

Issues of accountability

Discussion about accountability focused on questions of fiscal and managerial accountability and customer satisfaction. And these questions of accountability related primarily to localized policing arrangements. The Audit Commission stressed that police forces should be given control over their own budgets and that effective fiscal accountability could be ensured by new monitoring and evaluative procedures. The Commission also believed that internal accountability would be strengthened by the organizational changes it was proposing:

> Roles and responsibilities for contributing to its achievement at all levels have to be specified. Criteria for success have to be clarified. Managers have to be given the freedom and ability to manage, but also the responsibility for answering for their results (Davies 1990, p. 597)

The Home Office and the Inspectorate of Constabulary were fully supportive of such ideas. 'Crude' crime figures would no longer be the sole index of police performance. The Home Office wanted more systematic information on whether police forces were providing a fair and non-discriminatory service. Information would be demanded on police courtesy; ethnic and gender composition of arrests, caution rates and stop and searches; analysis of response times to telephone calls and the manner in which victims were helped and advised (Baker, 1991). It was argued that organizational accountability could be enhanced because in future there would be targets against which actual performance could be checked.

It was recognized that internal managerial control over the workforce was necessary if the proposed sea changes in policing were to be realized. Thus, 'post-Fordist' working practices were encouraged in the form of shifts towards more civilianization, more flexible working hours and the increasing individualization of work relationships and contractual issues. There were also moves to enhance internal accountability through the introduction of fixed term contracts, annual appraisal schemes and new disciplinary procedures.

A 'twin track' approach was mooted to make the police more accountable to the community. First, there was a renewed commitment to utilizing the Scarman-inspired local consultative groups as the arenas where 'customers' could articulate their concerns, and where the local police commander could report back on the issues of concern. Second, and perhaps more ideologically significantly, it was also argued that the reframing of policing as a service and the redesignation of the community as customers would make individual police officers more responsive. The ACPO 'mission statement' argued that this could only be achieved through the prioritization of customer needs, enhanced professionalism, a code of practice and customer contact surveys and independent surveys. As a consequence, it was hoped that the direct accountability of the police to its customers could be strengthened and discriminatory practices eradicated. Hence, the emphasis on customer satisfaction and the delivering of a 'total quality service' was intended to contribute towards the re-establishment of the 'traditional' consensus between the police and the local community.

There was no room within these proposals and reforms for formal structures of local democratic accountability. In the course of the discussions about the future of policing, it has become clear that there were plans to remove policing from the democratic 'gaze'. Modern 'new managerialist' systems and new customer/service approaches would make the 'politics of police accountability' an anachronistic irrelevance. Sir John Wheeler, for example, argued that people want an effective police force that is accountable directly to them, not to local politicians (Thames Television, 1991). In his discussions with local government representatives during 1989 and 1990, Wheeler stated bluntly that as far as he was concerned local political involvement in policing 'must go'. He subsequently advocated the setting up of regional Boards of Trustees, made up of a financial director from outside the police, and community representatives, to oversee policing matters. These Boards of Trustees would be accountable to the Home Secretary (*Police Review*, 8 November 1991).

Howard Davies, the then controller of the Audit Commission, also stated that politics had no role in policing and that the tripartite arrangement impeded the effective managerialization of policing:

> Chief Constables have...very little discretion over what the cash provided for policing will be spent on...They are not able to develop management roles which integrate financial and operational responsibilities (Davies, 1990, p. 597).

As far as he was concerned, police authorities had no role to play in decisions concerning police budgets. When the then Home Secretary, Kenneth Baker, addressed the 1991 Police Federation conference, he made an interesting statement about the constitutional arrangements governing the police: 'the tripartite system - the Home Secretary, the chief police officer and the community - has served this country well. Cap badge loyalty is loyalty to the community you serve. Let's leave it that way. We should keep party politics out of policing'.

Hence, the base-line of the official consensus that took shape in the late 1980s and early 1990s was that formal democratic political debate about policing was a hinderance to effective policing. It was only when the Sheehy inquiry, and the Home Office review of police structure funding and control were established in 1993 to give legislative shape to these various debates and ideas, that issues of democratic accountability were raised. And this was done mainly by chief police officers and their political allies, in a cynical attempt to derail the reform agenda. There was no public outcry on the issue.

What is clear is that recent developments, and indeed the reform agenda itself, have created the space and the contradictions necessary to imagine policing configurations that were unimaginable in the 1980s. It is up to those interested in the progressive transformation of policing to work with and through the contradictions unleashed by the managerialist reform proposals to democratize and pluralize that space and to deepen any changes rather, than resisting suggested reorganizations.

Local developments

In the first years of the 1990s, the Greater Manchester police authority, in addition to being in the vanguard of defending the constitutional status quo, was still grappling with the dilemmas posed by its liaison initiative. In 1992, a review of the police and community consultative groups (rechristened in 1989) took place. 'The Way Forward' argued that: 'it is now time to consider a fundamental change in the way we deliver the consultation to both members as clients and the communities as customers'. It recommended the jettisoning of its community representative model in order to dispense with time consuming and costly administrative procedures, and to make the group meetings more welcoming to the general public. An 'Open Forum' approach would allow all those attending to be actively involved in the meetings rather than having to listen to highly formal speeches and reports. It was hoped that this would allow participants to deliberate broadly and imaginatively about local issues, and lead to the participation of 'those currently disadvantaged and disenfranchised'. The consultation groups were reminded that they must make every effort to be as open and democratic as possible in order to be 'representative of their diverse communities' (Greater Manchester police authority, 1992). Thus, ten years on, questions of community representation and participation still troubled the liaison/consultation groups.

And what of Moss Side, the place where the debates about police-community consultation originated? One point must be stressed from the outset. This book has detailed how vibrant and autonomous local campaigns and struggles around racially unjust, ineffective and socially damaging policing issues materialized spontaneously in Moss Side, long before accountability became a formal political issue in Manchester, and continued to do so after it was politically decentred. After a series of meetings about the escalating violence in the area, the voluntary Moss Side and Hulme Community Forum was established in April 1991 'to empower and support members of the community in dealing with the fears and worries which they have in relation to the area and to enable them to work towards change'. Its remit was to conceive of practical policies to tackle drugs, violence, racism and produce a constructive dialogue with the police:

> on terms proposed and approved by the community. Any such relationship will require an acknowledgement by the police of the mistakes they have made in the policing of the community, and a willingness to work with the community (Moss Side and Hulme Community Forum, 1994, p. 1).

On 8 August 1991, the new chief constable, David Wilmott, met with the Community Forum to discuss the policing of the area. The chief constable conceded that there had been policing mistakes in the past, and both sides acknowledged the need for them to work together to resolve their differences. The next day it was reported that Steven Murphy, the chair of the police authority, attacked the Community Forum, claiming that it was undemocratic and unrepresentative and stated that the authority would inaugurate its own consultation process to 'ensure the widest possible representation of all groups in the area'. However, the police authority subsequently conceded that the Forum could function as the police-community liaison/consultation panel for the area. The reality was that any police authority attempt to impose a consultative group on the area would have met the same fate as previous efforts.

It is not clear whether this new dialogue can make any difference, given that the policing of the area still gives much cause for concern. In September 1991, John Samuels, a well-known outreach community development worker and methodist minister, was physically assaulted by police officers during a raid on a betting shop in Moss Side. This incident provoked another angry public meeting, and the setting up of another campaign to campaign for justice. As a consequence, all contact between the police and the Community Forum was suspended. In 1993, after another fatal shooting, considerable differences of opinion were expressed as to why police appeals for information were so unsuccessful. Local police spokespersons argued that fear of reprisals and misguided loyalties were the reasons for the wall of silence. However, there were counter-claims that many people in Moss Side still feared the police more than the gunmen:

> It is wrong to say people fear reprisals. The plain fact is that because of the way police behave, there is great distrust of the police in the community and that is the problem (*Manchester Evening News*, 4 January 1993).

And a recent article on a raid by Greater Manchester Police (which involved the force's specialist Armed Response Vehicles) provides another angle on how certain police officers prefer to communicate with the people of Moss Side in the 1990s:

> Some carry sub-machine-guns...shields and ladders...night-sticks. All wear automatic pistols on their hips and body armour on their chests...The two carrying the 'wham ram' move up to the target flat's door...It gives immediately...[a] bullet-resistant siege shield is slammed up against it and the officer behind it yells 'Armed police'. Then the 'talk-out' begins (Clarke, 1994, p. 28).

This, in many respects, brings us back to one of the main points of this book. It seems likely that struggles over the policing of areas like Moss Side will continue for the foreseeable future. How they are 'resolved' will depend on whether it is recognized that it is the people of these areas who have the democratic right to deliberate and decide on their policing requirements. If this had been recognized and acknowledged as a fundamental principle in 1981, perhaps there would not have been the escalating violence, and no need for the negotiations, at the end of a gun, that are characteristic of the 1990s.

Bibliography

ACC/AMA. (1975) 'The future development of the role of the police authority', *County Councils Gazette*, 9.
- (1980) 'Statutory responsibility for the police', *Working Party on Police Matters*.

ACPO. (1990) *Setting the Standards for Policing: Meeting Community Expectation*, London: Scotland Yard.

Alderson, J. (1984) *Law and Disorder*, London: Hamish Hamilton.

AMA. (1982) *Policies for the Police*, London: AMA.
- (1989) *Police Accountability*, London: AMA.

Anderson, B. (1983) *Imagined Communities*, London: Verso.

Anderton, J. (1977) *Violence and Delinquency in Large Cities*, Conference paper, June.
- (1979) 'Police practice and political power', *Royal Institute of Public Administration*, January.
- (1981a) 'Accountable to whom?', *Police*, 6 February.
- (1981b) 'The truth about the Moss Side meeting', *Police Review*, 18 September.
- (1981c) 'The truth about the Moss Side Meeting', *Police Review*, 18 September.
- (1981d) 'Serious incidents of public disorder in Greater Manchester 8th to 12th July 1981', Report to Greater Manchester Council.
- (1982) 'The reality of community policing', Press release, 12 March.
- (1985a) 'What price law and order?', *Police Review*, 14 June.
- (1985b) 'Community self-help in crime prevention', ACPO Conference Address, 7 June.
- (1985c) 'Constabulary duty should be left as it is', *Guardian*, 29 August.
- (1992) *James Anderton*, BBC 2, 1 August.

Arato, A. and Cohen, J. (1992) 'Civil Society and social theory' in P. Beilharz et al (eds) *Between Totalitarianism and Postmodernity*, Cambridge, Mass: MIT Press.

Arblaster, A. (1984) 'Police powers', *New Society*, 23 August.
- (1987) *Democracy*, Milton Keynes: Open University Press.

Aya, R. (1990) *Rethinking Revolutions and Collective Violence*, Amsterdam:

Het Spinhus.

BBC (1993) *Guns in Manchester*, Radio 4, 11 May.
Bachrach, P. and Botwinick (1992) *Power and Empowerment: A Radical Theory of Participatory Democracy*, Philadelphia: Temple University Press.
Baker, K. (1991) Lecture to the Police Foundation, 25 June.
Baldwin, R. and Kinsey, R. (1982) *Police Powers and Politics*, London: Quartet Books.
Banton, M. (1972) *Police Community Relations*, London: William Collins & Sons.
- (1975) 'A new approach to police authorities', *Police*, February.
Barber, B.R. (1984) *Strong Democracy: Participatory Democracy for a New Age*, California: California University Press.
Baudrillard, J. (1983) *In the Shadow of Silent Majorities*, New York: Semiotext(e).
Beetham, D. (1993) 'Liberal democracy and the limits of democratization', in D. Held (ed) *Prospects for Democracy*, Oxford: Blackwell.
Bell, C. and Newby, H. (1974) *The Sociology of Community*, London: Frank Cass and Co.
Benello, C. G. and Roussopoulos, D. (1971) *The Case For Participatory Democracy*, New York: Grossman.
Bentley, M. (1984) *Politics without Democracy*, London: Fontana.
Benyon, J.(ed) (1984) *Scarman and After*, Oxford: Pergamon Press.
Berki, R. (1989) 'Vocabularies of the state' in P. Lassman (ed) *Politics and Social Theory*, London: Routledge.
Berman, M. (1986) 'Take it to the streets: conflict and community in public space', *Dissent*, Summer.
Bernstein, R. J. (1991) *The New Constellation*, Oxford: Polity.
Bethnall Green and Stepney Trades Council (1978) *Blood on the Streets*, London.
Birley, D. and Bright, J. (1985) *Crime in the Community*, London: LCCJ.
Boaden, N (1982) *Public Participation in Local Services*, London: Longman.
Boddy, M. and Fudge, C. (eds) (1984) *Local Socialism*, London: MacMillan.
Bottoms, A. (1990) 'Crime prevention in the 1990s', *Policing and Society*, 1:1.
Bridges, L. (1982) 'Policing the urban wasteland', *Race and Class*.
- (1983) 'Extended views: the British Left and law and order', *Sage Race Relations Abstracts*, February.
- (1986) 'Beyond accountability: Labour and policing after the 1985 rebellions', *Race and Class*.
Bright, J. (1991) 'Crime prevention: the British experience' in K. Stenson and

D. Cowell (eds) *The Politics of Crime Control*, London: Sage.
Brogden, M. (1977) 'A police authority: the denial of conflict', *Sociological Review*, 25:2.
- (1982) *The Police: Autonomy and Consent*, London: Academic Press.
Brogden, M., Jefferson, T. and Walklate, S. (1988) *Introducing Policework*, London: Unwin Hyman.
Bundred, S. (1982) 'Accountability and the Metropolitan Police' in D. Cowell, T. Jones and J. Young (eds) *Policing the Riots*, London: Junction Books.
Bunyan, T. (1977) *The History and Practice of the Political Police*, London: Quartet Books.
- (1982) 'The police against the people', *Race and Class*.
Butcher, H. et al. (1990) *Local Government and Thatcherism*, London: Routledge.
Byford, L. (1975) 'Hands off the police authorities - and answer to Banton', *Police*, March.

Cain, M. (1972) 'Police professionalism: its meaning and consequences', *Anglo-American Law Review*, I.
- (1973) *Society and the Policeman's Role*, London: Routledge.
- (1977) 'An ironical departure: the dilemma of contemporary policing' in K. Jones (ed) *Yearbook of Social Policy in Britain*, London: Routledge.
- (1979) 'Trends in the sociology of police work', *International Journal of Sociology of Law*, 7:2.
Campbell, B. (1984) 'Town Hall Feminism', *New Socialist*, November.
Campbell, D. (1987) 'Policing: a power in the land', *New Statesman*, 8 May.
Campbell, T. (1983) *The Left and Rights*, London: Routledge.
Cawson, A. (1982) *Corporatism and Welfare*, London: Heinemann.
Centre for Contemporary Cultural Studies. (1982) *The Empire Strikes Back*, London: Hutchinson.
Clarke, M. (1994) 'Let us get on with it', *Police Review*, 18 February.
Clarke, R.V.G. and Hough, M. (1980) *The Effectiveness of Policing*, Aldershot, Gower.
Cohen, A. (1985) *Symbolic Construction of Community*, London: Tavistock.
Cohen, P. (1979) 'Policing the working class city', in B. Fine et. al., (eds) *Capitalism and the Rule of Law*, London: Hutchinson.
Cohen, S. (1979) 'Community control in a new utopia', *New Society*, 15 March.
- (1987) 'Taking decentralization seriously: values, visions and policies' in J. Lowman, R. Menzies and T. S Palys (eds) *Transactions: Essays in the Sociology of Social Control*, Aldershot: Gower.

Coleman, B. I. (1973) *The Idea of the City in the Nineteenth Century*, London: Routledge
Community Liaison Officer (1983) *Address to Jamaican Society*, 9 January. (1985) *Interview with Author*.
Conge, P. (1988) 'The concept of political participation', *Comparative Politics*, 4.
Costa-Dalla, M. and James, S. (1973) *Power of Women and Subversion of Community*, Bristol: Falling Wall Press.
Cowley, J et al. (1979) *Community or Class Struggle?*, London: Stage I Books.
Cox, A. and Scott, D. (1984) *GOTCHA: A Case Study of Covert Police Surveillance*, Manchester: Youth Development Trust.
Cox, B. (1975) *Civil Liberties in Britain*, Harmondsworth: Penguin.
Cox, G. (1982) 'It should be a two-way benefit', *Brief*.
- (1984a) 'Liaison panels for answering criticism', *Police Review*, 8 January.
- (1984b) 'Community priorities', *Police Review*, 16 November.
- (1985) *Interview with author*.
- (1986) 'Openness and accountability' in J. Benyon and C. Bourn (eds) *The Police: Powers, Procedures and Proprieties*, Oxford: Pergamon.
- 'The irresistible rise of the folk hero', *London Review of Books*, 3 March.
Cox, H. and Morgan D. (1973) *City Politics and the Press*, Cambridge: Cambridge University Press.

Dahl, R. (1989) *Democracy and its Critics*, New Haven: Yale University Press.
Davies, H. (1990) 'Effectiveness through delegation', *Policing*, 6:4.
Day, P, and Klein, R. (1987) *Accountabilities*, London: Tavistock.
Dean, M. (1982) 'The finger on the policeman's collar', *Political Quarterly*, 53.
Doherty, F. (1986) *The Stalker Affair*, Cork: Attic Press.
Donnison, H, et al (1986) *Neighbourhood Watch, Policing and the People*, London: Libertarian Research Trust.
Downes, D. and Ward, T. (1986) *Democratic Policing: Towards a Labour Party Policy on Police Accountability*, London: Labour Campaign for Criminal Justice.
Dunn, J. (1984) *The Politics of Socialism*, Cambridge: Cambridge University Press.

Elias, R. (1993) *Victims Still: The Political Manipulation of Crime Victims*, London: Sage.

Ewing, K. and Gearty, C. (1990) *Freedom Under Thatcher*, Oxford: Oxford University Press.

Fine, B. and Miller, R. (eds) (1985) *Policing the Miners Strike*, London: MacMillan.

Fishkin, J. S. (1992) *The Dialogue of Justice: Towards a Self-Reflective Society*, New Haven: Yale University Press.

Flynn, N. and Leach, S. (1986) *Abolition or Reform?*, London: Allen and Unwin.

Foley, M. (1991) *Rape: A Feminist Analysis of Recent Public Service Provision for Women*, Ph.D. University of Salford.

Foucault, M. (1977) *Discipline and Punish*, New York: Vintage Books.

- (1980) *Power/Knowledge*, Harvester: Brighton.
- (1981) *The History of Sexuality*, Vol I, Harmondsworth: Penguin.

Gamble, A. (1988) *The Free Economy and the Strong State*, London: MacMillan.

Garland, D. (1987) 'Review of "Losing the Fight Against Crime"', *Contemporary Crises*, 11:2.

Giddens, A. (1986) *The Nation-State and Violence*, Cambridge: Polity.

Gifford, Lord. (1986) *The Broadwater Farm Inquiry*, London: Karia Press.

Gifford, Lord, Brown, W. and Bundey, R. (1989) *Loosen the Shackles: First Report of the Liverpool 8 Inquiry into Race Relations in Liverpool*, London: Karia Press.

Gilroy, P. (1982) 'The myth of black criminality', in M. Eve and D. Musson. (eds) *The Socialist Register*, London: Merlin.

- (1983) 'Police and thieves', in Centre for Contemporary Cultural Studies (ed) *The Empire Strikes Back*, London: Hutchinson.
- (1987) *There Ain't No Black in the Union Jack*, London: Hutchinson.

Gilroy, P. and Sim, J. (1987) 'Law, order and the state of the Left' in P. Scraton (ed) *Law, Order and the Authoritarian State*, Milton Keynes: Open University Press.

Glassberg, A.D. (1981) *Representation and the Urban Community*, London: MacMillan.

Gordon, P. (1987) 'Community policing: towards the local police state?', in P. Scraton (ed) *Law, Order and the Authoritarian State*, Milton Keynes: Open University Press.

Goss, S. (1988) *Local Labour and Local Government*, Edinburgh: Edinburgh University Press.

Gramsci, A. (1971) *Selections from the Prison Notebooks*, London: Lawrence & Wishart.

Greater London Council. (1983) *A New Police Authority for London*, London:

GLC.
Greater Manchester Police Authority. (1992) *The Way Forward*, 2 October.
Grimshaw, R. and Jefferson, T. (1987) *Interpreting Policework*, London: Allen and Unwin.
Gusfield, J. R. (1975) *Community: A Critical Response*, Oxford: Blackwell.
Gutzmore, C. (1982) 'Capital, "black youth" and crime', *Race and Class*.
Gyford, J. (1985) *The Politics of Local Socialism*, London: Allen and Unwin.

HCRC (1983) *Policing in Hackney: A Record of HCRE's Experience - 1978-1982*, London: Hackney CRE.
Habermas, J. (1970) 'Towards a theory of communicative competence' *Inquiry*, 13.
- (1976) *Legitimation Crisis*, London: Heinemann.
- (1984) *The Theory of Communicative Action*, Vol I, Boston: Beacon.
Hain, P. (ed) (1979) *Policing the Police*, Vol I, London: J. Calder.
- (ed) (1980) *Policing the Police*, Vol II, London: J. Calder.
Hall, S. (1979) *Drifting into a Law and Order Society*, London: Cobden Trust.
- (1982) 'The lessons of Scarman', *Critical Social Policy*, 2:2.
- (1987) 'Urban unrest in Britain', in J. Benyon and J. Solomos (eds) *The Roots of Urban Unrest*, Oxford: Pergamon Press.
- (1988) *The Hard Road to Renewal*, London: Verso.
- (1990) 'Cultural identity and diaspora' in J. Rutherford (ed) *Identity, Community, Culture, Difference*, London: Lawrence Wishart.
Hall, S., Critcher, C., Clarke, J., Jefferson, T. and Roberts, B. (1978) *Policing the Crisis*, London: MacMillan.
Hamilton, R. and Barrett, M. (1986) *The Politics of Diversity*, London: Verso.
Hanmer, J, Radford, J, and Stanko, E. (1989) *Women, Policing and Male Violence*, London: MacMillan.
Haraway, D. (1985) 'A manifesto for cyborgs: science, technology and socialist feminism for the 1980s', *Socialist Review*, 80.
Harris, M. (1986) 'The last days of the mets', *New Society*, 21 March.
Harvey, D. (1990) *The Condition of Postmodernity*, Oxford: Blackwell.
Held, D. (ed) (1984) *States and Societies*, London: Martin Robertson.
Held, D. and Pollitt, C. (eds) (1986) *New Forms of Democracy*, Cambridge: Polity.
Hillering, G. A. (1955) 'Definitions of community', *Rural Sociology*, 20.
Hillyard, P. and Percy-Smith. J. (1988) *The Coercive State*, London: Fontana.
Hindess, B. (1983) *Parliamentary Democracy and Socialist Politics*, London: Routledge.
Hirst, P. (1988) 'Representative democracy and its limits', *Political Quarterly*,

Hobbs, D. (1988) *Doing the Business*, Oxford: Oxford University Press.
Hoggart, R. (1957) *The Uses of Literacy*, Harmondsworth: Penguin.
Holdaway, S. (1977) 'Changes in urban policing', *British Journal of Sociology*, 28:2.
- (1983) *Inside the British Police*, Oxford: Blackwell.
Home Office. (1981) *Racial Attacks*, London: HMSO.
- (1982) *Local Consultation Arrangements between the Police and the Community*, Circular 54/1982.
- (1983) *Manpower, Effectiveness and Efficiency in the Police Service*, Circular 114/1983.
- (1984) *Crime Prevention*, Circular 8/1984.
- (1985) *Arrangements for Local Consultation between the Police and the Community outside London*, Circular 2/1985.
- (1989) *Inter Departmental Racial Attacks Group Report*, London: HMSO.
- (1989) *Police Community Consultative Arrangements Under S106 of the PACE: Report of an Internal Home Office Review*, Circular 62/1989.
Hope, T. and Shaw, M. (eds) (1988) *Communities and Crime Reduction*, London: HMSO.
Horton, S. (1990) 'Local government', in S.Savage and L. Robins (eds) *Public Policy under Thatcher*, London: MacMillan.
Hough, M. and Mayhew, P. (1983) *The British Crime Survey: First Report*, London: HMSO.
Hough, M and Mayhew, P. (1985) *Taking Account of Crime: Key findings from the 1984 British Crime Survey*, London: HMSO.
Howe, D. (1988) *From Bobby to Babylon*, London: Race Today Publications.
Humphry, D. (1972) *Police Power and Black People*, London: Panther Books.
Humphry, D. and John, G. (1972) *Because They're Black*, London: Pelican.
Hunte, J. (1966) *Nigger Hunting in England?*, London: West Indian Standing Conference.
Hytner, B. (1981) *Report of the Moss Side Inquiry Panel*, Manchester: Greater Manchester Council.

Iannello, K. P. (1992) *Decisions Without Hierarchy*, New York: Routledge
Independent Committee of Inquiry. (1989) *Policing in Hackney 1945-1984: A Report Commissioned by the Roach Family Support Committee*, London: Karia Press.
Institute of Race Relations. (1979) *Police Against Black People*, London: Institute of Race Relations.
Institute of Race Relations. (1987) *Policing Against Black People*, London: Institute of Race Relations.

Jackson, B. (1968) *Working Class Community*, Harmondsworth: Penguin.
Jefferson, T. (1987) 'Controversies around police powers and accountability', *Delivering Justice*, Milton Keynes: The Open University.
Jefferson, T. and Grimshaw, R. (1984), *Controlling the Constable: Police Accountability in England and Wales*, London: Muller.
Jefferson, T, McLaughlin, E, and Robertson, L. (1988) 'Monitoring the monitors: accountability, democracy and policewatching in Britain', *Contemporary Crises*, 12.
Jessop, B. (1980) 'The transformation of the state in post-war Britain', in R. Scase (ed) *The State in Western Europe*, London: Croom Helm.
John, G. (1985) 'The trials of Jackie Berkeley', *Race Today*, May/June.
Johnson, L. (1990) *The Rebirth of Private Policing*, London: Routledge.
Johnson, N. (1990) *Restructuring the Welfare State*, London: Harvester.
Jones, T, et al. (1986) *The Islington Crime Survey*, Aldershot: Gower.
Jordan. B. (1988) *The State, Autonomy and Consent*, Oxford: Blackwell.
Joshua, H. and Wallace, T. (1983) *To Ride the Storm: the 1980 Bristol Riot and the State*, London: Heinemann.
Judge, T. (1976) 'Who gives the orders?', *Police*, September.

Keith, M. (1988) 'Squaring circles? consultation and inner city policing', *New Community*, 15:1.
Keith, M. and Murji, K (1990) 'Reifying crime, legitimising racism: policing, local authorities and left realism', in W. Ball and J. Solomos (eds) *Race and Local Politics*, London: MacMillan
Kettle, M. (1979) 'Anderton's way', *New Society*, 8 March.
- (1980) 'The politics of policing and the policing of politics' in P. Hain (ed) *Policing the Police*, Vol 2, London: J. Calder.
Kettle, M. and Hodges, L. (1982) *Uprising: The Police, the People and the Riots in Britain's Cities*, London: Pan Books.
Kettle, M. and Shirley, J. (1983) 'Revolution at the Yard', *Sunday Times*, 6 November.
Kinsey, R. (1984) *Merseyside Crime Survey: Ist Report*, Liverpool: Police Committee Support Unit.
Kinsey, R. and J. Young. (1982) 'Police autonomy and the politics of discretion', in D. Cowell, T. Jones and J Young (eds) *Policing the Riots*, London: Junction Books.
Kinsey, R., Lea, J. and Young, J. (1986) *Losing the Fight Against Crime*, Oxford: Blackwell.

Labour Party (1986) *Protecting Our People*, London: Labour Party.
Laclau, E. (1993) 'Power and representation' in M. Poster (ed) *Politics, Theory and Contemporary Culture*, New York: Columbia University

Press.
Laclau, E, and Mouffe, C. (1985) *Hegemony and Socialist Strategy*, London: Verso.
Lansley, S et al. (1989) *Councils in Conflict*, London: MacMillan.
Lash, S. and Urry, J. (1987) *The End of Organized Capitalism*, Oxford: Oxford University Press.
Lea, J. and Young, J. (1984) *What Is To Be Done About Law and Order*, Harmondsworth: Penguin.
Leach, S. et al. (1991) *After Abolition*, INLOGOV, University of Birmingham
Lee, K. (1988) 'Moss Side: aftermath of a murder', *New Society*, 13 May.
Levenson, H. (1981) 'Democracy and the police', *Poly Law Review*, 6:2.
Leys, C. (1984) 'The rise of the authoritarian state' in J. Curran (ed) *The Future of the Left*, Cambridge: Polity.
Lindblom, A. (1977) *Politics and Markets*, London: Basic Books.
London Strategic Policy Unit. (1986) *Policing Protest*, London: LSPU.
- (1988) *Collected Reports of the Police Monitoring and Research Unit*, London: LSPU.
Loney, M. (1983) *Community Against Development*, London: Heinemann.
Loveday, B. (1985) *The Role and Effectiveness of the Merseyside Police Committee*, Liverpool: Merseyside County Council.
- (1987) 'The joint boards', *Policing*, 3:3.
- (1988) 'Joint boards and the local accountability of the police in the metropolitan areas', INLOGOV, University of Birmingham.
Lukes, S. (1974) *Power*, London: MacMillan.
Lummis, C. D. (1992) 'The radicalization of democracy', *Democracy*, 2.
Lustgarten, L. (1986) *The Governance of the Police*, London: Sweet and Maxwell.
Lyall, S. and Soutter, L. (1993) *Los Angeles With a Map*, 4 June, London: ICA.
Lyotard, J. F. (1984) *The Postmodern Condition*, Manchester: Manchester University Press.

McCabe, S. and Wallington, P. with Alderson, J., Gostin, L and Mason, C. (1988) *The Police, Public Order and Civil Liberties*, London: Routledge.
McDonald, K. (1976) 'A police state in Britain?', *New Society*, 9 January.
MacKinnon, C. (1983) 'Feminism, marxism, method, and the state: toward feminist jurisprudence', *Signs*, 12.
McLaughlin, E. (1990) *Community, Policing and Accountability: A Case Study of Manchester, 1981-88*, Ph.D, Faculty of Law, University of Sheffield.
- (1991) 'Police accountability and black people: into the 1990s', in E.

Cashmore and E. McLaughlin (eds) *Out of Order?: Policing Black People*, London: Routledge.
- (1992) 'The democratic deficit: European union and the accountability of the British Police', *British Journal of Criminology*, 32:4.
- (1994) 'Policing', in E. Cashmore (ed) *Dictionary of Race Relations*, London: Routledge.

McLaughlin, E. and Muncie, J (1993) 'The Silent Revolution: Market-Based Criminal Justice in England', *The Socio-Legal Bulletin*, La Trobe.

McLaughlin, E. and Murji, K. (1993) 'Controlling the bill: restructuring the police in the 1990s', *Critical Social Policy*, 13:1.

McNee, D. (1983) *McNee's Law*, London: Collins.

Maguire, M and Pointing, J. (eds) (1988) *Victims of Crime*, Milton Keynes: Open University Press.

Manchester City Council. (1987) *Planning a Safer Environment for Women*, Manchester: City Council.

Manning, P. (1988) *Symbolic Communication*, Cambridge, Mass: MIT Press.

Mark, R. (1977) *Policing a Perplexed Society*, London: Allen and Unwin.

Marshall, G. (1960) 'Police responsibility' *Public Administration*, Spring.
- (1965) *The Police and the Government*, London: Methuen.
- (1978) 'Police accountability revisited' in D. Butler and A. H. Marshall (eds) *Policy and Politics*, London: MacMillan.

Massumi, B. (1992) *A User's Guide to Capitalism and Schizophrenia*, Cambridge, Mass: MIT Press.

Matthews, R. and Young, J. (eds) (1987) *Confronting Crime*, London: Sage.

Metropolitan Police (1986) *Public Order Review - Civil Disturbances, 1981-85*, London: Metropolitan Police.

Midgley, J. (1986) *Community Participation, Social Development and the State*, London: Metheun.

Morgan, R (1986) 'Police consultative groups: the implications for the governance of the police', *Political Quarterly*, 57:1.
- (1987) 'Police accountability: developing the local infrastructure', *British Journal of Criminology*, 27:1.
- (1992) 'Talking about policing', in D. Downes (ed) *Unravelling Criminal Justice*, London: MacMillan.

Morgan, R. and Maggs, C. (1984) *The Politics of Tranquillity: The Origins and Development of Police Liaison Committees*, University of Bath.
- (1985) *Setting the PACE: Police Community Consultation Arrangements in England and Wales*, University of Bath.

Morgan, R. and Swift, P. (1987) 'The future of police authorities: member's views', *Public Administration*, 65:3.

Morris, N. and Hawkins, G. (1977) *Letter to the President on Crime Control*, Chicago: Chicago University Press.

Morris, P. and Heal, K. (1981) *Crime Control and the Police: A Review of the Literature*, London: HMSO.
Morris, T. (1989) *Crime and Criminal Justice since 1945*, Oxford: Blackwell
Moss Side Community Forum. (1994) *Not Good Enough*, Manchester: MSCF.
Moss Side Defence Committee. (1981) *Hytner Myths*, Manchester: MSDC.
Mouffe, C. (1993) *The Return of the Political*, London: Verso.
Murphy, D. (1991) *The Stalker Affair and the Press*, London: Unwin and Hyman.

Nelson, J. M. (1975) *Access to Power: Politics and the Urban Poor in Developing Nations*, Princeton: Princeton University Press.
Newham Monitoring Project, (1989) *Into the 1990s: From Strength to Strength*, London: NMP Publications.
Newman, Sir, K. (1983) 'Policing London Post-Scarman', *Sir George Bean Memorial Lecture*.
Nisbet, R. (1970) *Quest for Communities*, Oxford: Oxford University Press.

Offe, C. (1980) *The Contradictions of the Welfare State*, London: Hutchinson.
Okojie, P. (1985) 'Chief constables and political interference: the case of Anderton and Greater Manchester', in B. Fine and R. Miller (eds) *Policing the Miners' Strike*, London: Lawrence and Wishart.
Okojie, P. and Noble, M. (1980) 'Police authorities and democratic control', Manchester Polytechnic Law Department.
Oliver, I (1987) *Police, Government and Accountability*, London: MacMillan.

Pahl, R. E. (1984) *Divisions of Labour*, Oxford: Blackwell.
Panitch, L. (1985) *Working Class Politics in Crisis*, London: Verso.
Pateman, C. (1970) *Participation and Democratic Theory*, Cambridge: Cambridge University Press.
Phillips, A. (1991) *Engendering Democracy*, Oxford: Blackwell.
- (1993) 'Must feminists give up on liberal democracy?' in D. Held (ed) *Prospects for Democracy*, Oxford: Blackwell.
Pilger, J. (1990) 'The dismantling of freedom', *Manchester Evening News*, 19 March.
Pinker, R. (1981) *The Barclay Committee*, London: Bedford Square Press.
Pitkin, H. F. (1967) *The Concept of Representation*, Berkeley: University of California Press.
Piven, F. and Cloward, R. A. (1971) *Regulating the Poor*, New York: Pantheon.
Plant, R. (1974) *Community and Ideology*, London: Routledge.
Platt, S. (1986) 'Return to Broadwater Farm', *New Socialist*, April.
Police Monitoring Research Unit. (1987) *Women and Violence Survey Report*,

Manchester: City Council.
Policy Studies Institute (1983) *The Police and People in London*, Vols I-IV, London: Policy Studies Institute.
Pranger, R. J. (1968) *The Eclipse of Citizenship*, New York: Holt Reinhart Wilson.
Probyn, E. (1993) *Sexing the Self*, London: Routledge.
Punch, M. (1979) 'The secret social service' in S. Holdaway (ed) *The British Police*, London: Edward Arnold.

Race Today (1985) 'The Moss Side police: a law unto itself', Editorial, May.
Regan, D. R. (1991) *Local Government Versus the Police: The Rise and Fall of Police Monitoring in Britain*, London: Hampden Trust.
Reiner, R. (1980) 'Forces of disorder', *New Society*, 10 April.
- (1983) 'The politicisation of the police in Britain'in M.Punch (ed) *Control in the Police Organisation*, Cambridge, Mass: MIT Press.
- (1985) *The Politics of the Police*, Brighton: Wheatsheaf.
- (1989) 'Whatever happened to police accountability?', *SAMIZDAT*, May/June.
Review Panel into Handsworth Rebellions. (1986) *A Different Reality*, West Midlands Council.
Ricci, D. M. (1975) *Community Power and Democratic Theory*, New York: Random House.
Richardson, A. (1983) *Participation*, London: Routledge.
Roarty, R. (1991) 'Habermas and Lyotard on Postmodernity' in I. Hoesterey (ed) *Zeitgeist in Babel*, Bloomington: Indiana University Press.
Robertson, D. (1985) *A Dictionary of Modern Politics*, London: Europa Publications.
Rock, P. (1990) *Helping Victims of Crime*, Oxford: Clarendon Press.
Rose, D. (1992) *Climate of Fear*, London: Bloomsbury.
Royal Commission. (1962) *Final Report of the Royal Commission on the Police*, Cmnd. 1728, London: HMSO.
Rustin, M. (1984) 'Opening to the future', *New Socialist*, October.
- (1985) *For a Pluralist Socialism*, London: Verso.

Samuels, H. (1993) *The Political Psyche*, London: Routledge.
Savage, S. (1984) 'Political control or community liaison?', *Political Quarterly*, 55:1.
- (1989) 'Crime control: the law and the community', *Talking Politics*, 2:1.
Savage, S. and Wilson, C. (1987) '"Ask a policeman": community consultation in practice', *Social Policy and Administration*, 21:3.
Scarman, Lord. (1981) *The Brixton Disorders 10-12 April 1981*, London:

HMSO.
Schmitter, P.C. (1977) *Trends towards Corporatist Inter-Mediation*, London: Sage.
Scraton, P. (1985) *The State of the Police*, London: Pluto.
- (ed) (1987) *Law, Order and the Authoritarian State*, Milton Keynes: Open University Press.
Sim, J. (1982) 'Scarman: The police counter-attack', in M. Eve and D. Musson (eds) *The Socialist Register*, London: Merlin Press.
Simey, M. (1976) 'All dressed up and no-where to go', *Police*, August.
- (1982) 'Police authorities and accountability' in D. Cowell et al (eds) *Policing the Riots*, London: Junction Books.
- (1988) *Democracy Rediscovered*, London: Pluto.
Smith, S. (1986) 'Police accountability and local democracy', *Area*, 18:2.
Spencer, S. (1985) *Called to Account: The Case for Police Accountability in England and Wales*, London: NCCL.
Spitz, E. (1984) *Majority Rule*, Chatham, NJ: Chatham House.
Stacy, M. (1969) 'The myth of community studies', *British Journal of Sociology*, 20:2.
Stalker, J. (1988) *Stalker*, London: Harrap.
State Research Bulletin. (1980) *Policing the 1980s: The Iron Fist*, London: State Research.
Stephens, M. (1988) *Policing*, Hemel Hempstead: Harvester.
Stringer, G. (1987) 'Stalking Stalker', *New Socialist*, February.
Sunstein, C. R. (ed) (1990) *Feminism and Political Theory*, Chicago: Chicago University Press.

Taylor, I. (1981) *Law and Order: Arguments for Socialism*, London: MacMillan.
Taylor, P. (1987) *Stalker: The Search for the Truth*, London: Faber and Faber.
Thames Television. (1991) *A Question for London: London's Crime Wave*, 8 January.
Thatchell, P. (1983) *Battle for Bermondsey*, London: Heretic Books.
Thorns, D. C. (1976) *The Quest for Community*, London: Allen and Unwin.
Titmus, R. (1968) *Commitment to Welfare*, London: Allen and Unwin.
Tuck, M. (1991) 'Community and the criminal justice system', *Policy Studies*, 12:3.
Tuck, M. and Southgate, P. (1981) *Ethnic Minorities, Crime and Policing*, Home Office Research Study No. 70, London: HMSO.

Unsworth, C. (1982) 'The riots of 1981: popular violence and the politics of law and order', *Journal of Law and Society*, 9:1.

Vogler, R. (1991) *Reading the Riot Act*, Milton Keynes: Open University Press.

Waddington, P. A. J. (1984) 'The role of the police authority: constitutional arrangements and social realities', *Local Government Studies*, 10:5.
Wainwright, H. (1987) *Labour: A Tale of Two Parties*, London: Hogarth.
Walker, M. (1986) *A Report To The Manchester City Council Police Monitoring Unit*, [unpublished report].
- (1986) *With Extreme Prejudice*, London: Canary.
Walklate, S. (1989) *Victimology: the Victim and the Criminal Justice Process*, London: Unwin Hyman.
Walters, T. (1981) 'Complaints against the police', *Poly Law Review*, 6:2.
Walzer, M. (1983) *Spheres of Justice*, New York: Basic Books.
Warren, R. L. (1957) 'Towards a reformulation of community theory', *Human Organization*, 15.
Williams, R. (1970) *The Country and the City*, London: Chatto and Windus.
- (1976) *Keywords*, London: Fontana.
Willmot, P. (ed) (1987) *Policing and the Community*, London: Policy Studies Institute.
- (1988) *Community in Social Policy in the 1990s*, London: Policy Studies Institute.
Windlesham, Lord. (1993) *Responses to Crime*, Vol II, Oxford: Clarendon Press.
Wolff Olins. (1988) *A Force for Change*, London: Wolff Olins.
Wolmar, C. (1988) 'The days of reckoning', *New Statesman*, 5 February.
Woodcock, Sir J. (1991) 'Overturning police culture', *Policing*, 7:3.
Wright, S. (1985) *Interview with author*, August.

Young, H (1989) *One of Us: A Biography of Margaret Thatcher*, London: MacMillan.
Young, I. (1990) 'The ideal of the community and the politics of difference', in L. Nicholson (ed) *Feminism and Postmodernism*, London: Routledge.
- (1990) *Justice - The Politics of Difference*, Princeton NJ: Princeton University Press.

Zander, M. (1985) *The Police and Criminal Evidence Act*, London: Sweet and Maxwell.

Main Reports and Formal Documentation Relating to the Politics of Policing in Manchester

a. Manchester City Council

    Police Monitoring Committee Minutes of Meetings, 1984-8.

    Police Monitoring Committee Working Party Minutes of Meetings, 1984-7.

    Police Monitoring Research Unit, 1984-8.

    Community Safety Unit, Reports 1988, 1990, 1992.

    PoliceWatch: Nos 1-9

b. Greater Manchester Council

    Police Committee Minutes of Meetings, 1983-6

    Community Liaison Officer's Reports, 1982-5

    Police Authority Annual Reports, 1986-88

    Community Liaison, Nos 1-12

    Community Liaison, Reports

c. Greater Manchester Police

    Annual Reports, 1977-92

    Greater Manchester Police Handbook

d. Youth and Allied Workers' Police Monitoring Group

    Minutes of Meetings/Training Days, 1982-6.

e. Gay Men's Police Monitoring Group

    Minutes of Meetings, 1985

Index

Accountability, 24-5
ACPO, 11
Active citizenship, 106, 108
Aids speech, 129-30
Anderton, 35-8, 39-56, 57-73, 97, 110, 120-7, 128-33, 144
Antagonism, 33
Arblaster, A, 25-31
Association of County Councils, 8
Association of Metropolitan Authorities, 14, 59
Barber, 29
Battle of Brittan, 70, 103, 122, 131, 135, 149
Baudrillard, 27
Beetham, D, 24
Berkeley, J, 70, 78, 103, 138
Borough watch committee, 5
Bridges, L, 18
Brixton, 106, 108
Broadwater Farm, 106
Brogden, M, 8
Bunyan, T, 10
Cain, M, 8
Chief constables, 5-10, 12-13, 121, 123-5
Communication theory, 31
Community, 21-3, 95-7, 134-46
Community Contact, 37, 48, 71
Community Liaison, 70-3, 79-95, 133-46
Community safety, 93, 161-5
Consultation, 15-8
Cox, G, 48, 62, 121
Crime Concern, 108
Crime control, 15
Crime Prevention, 102, 107-9, 112-115, 152-4, 161-5
Critical criminology, 16, 113
Day, P, 24-5

Democracy
    Participatory, 29-33
    Representative, 23-8
Dissensus, 33
Empowerment, 30
Ethnic minorities, 39, 74-5, 83, 140, 145

'Flaming', 33
Foucault, M, 29
Gay Men's Police Monitoring Group, 98
Gilroy, P, 11, 12, 18, 22
Greater London Council, 13, 94, 104, 149
Greater Manchester Police
    brutality, 49, 129
    paramilitary, 40, 66
    police band, 63-5
    public order 40
    racism, 39-42
    Tactical Aid Group, 39
Greater Manchester police authority, 127-33, 149, 177-8
Greater Manchester police committee, 42-3, 44-56, 57-73, 92-5, 120-7, 135-7, 144
Grimshaw, R, 6, 9, 11, 13, 18
Habermas, J, 31-2
Hall, S, 9, 11, 15, 17, 25
Hannaway, E, 138-9
Home Office, 6, 121, 124, 126, 128-33, 135-7, 140
Hytner Inquiry, 49-52
Inbert, P, 111
Institutional disruptions, 33
Jefferson, T, 6, 9, 11, 13, 18
Kettle, M, 9
Kinsey, R, 19
Laurence Scott dispute, 65-6
Lay visiting, 72-3
Lea, J, 16, 19
Left realism, 16-17, 113-4
Liverpool, 8, 106, 108
Local Government Act, 1972, 7
Local government elections, 1981, 13, 44; 1984, 90

Loveday, B, 8, 14
Lustgarten, L, 5
MacKinnon, C, 29
Magistrates, 6, 14, 59
Manchester City Council, 49-50, 56, 90-103, 127, 134, 136-8, 148-65
Manning, P, 10
Mendis, V, 138, 140
Metropolitan police, 13, 109-11, 171
Miners' strike 67, 102
Monitoring groups, 12
Morgan, R, 16, 82, 108
Moss Side, 45-8, 61-3, 136, 138, 178-9
Moss Side Defence Committee, 48, 72-3
Mouffe, C, 28, 171
Municipal socialism, 14, 91
Neighbourhood Watch, 152-3
Newman, K, 109-11
Noble, M, 7
Okojie, P, 7
Oliver, I, 7, 9, 13
Participation, 27, 28-33, 95-7, 134-46
Pateman, C, 30
Plastic bullets, 122-4
Plus Programme, 111, 174-5
Police accountability, 5-10, 11-19
Police and Criminal Evidence Act 1984, 14
Police committees, 5-10, 13-15, 17-18, 104-105
Police Federation, 11
Police Monitoring Committee, 97-103 73, 98, 148-61
Police Monitoring research unit, 97-103, 148-61
Policing
    community, 18
    community control of, 17
    corporate management, 9
    crisis in, 10-11
    managerialism, 175-6
    multi-agency, 18, 74, 77
    operational independence, 8-9, 13, 15-6, 36, 61, 121, 124, 126, 132
    politicization, 11
    professionalism, 8
    unrepresentative bureaucracy, 11
Politics of law and order, 12-15, 105-9, 111-15,

      150-1, 160-1
Post
      industrial, 22
      liberalism, 19
      marxism, 21
      modernism, 22
Popular justice, 19
Public meetings, 98-102
Racial violence, 74, 116-7
Reiner, R, 14, 35
Representation, 23-7, 95-7, 134-46
Riots, 14, 45-8, 61-3
Royal Commission, 5-6
Safer cities, 108
Salford City Council, 127
Scarman, Lord, 16, 18, 51
Scraton, P, 14, 19
Sexual violence, 116-7
Sim, J, 12, 18
Smith, S, 6
Stalker, J, 49, 124
Stalker Affair, 127-30, 135
Straw, J, 13
Superintendents Association, 11
Taylor, I, 12, 16, 17
Thatcherism, 19
Victim support, 116-7
Walker, M, 119
Williams, R, 22
Women, 85-6, 143-4, 146, 158-60
Young, I, 30
Young, J, 16, 19
Young people, 84-5, 141, 146
Youth and community workers, 53-5
Youth and Allied Workers' Police Monitoring Group, 54-6,